OXFORD STUDIES IN ISLAMIC ART
III

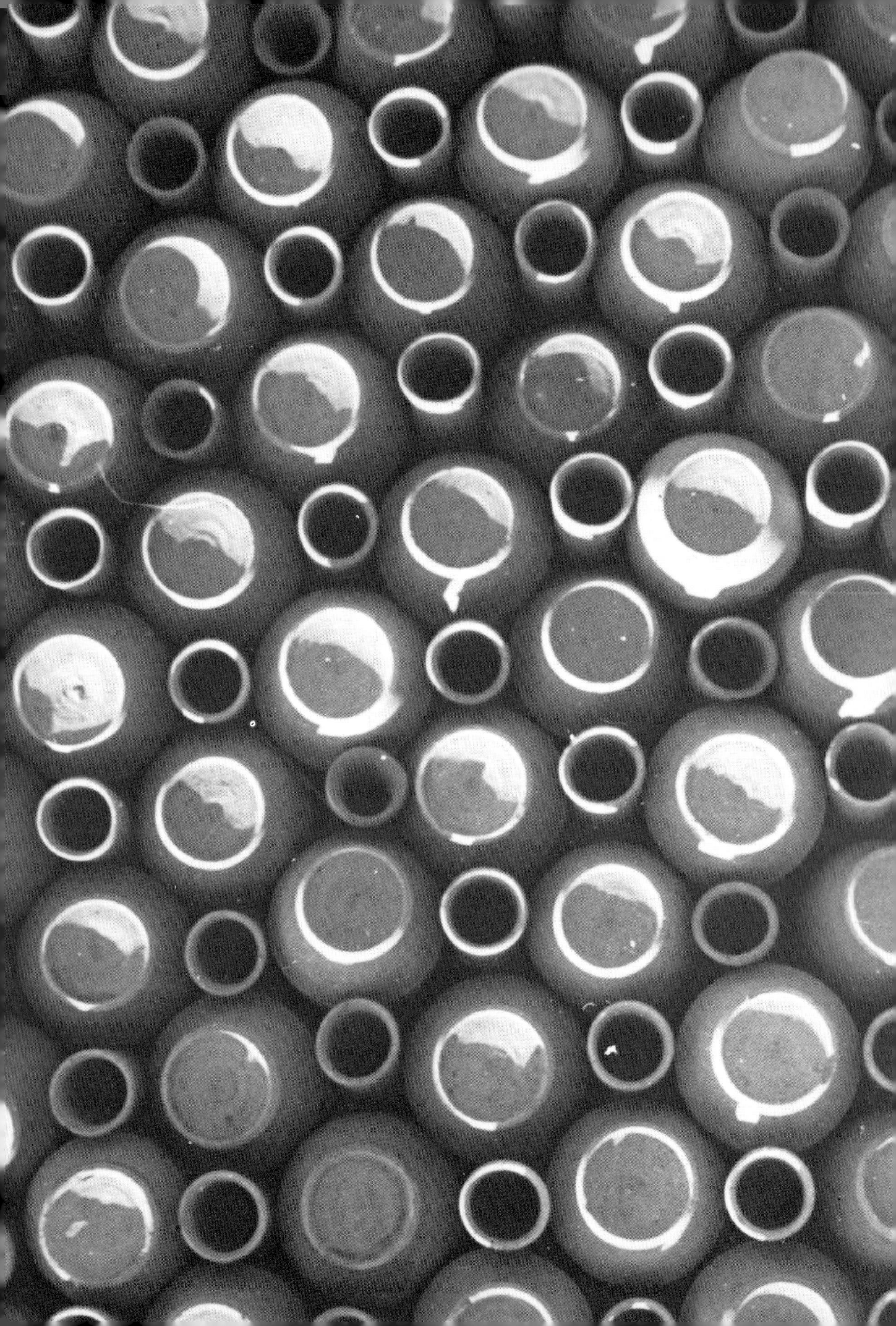

POTS & PANS

A Colloquium on Precious Metals and Ceramics
in the Muslim, Chinese and Graeco-Roman Worlds,
Oxford 1985

Edited by Michael Vickers

Published by Oxford University Press
for
the Board of the Faculty of Oriental Studies,
University of Oxford

Oxford University Press, Walton Street, Oxford OX2 6DP
London Glasgow New York Toronto
Delhi Bombay Calcutta Madras Karachi
Kuala Lumpur Singapore Hong Kong Tokyo
Nairobi Dar es Salaam Cape Town
Melbourne Auckland
and associate companies in
Beirut Berlin Ibadan Mexico City

British Library Cataloguing in Publication Data
Pots and pans: a colloquium on precious metals and ceramics in the Muslim, Chinese and Graeco-Roman worlds, Oxford 1985.—
(Oxford studies in Islamic art; 3)
1. Goldwork, Ancient 2. Silverwork, Ancient
I. University of Oxford. *Faculty of Oriental Studies*
739.2'09'01 NK7107

ISBN 0-19-728005-6
ISBN 0-19-728006-4 Pbk

Designed by Richard Foenander
Typeset on a Monotype Lasercomp at Oxford University Computing Service.
Printed in Great Britain by The Alden Press, Oxford

Contents

Preface

The eminent archaeologist V. Gordon Childe once wrote of the manufacture of vessels in one material intended to evoke the appearance of another that "skeuomorphism often gives us a glimpse into productive activities and artistic media of which no direct evidence survives". The Pots and Pans Colloquium held at the Ashmolean Museum, Oxford in March 1985, explored the phenomenon of "skeuomorphism"; surviving ceramics were treated as a reflection of gold- and silverworking traditions attested in the literary and epigraphic sources relating to ancient Greece and Rome, China and Medieval Islam, but of which few original specimens are now extant. Scholars of Near and Far Eastern cultures have no difficulty in accepting the view that precious metal objects might, as a matter of course, be imitated in cheaper materials; the dependence on the part of the manufacturers of fine pottery on forms and decorative effects originally created for another medium is not, however, as widely accepted as perhaps it should be by students of Graeco-Roman ceramics. One of the aims of the Colloquium was to redress this imbalance. Another was to employ the forms and decoration of pottery and porcelain to help us visualize the lost worlds described in our extant texts. These proceedings are arranged so that papers dealing with extant gold- and silverware are followed first by discussions of the relevant historical and literary sources, and then by some attempts at extrapolating from the evidence of the ceramic vessels themselves. A final paper examines some of the reasons for the comparative neglect by scholars of the topic under discussion.

An exhibition was mounted by the Ashmolean's Departments of Antiquities and Eastern Art in conjunction with the Colloquium, a permanent record of which has been published in the form of a Museum booklet—(M. Vickers, O, Impey and J. Allan, *From Silver to Ceramic*, Oxford, 1986).

Thanks are due to the speakers for making the Colloquium possible; to the chairpersons James Allan, Oliver Impey, Roger Moorey, Julian Raby, Jessica Rawson, and Brian Shefton for making the proceedings run smoothly; to the Jowett Trustees for a generous subvention towards the cost of publication; most of all, perhaps, to Caroline Roberts and Sally Purcell for their assiduous and painstaking work in ensuring that papers were properly edited, typeset and corrected.

Michael Vickers

Classical Greek Fictile Imitations of Precious Metal Vases

DAVID W.J. GILL

The imitation of precious metal vases in antiquity is well attested in the literary sources. Athenaeus, writing at the end of the second century A.D. about the potters in his home town of Naucratis, and perhaps recalling a much earlier period, states that they dipped, or literally baptized, their pottery to make it appear like silver.[1] For the classical Greek period this imitation is illustrated by the luxury thericleian vases, produced in the expensive media of terebinth wood, silver and sometimes gold, which were copied in considerably cheaper clay.[2] Theophrastus states that the luxury vases were so like their cheaper counterparts that "nobody was able to distinguish them from those made of clay".[3] A feature of all thericleians, luxury and imitation, was their black colour; this illustrates a newly read Oxyrhynchus Papyrus in which a pre-Socratic philosopher, Thrasyalces, states that "silver is black".[4] In addition Eubulus tells us that a characteristic of the thericleians was their metallic sheen.[5] Such a sheen on fictile vases became more common from the third quarter of the fifth century B.C. onwards, and in the light of the literary sources this need no longer be seen as a deterioration of workmanship but rather as an improvement in the skill of imitation—an interpretation which is now being more widely discussed and accepted.[6] Similar deception occurs in Etruria, where some early bucchero

1. Ath. xi.480.e. None of this pottery has been recognized as yet; cf. Edgar (1898-9), 65.

2. Ath. xi.470.e-472.d. cf. Bentley (1883), 160-89; Pottier (1912); Miller (1921); Wissowa (1934), 2367-8; Shefton (1971); Shefton (forthcoming). Bentley makes the useful observation that "...they were called Thericleian from the shape, whatsoever Artificier made them, or whether of Earth, or of Wood, or of Metal." Bentley (1883), 160. For thericleians in different media see e.g. Cic. *Verr.* II.iv.18.38 (metal), Theophr. *Hist.Pl.* v.iii.2 (wood) and Theophilos 2 (clay).

3. Theophr. *Hist.Pl.* v.iii.2.

4. Hughes & Parsons (1984), 3659. I am grateful to P.J. Parsons and Michael Vickers for drawing my attention to this reference. cf. Vickers (1985), 108-12.

5. Eubulus 56 (=Ath. xi.471.d; Kock (1884), 183).

6. cf. Noble (1965), 80; Vickers (1983a); Vickers (1985).

vases had a silver overlay which gave the appearance of a solid silver vase at a fraction of the cost.[7]

Despite influential objections by Dorothy Kent Hill on the grounds of technique, scholars have continued to see the norms of metalwork as influencing craftsmen who worked in clay.[8] Shefton has suggested that Achaemenid influence "started off early in the fifth century by Attic potters copying isolated oriental luxury vases."[9] Both Green and Sparkes have suggested that fictile stamped decoration was derived from metalwork, and this has been confirmed by patterns of tongues and linked palmettes found on metal stemlesses and cup-skyphoi.[10] Fictile figured decoration also has its counterparts in the techniques of incision and gold figure. The study of vases in precious metal is badly hampered by the melting down and re-use of plate in antiquity, which has given the impression that only a limited amount was produced; and the inference therefore, is that pottery was a valuable item. Yet the literary sources show that precious metal vases were in everyday use at symposia, and this may be illustrated by Alcibiades' raid on the house of Anytus, whose tables were full of gold and silver plate.[11] In addition, Johnston's study of commercial graffiti has confirmed that pottery was not considered to be valuable a commodity in antiquity, the highest recorded price for a fictile vase being three drachmae (**Fig. 1**), which pales into insignificance beside the 1,000 drachmae silver hydriae mentioned in the Acropolis inventories.[12] Indeed, a toy silver hydria in Oxford (**Fig. 2**) has a bullion value of six drachmae and four obols, more than double that of its much larger fictile counterparts.[13] Extant luxury vases show the variety of shapes used—cups, stemlesses, cup-skyphoi, mugs, kantharoi, stemmed dishes, askoi, perfume-pots, pyxides and rhyta—but only a small selection of these may be considered here.[14]

7. Ramage (1970), 17-18; Rasmussen (1979), 128.

8. Hill (1947), 248-56.

9. Shefton (1971), 111.

10. Green (1972), 6 and 13, n.34; Sparkes (1968), 12; Sparkes & Talcott (1970), 22. For the white-ground oinochoe, London D14, mentioned by Green, see Wehgartner (1983), pl.13. Stamped bronze stemlesses include Newcastle 577 and Würzburg H767, Züchner (1950-1), 175-7, figs.1-3; Mallwitz & Schiering (1964), 186, fig.59. For a stamped bronze cup-skyphos from Bulgaria, see Welkow (1940-2), 210, figs.292-3 and 211, fig.294.

11. Plut. *Alc.* 4.

12. For vase prices: Johnston (1979), 33. For comparison between fictile and silver vases, Vickers (1984), 90, n.26; Vickers (1985), 116.

13. Oxford 1971.894; Vickers (1983a), 36 and 44, fig.5.

14. For the range of luxury vases: von Bothmer (1984); British Museum (1976); Cologne (1979); Filow (1934); Gill (1987); Gorbunova (1971); Lordkipanidze (1971); Oliver (1977); Reeder (1974), 212-31; Strong (1966); Yalouris *et al.* (1980). Bronze vases are extremely common; cf. Weber (1983). For the pottery imitations of metal oinochoai, Krauskopf (1984).

Figure 1. Commercial graffito from Attic red-figured hydria from Camarina. 5th century B.C. Museo Nazionale, Syracuse, 23912. (After Johnston.)

Figure 2. Toy silver hydria. 5th century B.C. Ht. 5.9cm. Ashmolean Museum, 1971.894.

Several silver cups are known, mostly from the Seven Brothers' tumuli.[15] Each carries gold-figure or incised decoration, including a seated Nike (**Fig. 3**), satyrs and maenads, warriors outside the tondo of Bellerophon and the Chimaera, and two women and a man (**Fig. 4**). The silver cup from the Chmyrev mound has a concave lip, ribbed body, carefully worked foot, and on the floor an inlaid gold disc showing a Nereid on a hippocamp (**Figs. 5 and 6**). Its profile corresponds almost exactly with that of a fictile ribbed acrocup in Boston from Tanagra which shows, in red-figure technique, Sparte dismounting from her horse at an altar (**Figs. 7 and 8**).[16] Beazley was convinced that in the Sparte cup he was dealing with a cheap imitation, as he stated that "the shape is descended from the 'Acrocup', or rather it is an Acrocup influenced by metal originals such as the silver cup (with gold medallion) from the Chmyrev grave."[17] A further red-figure, ribbed example is known in New York and there are several black-glazed cups, sometimes decorated with incised and stamped decoration.[18] One is in Oxford and was a gift of Sir Arthur Evans (**Fig. 9**).[19] There is a note in the museum register that it was considered to have a metal prototype and Beazley described it as a

15. Seven Brothers' tumuli: Gorbunova (1971); Schefold (1931); Vickers (1983a), 43, fig.3. Chmyrev mound: Pharmakowsky (1910), 219-20, figs.18 and 19.

16. Boston 00.354: Beazley (1963), 1516, below; Beazley (1971), 500; Caskey & Beazley (1963), pl.106, 175.

17. Caskey & Beazley (1963), 90-1.

18. New York 06.1021.186: Beazley (1963), 1516, below; Richter & Hall (1936), pls.167, 172 and 181, 172. The tondo shows Eros driving a three-horse chariot. Richter & Hall (1936), 219, considered that the shape was derived from metalwork. For the shape in black glaze: Sparkes & Talcott (1970), 94-6.

19. Oxford 1917.63: Beazley (1927), pl.48, 140, 5.

Figure 3. Gold-figure tondo showing a seated Nike on a silver cup from the Seven Brothers' tumuli. 5th century B.C. Hermitage Museum. (After Gorbunova.)

Figure 4. Incised tondo showing two women and a man on a silver cup from the Seven Brothers' tumuli. 5th century B.C. Hermitage Museum. (After Gorbunova.)

"metalloid shape".[20] Similar fictile cups come from the grave of the Lacedaemonians in the Ceramicus, dating to 403, and from Motya, the Phoenician colony in Sicily which was sacked in 397 by Dionysius of Syracuse.[21] A date towards the end of the fifth century appears to be confirmed by the pro-Spartan iconography of the Sparte cup. Further fictile cups are known from Naucratis, Taranto and the south of France.[22] Beazley recognized that the potting of the bowl of the acrocups was extremely close to that found on fictile ribbed stemlesses (**Fig. 10**) and cup-skyphoi of the last quarter of the fifth century, which suggests that they came from the same workshops.[23]

A silver Rheneia cup from the Baschova mound at Duvanli in Bulgaria carries incised decoration showing Selene on a horse (**Figs.11 and 12**), and a second silver one is known from the Crimea.[24] There are no known figured, fictile Rheneia cups, although some later ones carry stamped patterns of

20. Beazley (1963), text 39.

21. Grave of the Lacedaemonians: Gebauer & Johannes (1937), 197-8, figs.14-15; Karo (1943), pl.35, 1. Motya: Isserlin *et al.* (1962-3), 121 and pl.13, 8; Coldstream (1970), 581, fig.19.

22. Naucratis: Oxford G.141.12, Bernand (1970), 708, no.766 and pl.25, 1 top left. Taranto: Taranto no number. Calvisson: Jully (1983), 1033, no.02-P. Castelnau/Lez: Jully (1983), 802, no.012-P.

23. cf. Caskey & Beazley (1963), 90-1.

24. Duvanli: Filow & Welkow (1930), 289, fig.9; Filow (1934), 64-5, figs.81-2 and pl.5; Webster (1939), pl.11, c; Rumpf (1953), pl.40, 6. Crimea: cf. Sparkes & Talcott (1970), 101, n.16.

Figure 5. Silver acrocup from the Chmyrev mound. 5th century B.C. Once Hermitage Museum.

Figure 6. Gold tondo showing a Nereid on a hippocamp from the Chmyrev mound. 5th century B.C. Once Hermitage Museum.

Figure 8. Red-figured tondo showing Sparte dismounting from her horse on an Attic acrocup from Tanagra. Museum of Fine Arts, Boston, 00.354. (After Caskey & Beazley.)

Figure 7. Attic red-figured acrocup from Tanagra. 5th century B.C. Ht. 9.8cm. Museum of Fine Arts, Boston, 00.354. (After Caskey & Beazley.)

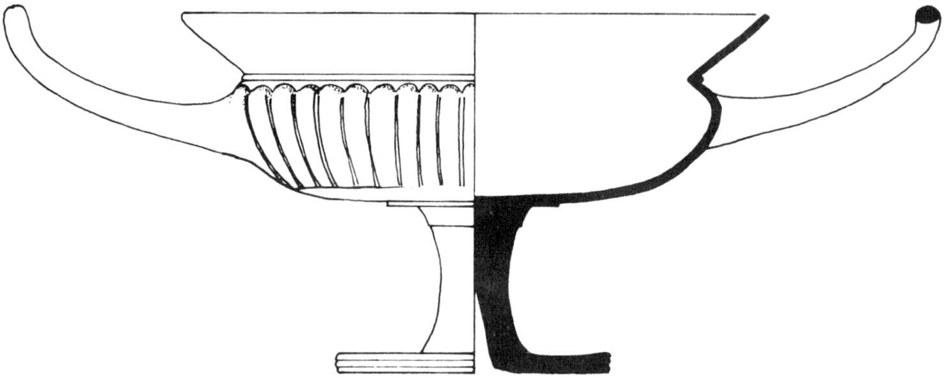

Figure 9. Attic black-glazed acrocup. 5th century B.C. Ht. 7.5cm. Ashmolean Museum, 1917.63.

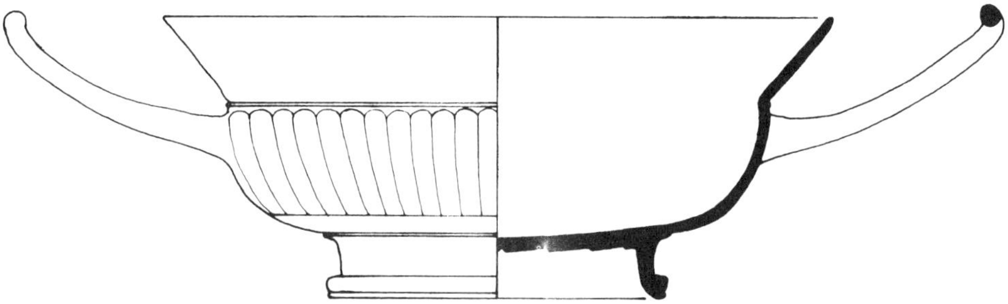

Figure 10. Attic black-glazed stemless cup. 5th century B.C. Ht. 5.9cm. Greek Museum, Newcastle upon Tyne, 642.

palmettes and ovules.[25] Both silver Rheneia cups have the later profile with the handles mounted on the bowl rather than on the lip. Sparkes and Talcott have pointed out that in itself the Duvanli cup does not provide evidence that there was a metal prototype for the clay version (**Fig. 13**).[26] Yet the forerunners of Rheneia cups were the coral red stemlesses of the class of Agora P10359, which may have been imitating gold cups captured during the Persian wars.[27] A related shape, the coral red, horizontally ribbed phiale, has been seen by Shefton as an imitation of Persian metalwork as it appears in the Persepolis frieze.[28] The present writer has shown that Rheneia cups were produced in the same workshops as bolsals, which are now known to have a metal prototype.[29]

25. For stamped Rheneia cups: Sparkes & Talcott (1970), 100-1; Gill (1984), 105.

26. Sparkes & Talcott (1970), 101.

27. For the coral red stemlesses: Sparkes & Talcott (1970), 99-100. Some appear in the upper fill of the Rectangular Rock-cut Shaft in the Agora which has now been shown to be a homogeneous deposit dumped after the Persian destruction of Athens; cf. Francis & Vickers (1982); Francis & Vickers (forthcoming).

28. This is conveniently illustrated by Shefton (1971), pl.20, figs.1-2.

29. Gill (1984), 105. The bronze bolsal is Amsterdam 10555; cf. Gill (1984), 103.

The cup-skyphos is another silver shape which has close parallels in the pottery and bronze workshops.[30] A silver example comes from the palace of Vouni on Cyprus, which was abandoned in the early fourth century (**Fig. 14**).[31] It has a steep wall which turns out slightly at the top, and two, high-rising U-shaped handles. The lower part of the foot is lipped with a thicker upper member and a thinner lower one. This shape was extremely popular in both the Attic and South Italian fictile workshops (**Fig. 15**) and we may presume that they were both using silver cup-skyphoi as prototypes. Very close in profile to the Vouni cup-skyphos is an Attic example from Marion on Cyprus, and several were found in the Thespian Polyandrion of 424, although the shape continued to be produced down to the second quarter of the fourth century.[32] Fictile cup-skyphoi are usually decorated with stamped and incised decorations which have a direct parallel in the bronze cup-skyphos from Bulgaria.[33] A possible name for the shape in antiquity was *kylix*, as is suggested by a graffito on an example in Zurich.[34] A second silver cup-skyphos from Nymphaion (**Fig. 16**) differs from the Vouni one by having an inset lip.[35] The underside is decorated with a centring mark and three concentric tooled ridges. This feature is aped on fictile vases throughout the fifth century and into the fourth. Before we leave the cup-skyphoi we should consider the values of silver and fictile examples. The Vouni cup-skyphos was worth 44 drachmae and one obol (191 g) in bullion value, and the Nymphaion one 66 drachmae and five obols (289 g). A fictile example from Nola now in the Louvre carries the graffito "twenty-five vases for sixteen drachmae" (**Fig. 17**), or five obols each, and thus we may obtain simple ratios of 1:53 and 1:80 between clay and silver.[36] Although Vickers has suggested that the clay to silver ratio may actually be as high as 1:1,000, the overall impression of a large difference between the values of the two media remains unchanged.[37]

30. Silver: Oxford 1885.485, from Nymphaion, Strong (1966), pl.17, a; Oliver (1977), 31, no.6; Vickers (1979), 42, fig.9 and pl.13, a, and one from Vouni, Woodward (1929), 238, fig.6; Gjerstad *et al.* (1937), pls.90, 5 and 92, d. Bronze: Reggio no number, from Medma, and one from Bulgaria, Welkow (1940-2), 210, figs.292-3 and 211, fig.294. Clay: Sparkes & Talcott (1970), 110-1.

31. Woodward (1929), 238, fig.6; Gjerstad *et al.* (1937), pls.90, 5 and 92, d.

32. Marion: Gjerstad *et al.* (1935), pl.142, 5. Thespian Polyandrion: Schilardi (1977), pl.35. For a late example: Agora P8191 B12:5, Corbett (1955), 184, fig.3, 24 and pl.71, 24; Sparkes & Talcott (1970), fig.6, 605.

33. Welkow (1940-2), 210, figs.292-3 and 211, fig.294.

34. Zurich 2531: Isler (1973), pls.29, 71, 6 and 12, text fig.12, 3.

35. Oxford 1885.486: Strong (1966), pl.17, a; Oliver (1977), 31, no.6; Vickers (1979), 42, fig.9 and pl.13, a.

36. Paris, Louvre N1840; cf. Gill (1986).

37. The clay to silver ratio of 1:333 originally proposed by Vickers (1983b), 303, has now been amended, Vickers (1984), 90, n.26; Vickers (1985), 116.

An unusual silver shape is the perfume-pot from the Selenskaya tumulus in the Taman and now in Leningrad (**Fig. 18**).[38] It has a handle which is square in profile and on the body there is a jog on the shoulder. As Sparkes has pointed out, this corresponds almost exactly with a class of fictile perfume-pots from Panticapaion in the Crimea, and on Cyprus a complete piece from Marion (**Fig. 19**) and a fragment from Chytroi.[39] One, once in Berlin and now lost, was decorated in red-figure.[40] On all there is a jog on the shoulder. A date in the early fourth century seems likely.

So-called "Pheidias shaped" mugs are also found in silver and clay and one of the best silver examples comes from the Baschova mound at Duvanli (**Fig. 20**).[41] It has a double-rolled handle with shouldering and a concave neck with a distinct junction where it meets the plump body. The shoulder is left undecorated but the body is decorated with narrow ribbing closed at the top by arcs. There is a distinct foot. In the same tumulus was found a slightly larger fictile mug of exactly the same shape (**Fig. 21**).[42] At the junction of neck and shoulder there is a rope pattern and the vertical ribbing extends to the shoulder. So close are they that one might suspect the existence of a mixed batch of silver and clay mugs from the Ceramicus, an idea proposed by Johnston in his study of the commercial graffito on the underside of a silver mug from Dalboki.[43] Other silver mugs of this shape are known from the Mogilanska mound near Vratsa, Boukyovtsi, and Paterno in Sicily (**Figs. 22-23**).[44] In addition there are numerous bronze mugs. Two replica, fictile "Pheidias shapes" mugs, one in Newcastle (**Fig. 24**) and the other in Reggio from Locri, are carefully decorated with moulded ribbing, closed at the top by arcs.[45] Shefton had seen this decoration as a fictile example of the thericleian technique and a "conscious and intended challenge to the oriental and luxury vases in precious metal".[46] He has noted that the ribbing is particularly close to that found on a silver kantharos in Leningrad (**Fig. 25**).[47] A further link

38. Leningrad Sel.39: Pharmakowsky (1913), 186, fig.16; Sparkes (1977), pl.9, 6.

39. Olynthus: Robinson (1933), pl.171, 798. Chauchitza: London 1919.11-19.184, Bailey (1969), 22, fig.1 and 23, fig.2, A1. Panticapaion: Leningrad B2219, Sparkes (1977), pl.7, 2-3. Marion: Cambridge GR 103.1890, Lamb (1930), pl.41, 279, 1. Chytroi: Oxford 1960.685. Hayes (1984), 74 under no.123, has also realized the close relationship between fictile and metal perfume-pots in the later fourth century B.C.

40. Beazley (1927-8), 213.

41. Plovdiv 1518: Filow (1934), 67, fig.84; Strong (1966), 84 and pl.17, b; Weber (1983), 451, C.II.17.

42. Plovdiv 1530: Filow (1934), 78, fig.100.

43. Johnston (1978), 79.

44. Mogilanska mound: Vratsa B.392, Nikolov (1967), 14, fig.4; Weber (1983), 451, C.II.18. Boukyovtsi: Sofia 6695, Cologne (1979), 131, no.265. Paterno: Berlin, 30 199, Mallwitz & Schiering (1964), 172, fig.47 and 175, fig.50; Oliver (1977), 58-9, no.25; Weber (1983), 450, C.II.12.

45. Newcastle 160, Shefton (1971), pl.21, fig.8, a-b and Reggio T.83, from Locri.

46. Shefton (1971), 110.

47. Strong (1966), pl.26, a; Shefton (1971), pl.21, fig.7.

ure 11. Silver Rheneia cup from Duvanli. 5th century B.C. Ht. cm. Plovdiv, 1516. (After Filow.)

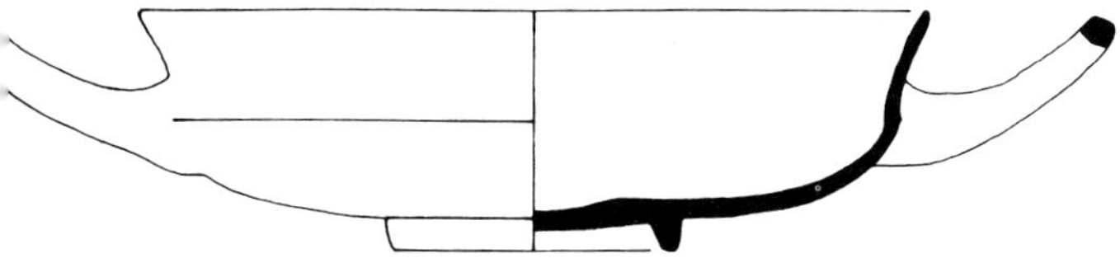

ure 13. Attic black-glazed Rheneia cup from Camarina. 5th cen-y B.C. Ht. 3.6cm. Museo Nazionale, Syracuse, 22936.

Figure 12. Incised tondo showing Selene on a horse on a silver Rheneia cup from Duvanli. 5th century B.C. Plovdiv, 1516. (After Filow.)

between fictile and metal mugs appears on a small class of "Pheidias shaped" mugs which are decorated on their walls with vertical petal-shaped ribbing.[48] They were produced in the last quarter of the fifth century. Corbett has made an important observation on the ribbing technique, that:

" ...the deeper segmentations of our vases involved an actual bending of the wall of the pot. Such ribbing increases the strength of a metal vase, but is a source of weakness in pottery; on many of the Agora examples the fabric has cracked on the inside along the lines of division between the ribs.[49] "

Two silver beakers and one silver mug come from Dalboki in Thrace and are now in Oxford (**Fig. 26**).[50] The mug has a wall which is in a continuous curve with a slightly concave neck, out-turned rim and a single loop handle hammered on to the rim. It has a flat bottom which protrudes around the base and at the centre there is a hole which must be original. Vickers has suggested that it may be for a rivet holding a base-plate in place. Fictile imitations are found on Siana cups. Brijder has stated that:

" ...the spike...is reminiscent of the nail driven through the centre of the bottom of the bowl and the ceiling of the foot in order to fix two parts of metal

48. e.g. Agora P10980 B 15:1, Corbett (1949), pl.93, 81, Agora P18288 B 19:12, Sparkes & Talcott (1958), fig.25 bottom right; Sparkes & Talcott (1970), pl.11, 215 and London 1978.1-21.60.

49. Corbett (1949), 333.

50. The silver mug is Oxford 1948.104: Prochorov (1880); Ashmolean Museum (1951), pl.50; Strong (1966), 85 and pl.18, b; British Museum (1976), 95, no.551; Oliver (1977), 30, no.5; Johnston (1978), 79-80; Weber (1983), 453 C.III 1. The two beakers are Oxford 1948.102 and 1948.103: Strong (1966), pl.18; British Museum (1976), 95, nos.549 and 550.

Figure 14. Silver cup-skyphos from Vouni. 5th century B.C. (After Gjerstad.)

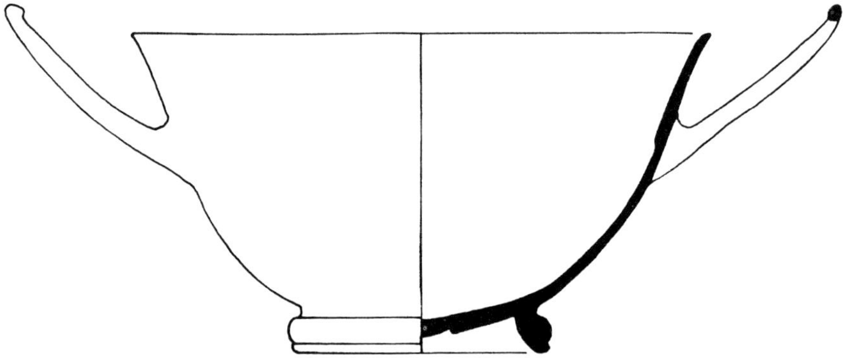

Figure 15. Local black-glazed cup-skyphos from Lipari Islands. 5th century B.C. Ht. 6.0cm. Ashmolean Museum, 1945.56.

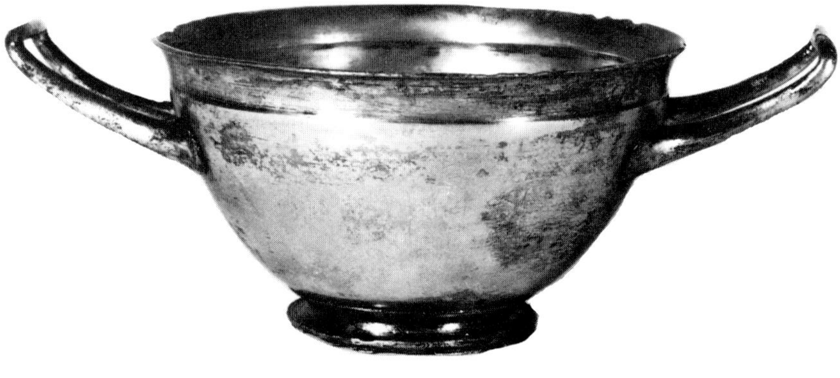

Figure 16. Silver cup-skyphos from Nymphaion. 5th century B.C. Ht. 5.6cm Ashmolean Museum, 1885.486.

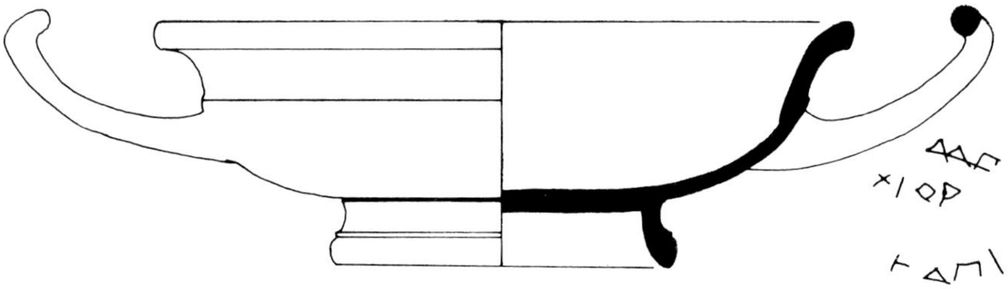

Figure 17. Attic black-glazed cup-skyphos and commercial graffito from Nola. 5th century B.C. Ht. 5.4cm. Louvre, N1840.

cups together.[51] " He also draws attention to a silver cup with a rosette in the centre of the floor, which he has compared to the painted tondos.[52] On the base of the Dalboki mug is the graffito *SKY* which has suggested that *skyphos* was the name for this shape in antiquity. The mug has been compared to its fictile counterparts and Scribner, commenting on a fictile example in Pittsburgh, has suggested an "imitation of metalware".[53] On fictile mugs of this shape the handle is usually mounted slightly below the rim, although one from Camarina and now in Syracuse (**Fig. 27**) has it mounted at the rim, as on the silver example.[54] The beakers have fictile parallels. One South Italian beaker from Nola and now in the Louvre (**Fig. 28**) has a plain wall decorated with impressed ovules and lines, and an Attic example in Carlsruhe (**Fig. 29**) has horizontal concave ribbing on the body, below which is a stamped frieze of meander separated by a saltire.[55] Shefton has seen possible Achaemenid influence on the Carlsruhe mug, and the ribbing is found not only on those portrayed on the Persepolis frieze, but also on a silver beaker from Boukyovtsi in Thrace (**Fig. 30**), which has a fillet of gold below the ribbing and on the lip a lotus and palmette frieze in gold-figure.[56] Similar horizontal, concave ribbing is also found on lower and broader mugs.[57]

A further shape to consider is the one-handled silver sessile kantharos from the Solokha tumulus near Melitopol (**Fig. 31**).[58] The lower body is ribbed and on the upper body a ritual scene and a frieze of ivy leaves are incised. Fictile versions of the shape are usually decorated with stamped patterns, three with figured scenes: two of these are replicas, one probably from Campania (**Fig. 32**) and the other from Pithecusae, with horses, and one from Perachora has a lion.[59] From graffiti on fictile versions of the shape we learn that its name in antiquity was the *karchesion*, a vase known in silver from the Acropolis inventories.[60]

A class of important luxury vases were the thericleians which are especially well attested in the writers of Middle Comedy. Shefton has done important work on the type, although a discrepancy appears to be growing between the literary and archaeological evidence which deserves some

51. Brijder (1983), 35 and n.139.

52. Brijder (1983), 36-7; Guzzo (1973), 58.

53. Scribner (1937), 346, no.6.

54. Syracuse 24007, from Camarina, 897.

55. Paris, Louvre N1947. Carlsruhe B881: Hafner (1951), pl.34, 332, 11.

56. Shefton (1971), 109. Sofia 6694, from Boukyovtsi: British Museum (1976), no.266, colour plate; Cologne (1979), 31, no.264.

57. e.g. Carlsruhe B882 and B889, Hafner (1951), pl.34, 332, 12-13, Lecce 2003, Bernardini (n.d.), pl.68, 8 and Oxford 1966.345, Ashmolean Museum (1967), pl.55, 393.

58. Strong (1966), pl.16, b.

59. Stamped horses: Newcastle 58, Sparkes (1968), 6, figs.5 and 6, pls.2, 4 and 8, 4 and its replica reported by Shefton. The one from Perachora is Dunbabin (1962), pl.151, 3861; Sparkes (1968), pls.3, 4 and 8, 4.

60. Boardman (1979), 150, n.1; Johnston (1979), 63, n.13. They appear in Acropolis inventories of 398/7, Köhler (1883), 649, 12 and 390/89, Köhler (1883), 660, 22-3.

comment.[61] As Athenaeus stated that Thericles, the creator of this type of vase, was a potter who came from Corinth and was active at the time of Aristophanes,[62] Shefton suggested that if we wish to identify thericleians then we should look at fictile vases. Following Pfuhl, he suggested that thericleians were linked with the ribbed "garland" kraters, hydriae and pelikai, now studied by Kopcke.[63]

Thericleians are usually recorded as being in luxury materials. Theophrastus, writing towards the end of the fourth century, records thericleians made from terebinth wood.[64] Pliny records that this wood was highly prized in antiquity.[65] It comes from the turpentine tree which is short-boled and up to five metres in diameter. The thericleians would have been made from the dark heart-wood. To obtain usable amounts of this commodity the trees must be cultivated for long periods of time in dry conditions—the slower the growth, the darker the wood—but even then a large tree may have little dark wood at the core. Thus terebinth wood was in short supply and became an expensive item. Cicero records that the silver thericleians in the possession of a man called Diodorus from Malta were coveted by Verres.[66] Plutarch records that Philopoemen of Megalopolis (c.253-182), to restrain the luxurious habits of his troops, had thericleians broken up in the workshops and breastplates gilded, and shields and bridles silvered, with the proceeds.[67] Although the usual colour of thericleians was black, Callixenus records gold ones in the Grand Procession of Ptolemy Philadelphus and Istrus, a pupil of Callimachus, speaks of gilded thericleians which may have had a wooden core.[68] Such valuable thericleians appear among the luxury vases in the triumph of Aemilius Paulus over Perseus, King of Macedon, after the victory at Pydna in 168.[69] Timaeus, writing at the end of the fourth or early third century, talks about an embassy from Taormina, including Polyxenus, who returned from Nicodemus with various gifts

61. Shefton (1971), 109-111; Shefton (forthcoming). The latter will be based on a paper delivered at the 1984 Amsterdam Symposium on Ancient Greek and Related Pottery. I am grateful to Brian Shefton for discussing these vases with me.

62. Ath. xi.470.f.

63. Pfuhl (1923), i. 46; Kopcke (1964).

64. Theophr.*Hist.Pl.* v.iii.2. Meiggs (1982), 298, disputes these references and suggests that such cups originated in Syria. For terebinth wood in antiquity: Wissowa (1934), 577-81. For the species: Zohary (1952); Tabatabai (1966); Yaltırık (1967); Huxley & Taylor (1977), 101; Sfikas (1978), 118, 101. I am grateful to the Commonwealth Forestry Institute, Oxford for giving me access to their collection of wood samples, and to Kathryn Gleason, Ian Gourlay and Michael Vickers for discussing the nature of the wood with me.

65. Pliny *HN* xvi.lxxvi.205.

66. Cic. *Verr.* II.iv.18.38.

67. Plut. *Phil.* ix.5.

68. Ath. xi.472.a; Callixenus 199.b, (=Ath. v.199.b; cf. Rice (1983), 73-4 and n.114); Istrus 47 (=Ath. xi.478.b). The Istrus fragment refers to pairs of vases which are often found in the archaeological record; cf. Sparkes & Talcott (1970), 13, n.19; Gill & Tomlinson (1985), 116, n.10.

69. Plut. *Aem.* xxxiii.2.

Figure 18. Silver perfume-pot from Selenskaya. 4th century B.C. Ht. 7.4cm. Hermitage Museum, Sel.39. (After Sparkes.)

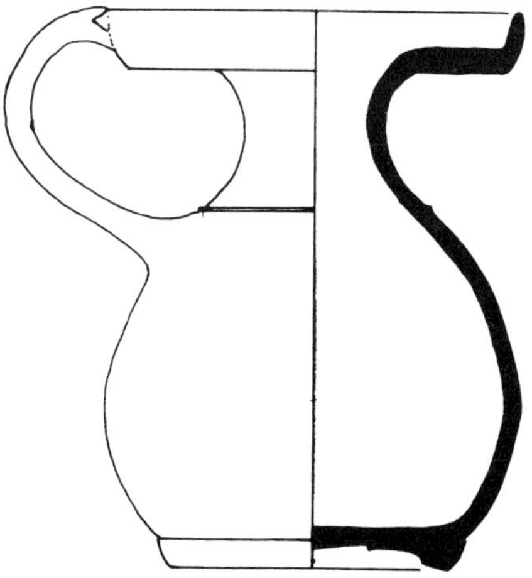

Figure 19. Attic black-glazed perfume-pot from Marion. 5th century B.C. Ht. 9.3cm. Fitzwilliam Museum, GR 103.1890.

including a thericleian kylix.[70] It is unlikely to have been a cheap terracotta one, and we may assume that it was valuable.

There are few instances of fictile thericleians in the literary sources. Theophilus, writing at the end of the fourth century and almost a century after thericleians were introduced, writes of a four kotylai thericleian potted of clay.[71] Eubulus in the *Kampylion* suggests that thericleians could be made of clay, but in the *Dolon* the crockery is contrasted with the thericleian kylices, which suggests that they were in another, presumably precious, material.[72] Theophrastus puts the right emphasis on fictile thericleians by stating that they were clever imitations of the ones made in terebinth wood.[73] One of the best observations on the relationship between metal and fictile thericleians has been made by Miller that:

" ...these cups [thericleians], highly prized by connoisseurs and by those who could afford to own them, gave rise to manifold imitations of them in clay; and that from these imitations, also called Thericleian, later writers spoke of Thericles as a potter, although his own art was exercised not at all in the field of ceramics but confined exclusively to that of toreutics.[74] "

The lack of evidence for thericleians in the archaeological record is partly due to the fact that they were luxury vases: the terebinth wood has rotted and the metal melted down and re-used. All we are left with are the considerably cheaper fictile vases, although literary sources show that they were considered

70. Timaeus 135 (=Ath. xi.471.f).

71. Theophilus 2 (=Ath. xi.472.d; Kock (1884), 473).

72. Eubulus 43 (=Ath. xi.471.e; Kock (1884), 179); Eubulus 31 (=Ath. xi.471.c-d; Kock (1884), 175).

73. Theophr. *Hist.Pl.* v.iii.2.

74. Miller (1921), 130.

Figure 20. Silver mug from Duvanli. 5th century B.C. Ht. 8.6cm. Plovdiv, 1518. (After Filow.)

Figure 21. Attic black-glazed mug from Duvanli. 5th century B.C. Ht. 13.3cm. Plovdiv, 1530. (After Filow.

Figure 22. Silver mug from Boukyovtsi. 5th century B.C. Ht. 8.6cm. Archaeological Museum, Sofia, 6695.

Figure 23. Silver mug from Paterno. 5th century B.C. Ht. 7.7cm. Staatliche Museen Antikenabteilung, Berlin, 30 19(
(After Oliver.)

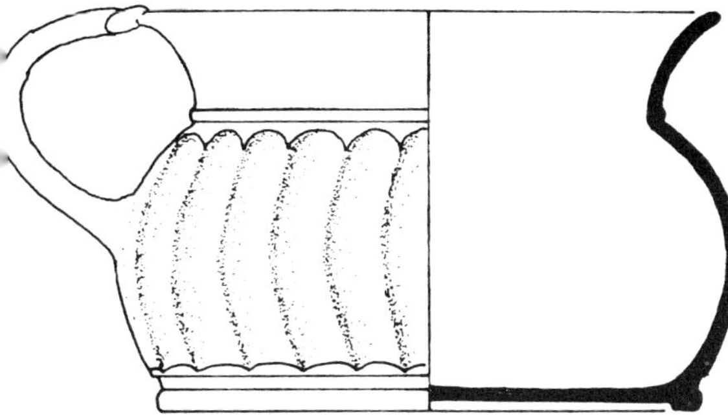

igure 24. Attic black-glazed mug. 5th century B.C. Ht. 8cm. Greek Museum, Newcastle upon Tyne, 160.

igure 25. Silver kantharos. 4th century B.C. Ht. 22cm. ermitage Museum. (After Strong.)

to be thericleians in their own right. Such fictile thericleians have been identified at Kafizin on Cyprus, where three black-glazed kantharoi, and possibly a lagynos, were all inscribed *thyreikleion* by officials of a flax company in the last quarter of the third century.[75] All are locally made and the kantharoi are decorated with heavy vertical ribbing on the lower body and equipped with double handles which are looped at the top and touch the slightly projecting rim. Each has a slightly concave and deep neck.

Many Attic fictile shapes have close parallels in the extant metalwork and the points of contact may be shown by profile, technique, finish and even figured decoration. Often the extant metalwork is not as early as the earliest fictile vases; yet this should not rule out possibilities of metal prototypes, as after all it is rare for a society to copy cheap objects in more costly materials. Old-fashioned or worn plate would be melted down and re-worked—indestructible pottery could only be placed in the grave or thrown away. The 1984 Amsterdam Symposium on Ancient Greek and Related Pottery confirmed that we live in a post-Beazley age and we must reconsider our approach to pottery studies.[76] The widespread distribution of Attic

75. Mitford (1980), 29-32, nos.40-42, (kantharoi) and 35-6, no.46, (lagynos).

76. Brijder (1984), 6.

Figure 26. Silver mug and beakers from Dalboki. 5th century B.C. Ht. 9cm. (mug), 11.3cm and 12.5cm. (beakers). Ashmolean Museum, 1948.102 (beaker), 103 (beaker) and 104 (mug).

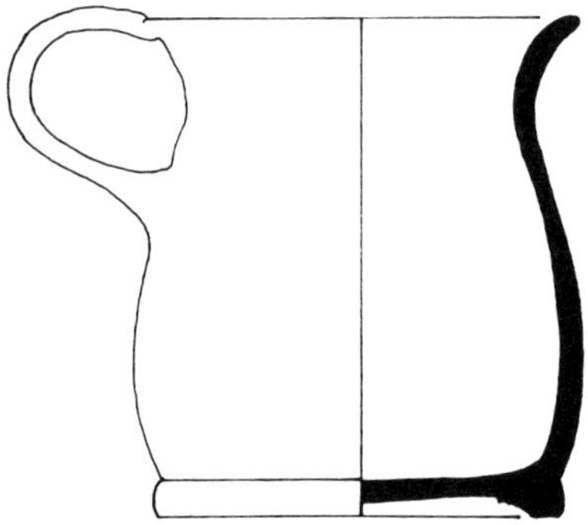

Figure 27. Attic black-glazed mug from Camarina. 5th century B.C. Ht. 6.9cm. Museo Nazionale, Syracuse, 24007.

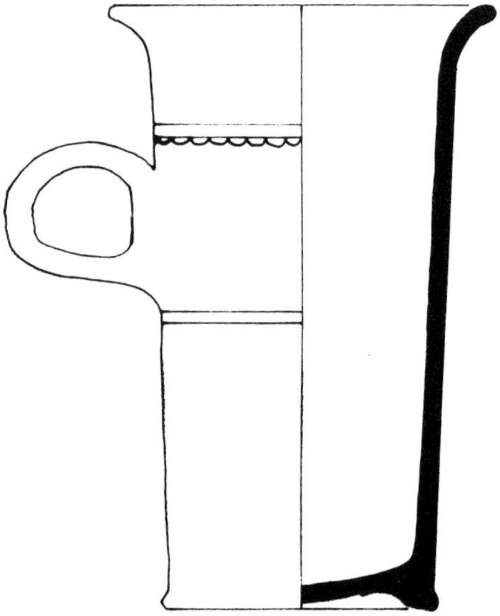

Figure 28. South Italian black-glazed beaker from Nola. 5th century B.C. Ht. 11.7cm. Louvre, N1947.

Figure 29. Attic black-glazed beaker. 5th century B.C. Ht. 9cm. Badisches Landesmuseum, Carlsruhe, B881. (After Hafner.)

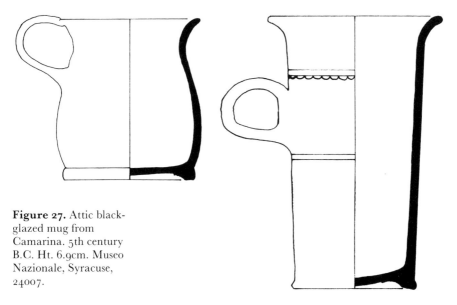

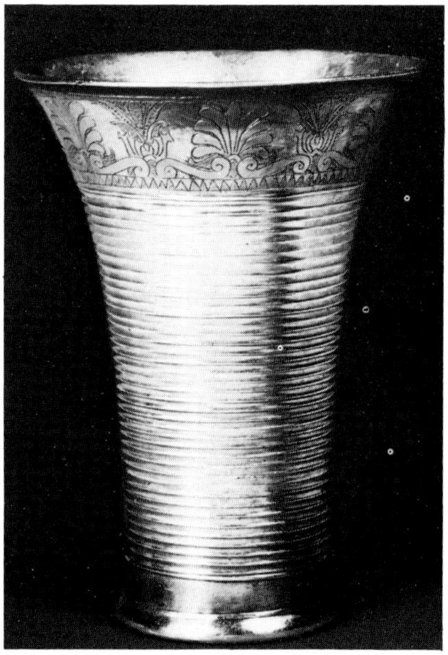

Figure 30. Silver beaker with gold-figure decoration from Boukyovtsi. 4th century B.C. Ht. 12.2cm. Archaeological Museum, Sofia, 6694.

Figure 31. Silver sessile kantharos from Solokha. 5th century B.C. Ht. 9.8cm. Hermitage Museum.

Figure 32. Attic black-glazed sessile kantharos with figured decoration. 5th century B.C. Ht. 9.7cm. Greek Museum, Newcastle upon Tyne, 58. (After Sparkes.)

pottery throughout the regions bordering the Mediterranean and Black Sea does not need to mean the export of a valuable commodity. One of the few mentions of the pottery trade in the literary sources is in pseudo-Scylax, where Phoenicians are recorded operating a method of exchange on the Atlantic coast of Africa.[77] Pottery was exported with more profitable cargoes, as can be seen, for example, in the Porticello wreck.[78] As Fulford has pointed out, the value of pottery lies in its being seen as an indicator of trade, and indeed there is:

" . . .no evidence that so-called fine wares were traded long distances on their own—rather they occur as space-fillers in more valuable cargoes.[79] " Pottery was cheap and its virtual absence from the literary records should warn us against giving it too exalted a place in Antiquity and especially at Athens, which was at times a very wealthy society having access not only to the Laurium silver mines, but also the wealth of an Empire.

Acknowledgements: I am grateful to Dr Michael Fulford, Prof. Brian Shefton and Mr Michael Vickers for their help and advice in the preparation of this paper.

77. Pseudo-Scylax 112: Müller (1882), 94.

78. Owen (1970); Owen (1971); Eiseman (1979).

79. Fulford (1980), 69; cf. Fulford (1984).

Bibliography

Ashmolean Museum (1951) — Ashmolean Museum, *Department of Antiquities, Summary Guide*, Oxford, 1951.

Ashmolean Museum (1967)	Ashmolean Museum, *Select Exhibition of Sir John and Lady Beazley's Gifts, 1912-1966*, London, 1967.
Bailey (1969)	Bailey, D.M., "Some Grave Groups from Chauchitza in Macedonia", *Opuscula Atheniensia*, 9, 1969, pp.21-40.
Beazley (1927)	Beazley, J.D., *Corpus Vasorum Antiquorum Great Britain, Oxford, Ashmolean Museum*, 1, (3), Oxford 1927.
Beazley (1927-8)	Beazley, J.D., "Aryballos", *Annual of the British School at Athens*, 29, 1927-8, pp.187-215.
Beazley (1963)	Beazley, J.D., *Attic Red-Figure Vase-Painters*, Oxford, 1963.
Beazley (1971)	Beazley, J.D., *Paralipomena*, Oxford, 1971.
Bentley (1883)	Bentley, R., *Dissertations upon the Epistles of Phalaris, Themistocles, Socrates, Euripides, and the Fables of Aesop*, London, 1883.
Bernand (1970)	Bernand, A., *Le Delta Egyptien d'Après les Textes Grecs*, i, 2, Cairo, 1970.
Bernardini (n.d.)	Bernardini, M., *Vasi dello Stile di Gnathia, Vasi a Vernice Nera*, Bari, n.d.
Boardman (1979)	Boardman, J., "The Karchesion of Herakles", *Journal of Hellenic Studies*, 99, 1979, pp.149-51.
von Bothmer (1984)	von Bothmer, D., "A Greek and Roman Treasury", *Bulletin of the Metropolitan Museum of Art*, 42, 1, 1984.
Brijder (1983)	Brijder, H.A.G., *Siana Cups I and Komast Cups, Allard Pierson Series*, iv, Amsterdam, 1983.
Brijder (1984)	Brijder, H.A.G., *Ancient Greek and Related Pottery, Proceedings of the International Vase Symposium in Amsterdam 12-15 April 1984, Allard Pierson Series*, v, Amsterdam, 1984.
British Museum (1976)	British Museum, *Thracian Treasures from Bulgaria*, London, 1976.
Caskey & Beazley (1963)	Caskey, L.D. and Beazley, J.D., *Attic Vase Paintings in the Museum of Fine Arts, Boston*, iii, Oxford, 1963.
Coldstream (1970)	Coldstream, J.N., "Motya: La Ceramica Greca", *Notizie degli Scavi di Antichità*, 1970, pp.580-2.
Cologne (1979)	Exhibition Catalogue, Cologne *Gold der Thraker. Archäologische Schätze aus Bulgarien*, Mainz, 1979.
Corbett (1949)	Corbett, P.E., "Attic Pottery of the Later Fifth Century from the Athenian Agora", *Hesperia*, 18, 1949, pp.298-345.
Corbett (1955)	Corbett, P.E., "Palmette Stamps from an Attic Black-Glaze Workshop", *Hesperia*, 24, 1955, pp.172-86.
Dunbabin (1962)	Dunbabin T.J., *Perachora*, ii, *The Sanctuaries of Hera Akraia and Limenia, 1930-1933*, Oxford, 1962.
Edgar (1898-9)	Edgar, C.C., "The Inscribed and Painted Pottery" in D.G. Hogarth, "Excavations at Naucratis", *Annual of the British School at Athens*, 5, 1898-9, pp.47-65.
Eiseman (1979)	Eiseman, C.J., *The Porticello Shipwreck: a Mediterranean Merchant Vessel of 415-385 B.C.*, Ann Arbor, 1979.
Filow (1934)	Filow, B.D., *Die Grabhügelnekropole bei Duvanlij in Südbulgarien*, Sofia, 1934.
Filow & Welkow (1930)	Filow, B., and Welkow, I., "Grabhügelfunde aus Duvanlii in Südbulgarien", *Jahrbuch des deutschen archäologischen Instituts*, 45, 1930, pp.281-322.

Francis & Vickers (1982)	Francis, E.D., and Vickers M., "Kaloi, Ostraca and the Wells of Athens", *American Journal of Archaeology*, 86, 1982, p.264.
Francis & Vickers (forthcoming)	Francis, E.D., and Vickers M., "The Agora Revisited", (forthcoming).
Fulford (1980)	Fulford, M.G., "Carthage: Overseas Trade and the Political Economy, c.A.D. 400-700", *Reading Medieval Studies*, 6, 1980, pp.68-80.
Fulford (1984)	Fulford, M.G., "Berenice and the Economy of Cyrenaica", *Libyan Studies*, 15, 1984, pp.161-3.
Gebauer & Johannes (1937)	Gebauer, K. and Johannes, H., "Ausgrabungen im Kerameikos", *Archäologischer Anzeiger*, 1937, pp.184-203.
Gill (1984)	Gill, D.W.J., "The Workshops of the Attic Bolsal" in Brijder (1984), pp.102-6.
Gill (1986)	Gill, D.W.J., "Two Herodotean Dedications from Naucratis", *Journal of Hellenic Studies*, 106, 1986, (forthcoming).
Gill (1987)	Gill, D.W.J., "Two New Silver Shapes from Semibratny", *Annual of the British School at Athens*, 82, (1987) (forthcoming).
Gill & Tomlinson (1985)	Gill, D.W.J., and Tomlinson R.A., "Two Type B Skyphoi in Birmingham", *Annual of the British School at Athens*, 80, 1985, pp.115-8.
Gjerstad *et al.* (1935)	Gjerstad, E., Lindros, J., Sjoqvist, E., and Westholm, A., *The Swedish Cyprus Expedition, Finds and Results of the Excavations in Cyprus*, ii, Stockholm 1935.
Gjerstad *et al.* (1935)	Gjerstad, E., Lindros, J., Sjoqvist, E., and Westholm, A., *The Swedish Cyprus Expedition, Finds and Results of the Excavations in Cyprus*, iii, Stockholm, 1937.
Gorbunova (1971)	Gorbunova, K.S., "Engraved Silver Kylikes from the Semibratny Barrows", *Kultura e Iskusstvo Antichnogo Mira*, Leningrad, 1971, pp.18-38 and p.123.
Green (1972)	Green J.R., "Oinochoe", *Bulletin of the Institute of Classical Studies*, 19, 1972, pp.1-16.
Guzzo (1973)	Guzzo, P.G., "Coppe Ioniche in Bronzo" *Mélanges de l'Ecole Française de Rome, Antiquité*, 85, 1973, pp.55-64.
Hafner (1951)	Hafner, G., *Corpus Vasorum Antiquorum Deutschland, Karlsruhe, Badisches Landesmuseum*, 1, (7), Munich, 1951.
Hayes (1984)	Hayes, J.W., *Greek and Italian Black-Gloss Wares and Related Wares in the Royal Ontario Museum: A Catalogue*, Toronto, 1984.
Hill (1947)	Hill, D.K., "The Technique of Greek Metal Vases and its Bearing on Vase Forms in Metal and Pottery", *American Journal of Archaeology*, 51, 1947, pp.248-56.
Hughes & Parsons (1984)	Hughes, D., and Parsons, P.J., *Oxyrhynchus Papyri*, 52, 1984.
Huxley & Taylor (1977)	Huxley, A. and Taylor, W., *Flowers of Greece and the Aegean*, London, 1977.
Isler (1973)	Isler, H.P., *Corpus Vasorum Antiquorum Schweiz, Zürich, Öffentliche Sammlungen*, Bern, 1973.

Isserlin *et al.* (1962-3)	Isserlin, B.S.J., MacNamara, E., Coldstream, J.N., Pike, G., du Plat Taylor, J., Snodgrass, A.M., "Motya, a Phoenician-Punic Site near Marsala, Sicily", *Annual of the Leeds University Oriental Society*, 4, 1962-3, pp.84-131.
Johnston (1978)	Johnston, A.W., "Some non-Greek Ghosts", *Bulletin of the Institute of Classical Studies*, 25, 1978, pp.79-84.
Johnston (1979)	Johnston A.W., *Trademarks on Greek Vases*, Warminster, 1979.
Jully (1983)	Jully, J.J., *Céramiques Grecques ou de Type Grec et autres Céramiques en Languedoc Méditerranéen, Roussillon et Catalogne*, ii, 1, Paris, 1983.
Karo (1943)	Karo, G., *An Attic Cemetery*, Philadelphia, 1943.
Kock (1884)	Kock, T., *Comicorum Atticorum Fragmenta*, ii, Leipzig, 1884.
Köhler (1883)	Köhler, U., *Inscriptiones Atticae aetatis quae est inter Euclidis annum et Augusti temporam, Inscriptiones Graecae*, ii, 2, Berlin, 1883.
Kopcke (1964)	Kopcke, G., "Golddekorierte attische Schwarzfirniskeramik des vierten Jahrhunderts v.chr.", *Athenische Mitteilungen*, 79, 1964, pp.22-84.
Krauskopf (1984)	Krauskopf, I., "Terrakotta-Imitationen der Bronzekannen der Form Beazley VI in Athen, Westgriechenland und Etruria" in Brijder (1984), pp.83-7.
Lamb (1930)	Lamb, W., *Corpus Vasorum Antiquorum Great Britain, Cambridge, Fitzwilliam Museum*, 1, (6), Oxford, 1930.
Lordkipanidze (1971)	Lordkipanidze, O., "La Civilisation de l'Ancienne Colchide aux Ve-IVe Siècles (à la Lumière des Plus Récentes Découvertes Archéologiques)", *Revue Archéologique*, 1971, pp.259-88.
Mallwitz & Schiering (1964)	Mallwitz, A., and Schiering, W., *Die Werkstatt des Pheidias in Olympia, Olympische Forschungen*, v, Berlin, 1964.
Meiggs (1982)	Meiggs, R., *Trees and Timber in the Ancient Mediterranean World*, Oxford, 1982.
Miller (1921)	Miller, W., "Thericles, Potter, in the Light of the Greek Drama", *Transactions of the American Philological Association*, 52, 1921, pp.119-31.
Mitford (1980)	Mitford, T.B., *The Nymphaeum of Kafizin, Kadmos*, Berlin/New York, 1980.
Müller (1882)	Müller, C., *Geographi Graeci Minores*, i, Paris, 1882.
Nikolov (1967)	Nikolov, B., "Tombe III du Tumulus di 'Mogilanska Mogila' près de Vraca", *Arkeologia*, 9, 1967, pp.11-8.
Noble (1965)	Noble, J.V., *Techniques of Painted Attic Pottery*, New York, 1965.
Oliver (1977)	Oliver, Jr., A., *Silver for the Gods: 800 Years of Greek and Roman Silver*, Toledo, 1977.
Owen (1970)	Owen, D.I., "Picking up the Pieces: the Salvage Excavations of a Looted Fifth Century B.C., Shipwreck in the Straits of Messina", *Expedition*, 13, 1, 1970, pp.24-29.
Owen (1971)	Owen, D.I., "Excavating a Classical Shipwreck", *Archaeology*, 24, 1971, pp.118-29.
Pfuhl (1923)	Pfuhl, E., *Malerei und Zeichnung der Griechen*, Munich, 1923.
Pharmakowsky (1910)	Pharmakowsky, B., "Archäologische Funde in Jahre 1909: Russland", *Archäologischer Anzeiger*, 1910, pp.178-234.

Pharmakowsky (1913) Pharmakowsky, B., "Archäologische Funde in Jahre 1912: Russland", *Archäologischer Anzeiger*, 1913, pp.195-244.

Pottier (1912) Pottier, E., "Thericleia Vasa" in C. Daremberg and M.E. Saglio, *Dictionnaire des Antiquités Grecques et Romaines d'Après les Textes et les Monuments*, Paris, 1912, vol.T-Z, pp.212-4.

Prochorov (1880) Prochorov, V., *Bulgarian Excavations in the Neighbourhood of Eski-Zagora*, St. Petersburg, 1880.

Ramage (1970) Ramage, N.H., "Studies in Early Etruscan Bucchero" *Papers of the British School at Rome*, 38, 1970, pp.1-61.

Rasmussen (1979) Rasmussen, T., *Bucchero Pottery from Southern Etruria*, Cambridge, 1979.

Reeder (1974) Reeder, E.D., *Clay Impressions from Attic Metalwork*, Ann Arbor, 1974.

Rice (1983) Rice, E.E., *The Grand Procession of Ptolemy Philadelphus*, Oxford, 1983.

Richter & Hall (1963) Richter, G.M.A., and Hall, L.F., *Red-Figured Athenian Vases in the Metropolitan Museum of Art*, New Haven, 1936.

Robinson (1933) Robinson, D.M., *Mosaics, Vases, and Lamps of Olynthus found in 1928 and 1931, Excavations at Olynthus*, v, Baltimore, 1933.

Rumpf (1953) Rumpf, A., *Malerei und Zeichung der Griechen*, Munich, 1953.

Schefold (1931) Schefold, K., "Attische Silberschale", *Römische Mitteilungen*, 46, 1931, pp.119-29.

Schilardi (1977) Schilardi, D.U., *The Thespian Polyandrion (424 B.C.): The Excavations and Finds from a Thespian State Burial*, PhD thesis, Princeton, 1977.

Scribner (1937) Scribner, H.S., *A Catalogue of the Spang Collection of Greek and Italian Vases and Etruscan Urns in the Carnegie Museum*, Pittsburgh, 1937.

Sfikas (1978) Sfikas, G., *Trees and Shrubs of Greece*, Athens, 1978.

Shefton (1971) Shefton, B.B., "Persian Gold and Attic Black Glaze, Achaemenid Influences on Attic Pottery of the 5th and 4th Centuries B.C.", *IXth International Congress of Classical Archaeology, Damascus 11-20 October 1969*, Damascus, 1971, pp.109-11.

Shefton (forthcoming) Shefton, B.B., "Therikleia", (forthcoming).

Sparkes (1968) Sparkes, B.A., "Black Perseus", *Antike Kunst*, 11, 1968, pp.3-16.

Sparkes (1977) Sparkes, B.A., "Quintain and the Talcott Class", *Antike Kunst*, 20, 1977, pp.8-25.

Sparkes & Talcott (1958) Sparkes, B.A. and Talcott, L., *Pots and Pans of Classical Athens, Agora Picture Book*, i, Princeton, 1958.

Sparkes & Talcott (1970) Sparkes, B.A. and Talcott, L., *Black and Plain Pottery of the 6th, 5th and 4th Centuries B.C., Athenian Agora*, xii, Princeton, 1970.

Strong (1966) Strong, D.E., *Greek and Roman Gold and Silver Plate*, London, 1966.

Tabatabai (1966) Tabatabai, M., *Pistachio and its Importance in Iran*, Tehran, 1966.

Vickers (1979) Vickers, M., *Scythian Treasures in Oxford*, Oxford, 1979.

Vickers (1983a) Vickers, M., "Les Vases Peints: Image ou Mirage?" in F. Lissarague and F. Thelamon, *Image et Céramique Grecque. Actes du Colloque de Rouen 25-26 Novembre 1982*, Rouen, 1983, pp.29-44.

Vickers (1983b) Vickers, M., review of R.D. Barnett, *Ancient Ivories in the Middle East*, *Burlington Magazine*, 1983, p.303.

Vickers (1984) Vickers, M., "The Influence of Exotic Materials on Attic White-Ground Pottery" in Brijder (1984), pp.88-97.

Vickers (1985) Vickers, M., "Artful Crafts: the Influence of Metalwork on Athenian Painted Pottery", *Journal of Hellenic Studies*, 105, 1985.

Weber (1983) Weber, T., *Bronzekannen. Studien zu ausgewählten archäischen und klassischen Oinochoenformen aus Metall in Griechenland und Etruria*, Frankfurt/Bern, 1983.

Webster (1939) Webster, T.B.L., "Tondo Composition in Greek Art", *Journal of Hellenic Studies*, 59, 1939, pp.103-23.

Wehgartner (1983) Wehgartner, I., *Attisch Weissgrundige Keramik*, Mainz, 1983.

Welkow (1940-2) Welkow, I., "Grabfund aus Belila", *Bulletin de l'Institut Archéologique Bulgare*, 14, 1940-2, pp.210-1.

Wissowa (1934) Wissowa, G., *Paulys Real-Encyclopädie der classisches Altertumwissenschaft*, Stuttgart, 1934.

Woodward (1929) Woodward, A.M., "Archaeology in Greece, 1928-1929", *Journal of Hellenic Studies*, 49, 1929, pp.220-39.

Yalouris *et al.* (1980) Yalouris, N., Andronikos, M., Rhomiopoulou, K., Herrmann, A., and Vermeule, C., *The Search for Alexander: An Exhibition*, New York, 1980.

Yaltırık (1967) Yaltırık, F., "Türkiye florası için yeni bir tür: *Pistacia eurycarpa* Yalt.", *Istanbul Üniversitesi Orman Fakültesi Dergisi*, 17, 1, 1967, pp.148-55.

Zohary (1952) Zohary, M., "A Monographical Study of the Genus *Pistachia*", *Palestine Journal of Botany Jerusalem Series*, 5, 1952, pp.187-228.

Züchner (1950-1) Züchner, W., "Von Toreuten und Topfern", *Jahrbuch des deutschen archäologischen Instituts*, 65-6, 1950-1, pp.175-205.

Tombs or Hoards: The Survival of Chinese Silver of the Tang and Song Periods, Seventh to Thirteenth Centuries A.D.

JESSICA RAWSON

In China gold and silver were used occasionally for eating and drinking vessels from at least the late fifth century B.C.; however, only from the Tang dynasty (A.D. 618-906) were cups and dishes quite frequently made of these precious metals. Several large Tang dynasty hoards of silver vessels have been excavated in recent years. These finds, together with excavated material from the succeeding centuries, are listed as an Appendix to the present article. The period covered includes the successor dynasties to the Tang: the Liao dynasty of the Khitan tribes ruling northern China (907-1125), and the minor dynasties, known as the Five Dynasties, who controlled the rest of the country in the tenth century. The Song dynasty was established in 960, but in 1126 was driven from the northern capital of Kaifeng by the Jurchen tribes. While the Song, now described as the Southern Song (1127-1279), re-established themselves at Hanghzou, the Jurchen took over the north as the Jin dynasty (1115-1234). Southern Song material is included in this account, but silver of the Jin has been excluded. Gold has not been separately considered as gold vessels are very rare.

Most of the excavated material has come from hoards, but a few burials that include silver vessels have also been found. A comparison of the numbers and types of silver found in these two different kinds of site contributes to our understanding of the status and role of silver in Chinese society. Further, the juxtaposition of the two materials in these few tombs is helpful in illuminating the relative positions of silver and ceramics. In the present account finds of silver ingots and of jewellery have been omitted.

Pre-Tang Production

The history of the use of silver in China is comparatively short and will be summarized here to provide a context for the dramatic increase in production under the Tang. During the Shang and Zhou periods (c.1700-221 B.C.), bronze and jade seem to have been regarded as the most precious materials, being employed for ritual vessels and for ceremonial discs, pendants and sceptres. At some periods lacquer may have been equally valued, but because it perishes easily its significance is probably often underestimated. From the Eastern Zhou period (770-221 B.C.) gold and silver were used as inlays, following perhaps the customs of the nomadic tribes on China's northern and western borders.[1] A cast gold dish and a cup from the fifth-century tomb of the Marquis Yi of Zeng, excavated at Sui Xian in Hubei province, are rare examples of vessels made of precious metal.[2] These pieces are probably not the survivors of a large industry. Their shapes, and in the case of the bowl or dish, the decoration, reflect bronze prototypes, suggesting that techniques of working gold or silver were not yet well developed in the fifth century.

Under the Han dynasty (206B.C. - A.D.220) there was a change of practice. Large numbers of Han period silvered bronze vessels decorated with gilded cloud scrolls were made. The silver background to the gold design suggests that these bronzes were substitutes for more expensive containers in silver. Three silver dishes have come from a pit adjacent to the tomb of one of the kings of the petty Qi state in present-day Shandong province, buried in the second century B.C. (**Fig. 1**).[3] These dishes, which are shallow, indeed almost flat, and have flat flanged lips, were the prototypes for bronze examples. Dishes of similar shape and decoration were also made in lacquer, and all were descended from bronze and pottery basins and dishes which had been in use in China for some centuries. On the other hand, a silver box found with the dishes exhibits distinctly foreign traits. It stands on a high foot and its lid is surmounted by three crouching animals (**Fig. 1**). Lobes around both the body and lid are reminiscent of the decoration of Achaemenid silver and must have been based upon a provincial Iranian model. This box is one of a number of silver pieces, excavated in recent years, that were imported into China or were made in China in imitation of foreign silverwork.

Foreign metalwork is especially associated with the period of the Northern Wei dynasty (A.D. 386-534). A bowl from an early sixth-century tomb of one Feng Hetu is decorated with a figure hunting a boar in a style that recalls

1. Contact with the metal-working practices of the nomadic peoples to the north and north-west of China is discussed by So (1980).

2. The gold vessels from the tomb of the Marquis Yi of Zeng are illustrated in Beijing (1980a), pls.94-6.

3. The silver dishes can be compared with lacquerware from Mawangdui tomb no.1, Beijing (1973), 86, fig.80.

Figure 1. Drawings of silver vessels found in Pit 1 near a tomb of the Qi state at Linzi Xian, Shandong province. 2nd century B.C. Ht. of the covered box 11cm., diam. of the dish 23.5cm. (After *Kaogu xuebao*, 2, (1985), 258, fig.29.)

Sasanian or provincial Iranian work.[4] Another vessel from a tomb of similar date displays a small relief lotus at its centre, surrounded by radiating wavy lines (**Fig. 2**). These lines are an interpretation of curved fluting seen on late Roman silverwork. Intermediaries between Rome and China are found in silver bowls from Georgia and from sites on the north-west frontier of the Indian sub-continent.[5] Other pieces in foreign styles found in China are listed in the Appendix. To these examples can be added some unusual gilt-bronzes

4. The dish from the tomb of Feng Hetu is illustrated in *Wenwu*, 8, (1983), 1-4, figs.4, 5. I am indebted to comments from Prudence O. Harper in identifying the Iranian origins of this dish and also the box from the Qi state tomb.

5. Roman silver vessels decorated with curved fluting are illustrated in Walters (1921), no.73, pl.ix, no.140, pl.xxii. I am grateful to Dieter Metzler for a reference to Matchabely (1976), fig.33, illustrating silver from Georgia. A dish with curved fluting said to have come from Buddigharra in the Punjab and now in the British Museum is illustrated in Dalton (1964), no.204, pl.xxxiii.

excavated at Datong in Shanxi and a silver ewer from a Northern Zhou tomb.[6] Such foreign imports not only stimulated an interest in gold and silver as appropriate materials for fine eating and drinking vessels, but also established in China a range of foreign vessel shapes, including stem-cups, cups with flanged handles, lobed bowls and slender ewers, and a series of foreign decorative schemes, among which centrally placed animal designs are the most conspicuous.[7]

The Production of the Tang and Song Periods

While these pre-Tang finds are scarce and decidedly exotic, the large numbers of vessels surviving from the Tang period indicate that from the seventh century silver became quite common. Particularly large hoards have been found at Hejiacun, near the present-day city of Xi'an (formerly the capital of the Tang, Chang'an), and at Dingmaoqiao at Dantu in the south-eastern province of Jiangsu. Most of the other hoards come from the area of Xi'an (**Fig. 3**), but a few pieces have been found in different parts of Shaanxi province or even much further afield in Liaoning province.[8]

It is argued that the Hejiacun hoard was buried at the time of the An Lushan rebellion in 755, and these views together with evidence from a number of pieces with datable inscriptions, have made it possible to propose chronological developments for both silver vessel shapes and ornament. From the Tang period, foreign vessel types and decoration were modified, establishing for the first time a distinctly Chinese treatment of silverware. The principal vessel types were ewers and jars, lobed bowls, cupstands, cups of foreign origin, including stem-cups, waisted cups, cups with flanged handles and oval cups of a type favoured by the Sasanians, dishes with flat rims of circular, lobed or bracketed shapes, and small boxes of many different shapes. Early Tang decoration consisted of two contrasting types: miniature flower and animal motifs against a ring-punched ground, and large animals in repoussé. Over the following centuries the small-scale motifs were replaced by larger sprays of flowers and these bold patterns were combined with the large animal figures to establish one of the most enduring of all Chinese ornamental

6. Although of bronze rather than gold or silver, the gilded cups from Datong were evidently based on provincial Central Asian copies of Hellenistic or Roman plate. They are illustrated in Beijing (1972), 149-52. The Northern Zhou period ewer has recently been published in *Wenwu*, 10, (1985), 1-20, pl.1, fig.23.

7. Decoration on Tang dynasty silver is discussed in Rawson (1982).

8. Tang dynasty hoards are listed in the Appendix sections: "Hoards of Gold and Silver Vessels from Sites in the Present-Day City of Xi'an in Shaanxi Province and the Surrounding Area", "Hoards that Contain Silver Vessels with *Jinfeng* (Dedication) Inscriptions" and "Tang Dynasty Hoards from Other Parts of China".

Figure 2. Silver wine cup from the tomb of Li Xisong at Zanhuang Xian, Hebei province. 6th century A.D. Diam. 9.2cm. (After *Kaogu*, 6, (1977), 382-90, pl.5:4.)

schemes: centrally placed animal figures surrounded by flowers.[9]

Under the Tang, silver vessels were rarely, if ever, buried in tombs. However, with the establishment of the foreign dynasty of the Liao and the smaller southern kingdoms, Tang burial customs were ignored and silver was included in a few tombs. Such finds are meagre and larger numbers of pieces have come from a Liao dynasty hoard at Balinyouqi in Inner Mongolia, and later Song period hoards from Junan Xian in Shandong provinces, Deyang, in Sichuan province, and Le'an in Jiangxi province (**Fig. 4**). For the Southern Song the tomb of Zhang Tongzhi's wife (buried in 1199) provides a small but significant assemblage of silver (**Fig. 5**).[10]

The typology just outlined for the Tang period can now be extended into the tenth century and Song periods. During the ninth and tenth centuries simple foliate and flower-shaped bowls replaced the intricate vessels of the early Tang, and after the tenth century some of the rather foreign shapes such as stem-cups and oval cups declined in use. Other vessel types, including ewers, foliate and bracketed bowls and cups, were retained and developed. The decoration of later silver is generally much less elaborate than the finely chased ornament of early Tang vessels. Liao pieces, however, bear quite complex designs and repoussé seems to have been particularly popular in the north. On the silver from Deyang and Mianyang (**Fig. 13**) in Sichuan and the

9. The development of such decorative schemes is discussed in Rawson (1984), 90-120.

10. Song dynasty tombs and hoards are listed in the Appendix: "Tombs and Hoards of the Song Period (960-1279)".

sets of bowls from Le'an in Jiangxi, pictorial animal and figure subjects surrounded by borders of flowers, later to dominate ceramic decoration, are seen to be common Song silver designs (**Fig. 4**).[11]

Many Chinese silver vessels must have been melted down and turned into silver ingots, which survive in considerable numbers. The remaining vessels are, therefore, impressive evidence of the abundance of silver utensils in the period under discussion. The quantities of vessels in the larger hoards are particularly interesting. For example, the hoard from Hejiacun contained a number of highly-wrought exotic cups and bowls, which were lobed or faceted and decorated with repoussé figures or intricate scrolls. Such pieces were generally singletons, obviously much prized. But forty-five plain bowls and fifty-one plain dishes are another matter.[12] They can really only be explained as sets of pieces required for parties or feasts. Similarly, much later in date, the hoard found at Le'an in Jiangxi province contained thirty-eight dishes decorated with fishes (**Fig. 4**), twenty high-footed cups, twenty-two spoons and twenty-three pairs of chopsticks. Once again, such quantities must have been the sets of utensils belonging to a wealthy family used for entertaining guests.

Much of the silver described seems to have been intended for wine parties; many of the early pieces in foreign style were wine cups. The bowl from the tomb of Li Xisong (**Fig. 2**), for example, was joined with green-glazed ceramic cups and placed on a large bronze tray with a gilt-bronze bottle and a gilt-bronze pouring vessel as a wine set. It seems likely that the silver bowl was the personal cup of the occupant of the tomb and that for burial it was placed with less valuable cups on the bronze tray.[13] This use of a single cup in a burial can be contrasted with the many identical cups and bowls for daily use found at Hejiacun, Dingmaoqiao or Le'an.

The hoard from Dingmaoqiao seems to have consisted of vessels made specifically for wine parties. The excavators argue that the pieces were made as a set in the mid-Tang period, and they establish a connection with wine drinking on account of a large number of counters in the set, inscribed with well-known sayings from the classics, which were used in wine-drinking

11. The pictorial scenes on Chinese silver are related to Tang and Song period lacquer decoration. Trays and boxes were painted in lacquer with scenes borrowed from decorative painting on screens or similar items. Trays of the Tang period in the Shōsōin illustrate the early use of pictorial motifs on painted lacquer, Rawson (1985), 226, fig. 14. The repertories of silver and lacquer designs seems to have been to some extent interchangeable. Thus pictorial scenes known at an earlier date in lacquer appear on the Mianyang bowls (**Fig. 13**).

12. *Wenwu*, 1, (1972), 30-42. Attention is generally focused on the elaborately decorated silver and gold pieces in the Hejiacun hoard. However, the survival of large numbers of undecorated pieces may be more important to our understanding of the employment of silver.

13. The arrangement of the bowls and tray is discussed in the excavation report, *Kaogu*, 6, (1977), 382-90, 372.

games.[14] The other items included twenty-eight boxes, eight cupstands, two large platters, ten bowls, six small platters, several bottles and ewers, an incense burner, eighteen pairs of chopsticks and ten spoons.

If the range of vessels used and the significant quantities in which they are found show silver as an appropriate material for wine parties or feasts, a number of silver dishes with donation inscriptions confirm the high status of silver in Tang society. There inscriptions record gifts in the eighth and ninth centuries of dishes and ingots from high officials to the Emperor (**Fig. 3**). Such gifts were taken into the personal use of the Emperor, indicating that the Imperial household led the fashion for eating and drinking off silver. The geographical distribution of finds dating after the fall of the Tang illustrates a spread in the use of silver, suggesting that a taste established at the Tang court was later adopted by the high-ranking and wealthy in all parts of China. This development was probably accentuated by the overthrow of the Tang, with their centre of power at Xi'an, Chang'an, and the rise of several competing courts and capitals.

Silver Recovered from Tombs

While large hoards, such as the group from Hejiacun, and the smaller deposits with donation inscriptions indicate that gold and silver vessels were used in the Tang by the Imperial family and high-ranking officials, as yet such cups and bowls have not been found in their tombs. Several reasons may account for this lack. First, the major Imperial tombs have not been excavated. Secondly, some of the lesser tombs that have been examined have been partially robbed. However, more importantly, it appears that at the beginning of the Tang period efforts were made to restrict burial of precious materials.[15]

In place of gold or silver, early Tang period tombs were supplied with vessels in low-fired ceramic decorated with brilliant lead-glaze. Many of these bowls, dishes and ewers reproduced shapes that were first developed in silver. A small bowl or cup from the tomb of the Princess Yongtai is a typical example (**Fig. 7**). Its double curved profile, with a convex belly rising into a

14. *Wenwu*, 11, (1982), 15-27.

15. Burial practices of the Tang have not yet been systematically studied. Wechsler (1985), 142-60, drawing on the *Tang huiyao* and other historical sources, mentions attempts by the early Tang Emperors to restrict the burial of precious materials by example. However, despite good intentions of restraint, precious materials were buried in some if not all Imperial tombs. Subsequently such famous tombs were systematically robbed, which makes it very difficult to establish what was interred in these major burials. It is possible that burials of high-ranking individuals were supplied with gold and silver as well as replicas, *mingqi*, in earthenware, but that the items in precious metals or stones were stolen soon after burial.

Figure 3. Drawing of a silver dish decorated with two fishes and a floral border, found in the suburbs of Xi'an. Offered by Li Mian between A.D.760-67. Diam. 17cm. (After *Kaogu yu wenwu*, 4, (1984), 29-31, fig.1.)

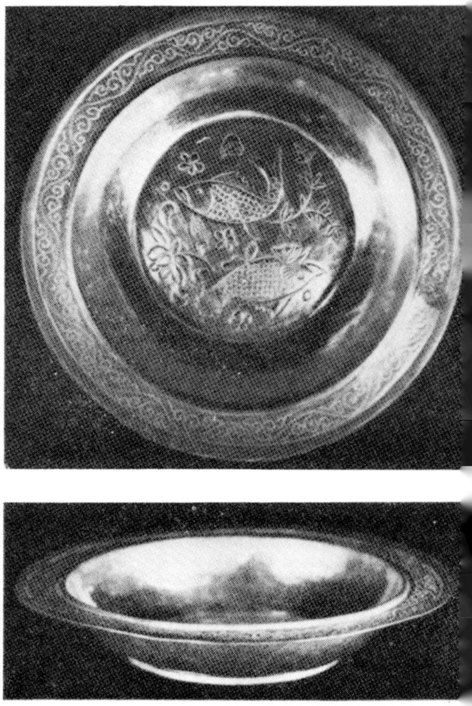

Figure 4. Silver dish decorated with fish, founc at Gongxi, Le'an Xian, in Jiangxi province. Song dynasty, 11th-12th century A.D. Diam. 11.9cm. (After *Wenwu ziliao congkan*, 8, (1983), 116-20.)

widely splayed lip, is a metal shape, which can be matched exactly by a small cup in the British Museum (**Fig. 6**). Such lead-glazed wares were not for daily life but were intended simply for conspicuous display at a funeral and to provide the dead person with the appropriate vessels. The consistent reproduction of silverware shapes and decoration in ceramics for the dead underlines the importance that silver must have had for the living.[16]

From the tenth century some silver vessels were placed in tombs. This change may have followed a relaxation of Tang practices, with the decline and collapse of the dynasty in the early tenth century. In addition, the tombs now to be described were constructed for rulers of minor states who first challenged, and then succeeded to Tang power. The inclusion of silver in these tombs indicated perhaps the aspirations of such rulers.

The tomb of Wang Jian, the ruler of the petty state of Shu in Sichuan province, who died in 918, must have been sumptuously equipped but was unfortunately robbed, leaving only finely decorated lacquer with silver

16. Lead-glazed ceramics of the Tang period are discussed by W. Watson in another paper in this volume.

overlays to hint at its former riches.[17] Other burials of the early tenth century have survived better. The tombs of Qian Kuan, ruler of the Wū-Yue state, and of his mother, Qiu Shuishi, represent burials of the last years of the Tang period in southern China. The two tombs are situated in Lin'an Xian in Zhejiang province.[18]

As the tomb of Qian Kuan was partially robbed, the tomb of his mother will be considered first. The substantial structure was equipped with silver, ceramics, bronze and iron utensils. Among the thirty-eight silver items only some were made for actual use, others were miniature replicas, *mingqi*, intended for burial. The principal silver vessels were as follows: a covered jar, a high footed covered cup (*dou*), a ewer, a basin, a deep bowl (*bo*), a pouring vessel (*yi*) a round box, a butterfly-shaped box, a spittoon, an incense burner, a basin, foliate lobed bowls, a cup, four dishes, a spoon and a pair of chopsticks. The presence of the single spoon and the pair of chopsticks is most suggestive, indicating that these pieces of silver were for the personal use of the occupant of the tomb.

The ceramics from the tomb are also most interesting. The green wares included such large items as a deep bowl and covered jar and an incense burner of metal shape. The seventeen white wares were of finest quality; among them were nine foliate bowls, similar to the example in Figure 10. Two cups were of decidedly silver shape, one with a flanged handle in Tang style and the other, an oval cup with lobes of a type associated with Sasanian Iran. This cup is described in Chinese as a *haitang bei*. In addition there were four bowls, three ewers and one cupstand. Many of the pieces were bound at the lip and foot with gold or silver, and some were inscribed on the base with the characters *guan* "official" or *xin guan* "new official". The kiln site at which these white wares were made has not been identified. However, Li Huibing has argued that most of the known white ceramics with these inscriptions were made at the Ding kilns in Hebei province.[19]

Although most of the silver had been robbed from Qian Kuan's tomb, white and green ceramics similar to those from his mother's tomb were left behind (**Fig. 9**). These ceramics included ten dishes similar to those in Figure 10, two bowls, a vase, a ewer, a *haitang bei* and a dish with a flat rim illustrated in Figure 9. The white pieces in Figure 9 also include a ewer with a stepped handled and the *haitang bei*. They are shown next to silver examples of the same vessel types from the British Museum (**Fig. 8**) to illustrate their dependence on such silver models. Although the white wares in both tombs

17. Two small silver boxes and a silver bowl were also retrieved, Beijing (1964), fig.34, pl.37. For the lacquer remains inlaid with silver, see Beijing (1964), pls.xl, xlvi, xlix, liii-lvii.

18. Appendix: "Tenth-Century Tombs and Hoards in Southern China".

19. Recent contributions to the study of porcelains marked *guan* or *xin guan* have been made by Feng Xianming (1984) and Li Huibing (1984).

were of the highest quality they were obviously subordinate to the silver; for while the silver vessels were placed near the coffin in Qiu Shuishi's tomb, the ceramics were sited further away. Allocation of one *haitang bei* to each of the two tombs suggests that they were the personal possessions of the two occupants and perhaps only slightly less valuable than the silver. Gold and silver bindings on many of these wares must have been intended to increase their value.

Exactly the same juxtapositions of silver eating vessels, a spoon and a pair of chopsticks, with fine white wares in silver shapes inscribed with the characters *guan* or *xin guan*, have been found in a number of slightly later tombs constructed for high-ranking individuals in the Liao territory. The tomb of Fuma Zeng, Prince of Wei, dated 959, excavated at Dayingzi near Chifeng in Inner Mongolia, can be taken to represent these Liao burials.[20] The coffin was placed in a central chamber with, in a rear chamber, silver vessels comprising a bowl decorated with a dragon, a silver pouring vessel (*yi*), a wine ewer, a cupstand and a spoon and a pair of chopsticks.[21] This wine set was accompanied by a number of ceramics including a white bowl and bowl stand. Two foliate dishes marked *guan* (**Fig. 10**), with two similar unmarked bowls, a white ceramic ewer and a number of green wares were placed in a subordinate southern chamber.

Other Liao tombs reveal fewer silver vessels, although the practice of supplying a tomb with some silver and some fine ceramics continued in the north. Two related groups dated to the late tenth century come from the foundation deposits of pagodas in Ding Xian in Hebei province. As in the Liao tombs, silver vessels and boxes were supplemented with a number of fine Ding wares, many of them with the *guan* or *xin guan* inscriptions. The excavators of the deposits have noted that many of the ceramics were made in metal, especially silver, shapes.[22]

Most of the Song period tombs excavated so far have been supplied with ceramic rather than silver vessels. The principal exception is the tomb of the wife of one Zhang Tongzhi, buried at Huangyueling in Jiangpu Xian in Jiangsu province: here eating and drinking vessels appropriate to a tomb were made of silver (**Fig. 5**). These items were supplemented by four pieces of Ding ware bound in silver. Three other tombs listed in the Appendix were also supplied with silver or gold items.[23] As this practice continued into Yuan times, it can be argued that where the families could afford silver vessels and

20. Some items from the tomb of Fuma Zeng were shown in London in the exhibition *The Genius of China*, Watson (1973), nos.348-55.

21. For the plan of the tomb of Fuma Zeng see *Kaogu xuebao*, 3, (1956), 1-32, figs.1-6.

22. Finds from the Ding Xian pagodas are described in *Wenwu*, 8, (1982), 39-51; the imitation in Ding ware of gold and silver shapes is mentioned on page 44.

23. Appendix: "Tombs and Hoards of the Song Period (960-1279)".

Figure 5. Four silver vessels and two Ding ware bowls bound in silver from the tomb of the wife of Zhang Tongzhi (d.A.D.1199) at Huangyueling, Jiangpu Xian, in Jiangsu province. (After *Wenwu*, 4, (1973), 59-66.)

deemed it appropriate to bury items in precious metals, silver or even gold vessels were interred in tombs.[24]

The tomb of the wife of Zhang Tongzhi illustrates the continuing role of white ceramics, especially Ding ware, as a supplement to silver. In all the tombs examined the white wares were to a greater or lesser extent modelled on silver, and many of them were bound in silver or gold, suggesting a close relationship between the materials.[25] In the tenth century the Wū-Yue tombs at Lin'an and the Liao tombs in the north illustrate the careful match achieved between early white wares of a Ding type and silver (**Figs. 8-10**). As the manufacture of Ding ware progressed, the potters did not deviate from the silver that had inspired some of their early vessel types, but rather over the centuries of the Northern Song they developed new techniques that made possible a closer imitation of silver shapes and decoration in Ding ware.

A foliate dish with decoration of birds on a rock amid flowers, in the Percival David Foundation (**Fig. 12**), is a product of the complex moulding and firing techniques which were among the outstanding achievements of the Ding potters. The dish is closely based on a silver vessel, such as those excavated at Mianyang Xian in Sichuan province (**Figs. 11, 13**), and this very intimate relationship suggests that in large measure the techniques that made possible the successful manufacture and firing of the dish arose from an endeavour to continue making porcelains based upon silver models.[26] If gold and silver were highly valued, such fine porcelains can have stood only just below them in the estimation of those who made and used them.

Conclusion

The use of silver and gold in China for eating and drinking vessels was a relatively late development. However, once established, vessels in these precious metals were employed by the Imperial family and high-ranking officials of the Tang. During the tenth century and Song periods, silver was more widely used both geographically and socially. The few pieces of silver

24. Yuan dynasty tombs containing silver vessels are reported in *Wenwu*, 12, (1964), 52-60; *Wenwu*, 7, (1982), 54-60.

25. In the late Northern Song period, Ding wares and southern *yingqing*-glazed porcelains were fired upside down on bare rims. These rims were subsequently bound in metal. However, porcelains were bound in metal long before the development of the firing techniques that left porcelains with bare rims. These early bindings must have been directed to enriching the porcelains. Subsequently, the bound rims could be used to hide defects. This topic will be expanded in a forthcoming paper to be presented at the 2nd International Conference on Ancient Chinese Pottery and Porcelain to be held in Beijing, 15-19 November, 1985.

26. Although not considered in the present discussion, it can be argued that silver vessels were as much the model for Tang and Song period lacquers as they were for ceramics. Lacquer vessels in silver shapes are illustrated in *Wenwu*, 2, (1982), 93; *Wenwu*, 5, (1966), 56-9.

Figure 6. Silver bowl. Tang dynasty (A.D.618-906.) Ht. 4cm., diam. 8.5cm. British Museum, 1938.5-24.705.

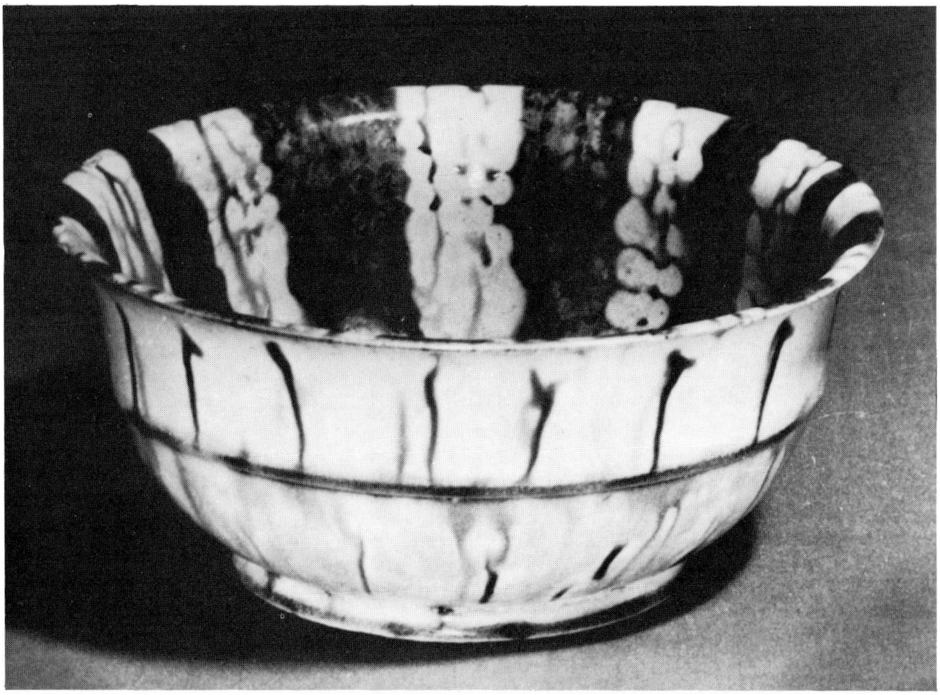

Figure 7. Earthenware bowl with three-coloured lead glaze, from the tomb of the Princess Yongtai (buried A.D.706) at Qian Xian in Shaanxi province. Ht. 7.4cm. (After *Wenwu* 1, (1964), 7-33, fig.32.)

surviving in burials indicate the use of silver eating and drinking vessels by the high-ranking and wealthy from the tenth to the thirteenth centuries. Such silverware was supplemented by ceramics, which in many cases imitated the shapes and decoration of contemporary silver. The history of certain ceramic types has therefore to be considered as developing in response to a standard set by silver. This silver model accounts for some of the refined qualities of porcelain sought and achieved by the Chinese potters of the Tang to Song periods.

Appendix

Silver Vessels from Pre-Tang Dynasty Tombs

1. **Site** Pits around a royal tomb of the state of Qi in Linzi Xian in Shandong province; second century B.C.
Contents A silver box on a high foot with three crouching beasts on the lid; the lid and body are lobed in Achemenid style; three shallow silver dishes with flat rims, decorated in gold with cloud scrolls.
Published *Kaogu xuebao*, 2, (1985), 223-66.
Five pits arranged around the tomb contained as follows:
1. Ritual vessels and daily-use utensils.
2. Dogs.
3. Weapons for the guard of honour.
4. Chariots and horses.
5. Weapons and daily-use utensils.

The silver items were included in Pit 1.

2. **Site** Tombs of Feng Hetu (d.501, buried 504), five kilometres west of the city of Datong, Shaanxi province.
Contents A gilded bowl with repoussé decoration of a figure hunting a boar, in provincial Sasanian style, and a silver oval-eared cup in Chinese taste.
Published *Wenwu*, 8, (1983), 1-4.

3. **Site** Tomb of Li Xisong (501-40) and his wife at Zanhuang Xian, Hebei province.
Contents A wine set consisting of a large bronze tray, a silver wine cup decorated with a lotus flower surrounded by wavy lines, a gilt-bronze pouring vessel, a gilt-bronze bottle and a number of grey-green glazed cups; a gold ring set with a seal stone and Byzantine coins.
Published *Kaogu*, 6, (1977), 382-90, 372; *Wenwu ziliao congkan*, 1, (1977), 152-3.

gure 8. Silver dish, ewer and cup from a hoard said to have come from Beihuangshan in Shaanxi province. 9th-10th ntury A.D. Dimensions from left to right: ht. 4.3cm., width 23.8cm., ht. 25.2cm., ht. 6.7cm., width 14cm. British useum, 1962.3-19.10, 3, 4.

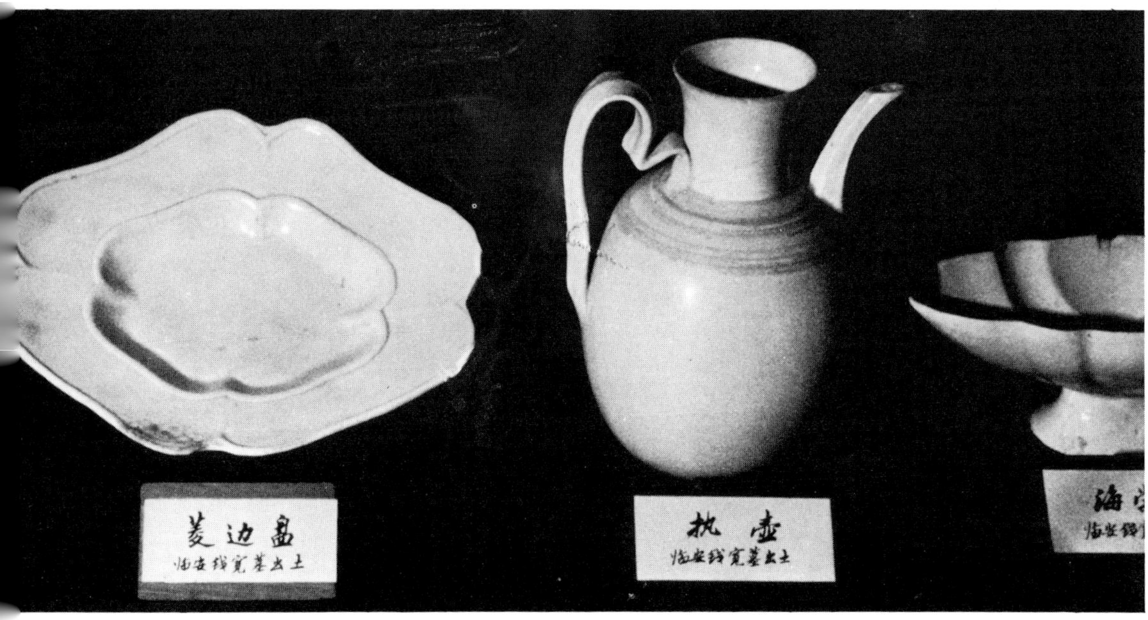

ure 9. Ceramics from the tomb of Qian Kuan, buried A.D.900. Zhejiang Province Museum.

4. **Site** Remains of two tombs, thought to date to the early Liao period (tenth century), at Lijiayingzi in the Aohan Banner in Inner Mongolia.
Contents Tomb 1 contained five silver items, a ewer in Sasanian style crowned with a small modelled head, a dish with a prowling feline in relief, an oval wine cup, a small wine container with a ring handle and a ladle. The second tomb contained some belt fittings. The contents of both tombs seem to be earlier than the Liao date assigned to the tombs by the excavators.
Published *Kaogu*, 2, (1978), 117-8.

5. **Site** Tomb of Li Jingxun (buried 608) west of the city of Xi'an in Shaanxi province.
Contents A gold necklace and other jewellery in foreign style, a gold stem-cup and jade cup with a gold binding around the lip, and nineteen silver items, including cups, boxes, a platter and a spoon.
Published Beijing (1980b), 3-28.

Hoards of Gold and Silver Vessels from Sites in the Present-Day City of Xi'an in Shaanxi Province and the Surrounding Area

1. **Site** Hejiacun in the southern suburbs of Xi'an; contained in two earthenware jars buried in a pit.
Contents More than a thousand items, which included two hundred and seventy gold and silver vessels, together with glass and jade vessels and ornaments, coins and minerals.
Published *Wenwu*, 1, (1972), 30-42; *Wenwu*, 6, (1972), 52-5; Beijing (1972), 44-70; Qian Hao (1981), 168-71.

The hoard was found at the site of the residence of Li Shouli, son of Li Xian—the Prince Zhanghuai (654-34), and cousin of the Emperor Xuanzong (712-56). Li Shouli died in 741 and his son inherited his title, Prince of Bin (or Fen). The hoard was probably buried after 755 at the time of the An Lushan rebellion. The large numbers of plain silver vessels—forty-five bowls and fifty-one small dishes—were probably used for feasts and wine parties.

2. **Site** Shapocun in the eastern suburbs of Xi'an.
Contents Fifteen silver pieces, including a number of cups of Chinese manufacture in distinctly foreign shapes. Both vessels shapes and decoration are closely related to material in the Hejiacun hoard.
Published *Wenwu*, 6, (1964), 30-2.

3. **Site** Hansenzhai on the site of the Xingqing palace built by the Emperor Xuanzong (713-56).

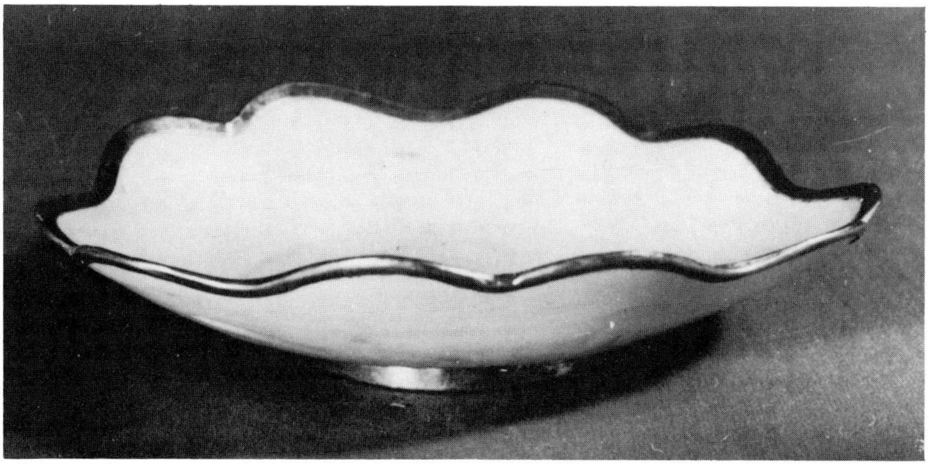

Figure 10. Porcelain dish with a gold binding at the rim, from the tomb of Fuma Zeng, Prince of Wei (d.A.D.959), found at Dayingzi near Chifeng in Inner Mongolia. Diam. 21.3cm. (After Beijing (1958), pl.119:1.)

Contents Part of a large platter, 84 cm.in diameter, decorated in the centre with a phoenix; also reported from nearby sites: two lobed boxes, a number of hairpins, and other jewellery.
Published *Wenwu*, 8, (1959), 34-5; Akiyama (1968), pls.170, 181-3.

4. **Site** Bafuzhuang, north-east of Xi'an, on the site of the Eastern Inner Park of the Daming Gong.
Contents Lobed platter on three feet, decorated at the centre with a lion, and around the rim with a floral border, all in repoussé; found with four spoons, two of which bear dates equivalent to 743 and 751.
Published *Wenwu*, 4, (1957), 11; Akiyama (1968), pl.180.

5. **Site** Taiyi street in Xi'an, during construction work.
Contents A small lobed dish with petalled borders enclosing a design of *makara*.
Published *Wenwu*, 9, (1983), 14.

6. **Site** Suburbs of Xi'an.
Contents Three lobed boxes.
Published *Kaogu yu wenwu*, 4, (1984), 22-6.

7. **Site** Heping gate at Xi'an.
Contents Seven cupstands, one dated to 860.
Published *Kaogu*, 12, (1959), 679-81; Akiyama, (1968), pls.178-9.

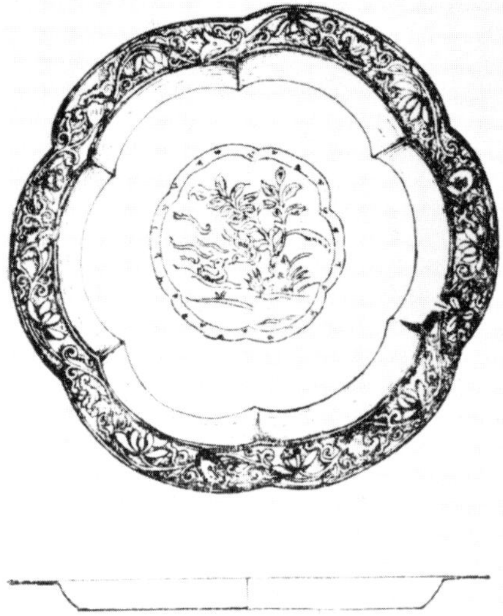

Figure 11. Drawing of silver dish from a hoard found at Mianyang Xian in Sichuan province. 11th-12th century A.D. Diam. 17.8cm. (After *Wenwu*, 4, (1974), 78.)

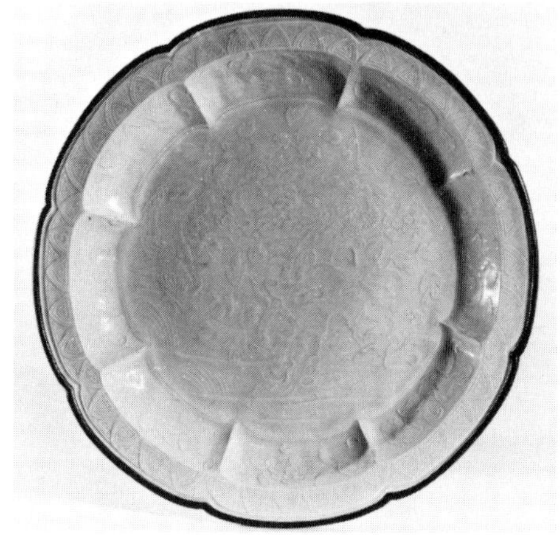

Figure 12. Porcelain dish decorated with a scene of birds on a rock, Ding ware. 13th century A.D. Diam. 21.5cm. Percival David Foundation.

8. **Site** Western suburbs of Xi'an.
Contents Wine jug dated to 872, made for use in the Xuanhui jiufang.
Published *Kaogu yu wenwu*, 1, (1982), 51-2, pl.10:2.

9. **Site** Eastern suburbs of Xi'an.
Contents A spittoon and dish found with an ingot dated to 879.
Published *Kaogu yu wenwu*, 4, (1984), 27-8.

10. **Site** Xianyang.
Contents A gold wine ewer.
Published *Kaogu yu wenwu*, 1, (1982), 53, 43.
In addition various small hoards and tomb groups are surveyed in *Kaogu yu wenwu*, 1, (1982), 54-8.

Hoards that Contain Silver Vessels with *Jinfeng* (Dedication) Inscriptions

The following summary is based upon an account of *jinfeng* inscriptions by Lu Zhaoyin, published in *Kaogu*, 2, (1983), pp.173-9. The inscriptions, which end with the character *jin*, record the presentation of silver vessels or silver ingots by high officials, presumably in return for favours received. The inscriptions name the donors and their titles. As most of these individuals and the dates

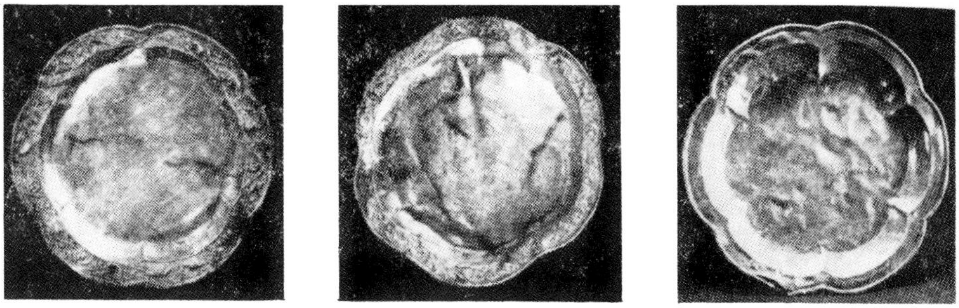

Figure 13. Silver dishes from a hoard found at Mianyang Xian. Diam. 17.8cm. (After *Wenwu*, 4, (1974), 78.)

when they held particular offices are known from the Tang official histories, this information makes it possible to date the silver fairly precisely.

Unlike taxes or tribute, these offerings went to the palace (*neiku*) for the Emperor's use. The custom started during the reign of Gaozong (650-83) and reached its peak under Dezong (780-804). Two special storehouses were established in 784 to receive the gifts, which included other valuable items as well as silver and gold. The excavations of silver with the donation inscriptions suggest either that the surviving pieces were never presented to the Emperor, or that after presentation they were given to other officials and courtiers. The gifts recorded range in date from 757 to 880; the silver vessels found with the inscribed pieces appear on stylistic grounds to belong to the same period. With one exception the silver ingots similarly inscribed will not be considered.

1. **Site** Southern suburbs of Xi'an.
Inscribed Piece Shallow dish decorated with a pair of fish among flowers.
Donor Li Mian, when he was Hongzhou Cishi.
Date Offered between 760 and 767.
Other Contents Three other silver dishes decorated with birds and flowers.
Published *Kaogu yu wenwu*, 4, (1984), 29-31.

2. **Site** Karachin Banner in Liaoning province.
Inscribed Piece Large platter decorated with a crouched deer among flowers.
Donor Liu Zan when he held the offices of Xuanzhou Cishi, Xuanshechi Guancha shi, Yushi zhongcheng.
Date Offered between 787 and 796.
Other Contents Three similar large dishes with gold decoration: two with

makara-like fishes and one with a lion; a *hu* in the shape of a pair of fish, and parts of a damaged container decorated with flowers.
Published *Kaogu*, 5, (1977), 327-334.

3. **Site** Northern suburbs of Xi'an.
Inscribed Piece A large platter decorated with a pair of phoenixes.
Donor Pei Su when he held the offices of Yuezhou Cishi, Zhendong Guancha shi and Yushi dafu.
Date Offered between 799 and 802.
Published *Wenwu*, 10, (1963), 60.

4. **Site** Liulin Beiyincun in Yao Xian, Shaanxi province.
Inscribed Piece A foliate dish decorated with flowers.
Donor Jing Mei when he was Lan Tie shi.
Date Offered between 849 and 851.
Other Contents A jar, bowls, dishes and cups in silver were found buried in an earthenware jar.
Published *Wenwu*, 1, (1966), 46-7, 33.

5. **Site** Lantian Xian, Shaanxi province.
Inscribed Piece A foliate bowl decorated with mandarin ducks.
Donor Li Gan when he was Giuguan chen.
Date Li Gan is not known from the official histories, so this inscription cannot be used to date the piece. A box dated to 866 was found with the bowl.
Other Contents Three silver ingots and nine other vessels and boxes.
Published *Kaogu yu wenwu*, 1 (1982), 46-50.

Tang Dynasty Hoards from Other Parts of China

1. **Site** Dingmaoqiao in Dantu Xian, Jiangsu province.
Contents Nine hundred and sixty items, including ingots, hairpins, combs, jewellery, as well as vessels. These latter include twenty-eight boxes, eight cupstands, two large platters, six small platters, bottles, ewers, an incense burner, eighteen pairs of chopsticks, and ten spoons. Inscribed counters suggest that the vessels in this hoards were used for wine drinking, with the counters being used in drinking games.
Published *Wenwu*, 11, (1982), 15-27.
From the shapes and decoration of the pieces and inscriptions on them the excavators argue that the majority of the items in this hoard were made as a set in the mid-Tang period.

2. **Site** Changxian Xian in Zhejiang province.
Contents Three cups, a bowl, a Sasanian-type bowl, twenty-two spoons,

various ladles, fifteen pairs pairs of chopsticks, hairpins and other jewellery.
Published *Wenwu*, 11, (1982), 38-42.

Tenth-Century Tombs and Hoards in Southern China

1. **Site** Tomb of Wang Jian (d.918) in the outskirts of Chengdu, Sichuan province.
Contents The tomb had been robbed, but two silver boxes and a silver bowl, a lacquer bowl with a silver lining and lacquer boxes set with silver survived these incursions.
Published Beijing (1964).

2. **Site** Tomb of M24 of Shui Qiushi (d.90), mother of Qian Kuan, a ruler of the Wū-Yue state, at Lin'an Xian, Zhejiang province.
Contents More than a hundred items, including forty-two green or white ceramics and thirty-eight silver items. Among the silver were a covered jar, a covered cup (*dou*), a basin, a pouring vessel (*yi*), a box, a spittoon, an incense burner, a tray, a bowl, a cup, four dishes, a spoon, and a pair of chopsticks, and also miniatures vessels or *mingqi*, intended as replicas for burials. The ceramics were of high quality and both green and white wares reproduced metal shapes. The seventeen white pieces included two cups, nine dishes, three ewers, two bowls, a cupstand. Many were marked *guan* or *xin guan*.
Published *Zhejiang sheng wenwu kaogu kan*, 1981, 94-104.

3. **Site** Tomb M23 of Qian Kuan, a ruler of the Wū-Yue state, at Lin'an (d.895 and buried 900), Zhejiang province.
Contents The tomb had been robbed and most of the silver and other precious material removed. Fifteen fine white ceramics were found similar to those in the tomb of his mother, including an elongated oval cup, a *haitang bei*, in Sasanian style, matching the one belonging to Shiu Qiushi. In addition there were ten foliate dishes, two bowls, an elongated dish, and one ewer. Several pieces were marked *guan* or *xin guan*.
Published *Wenwu*, 12, (1979), 18-23.

4. **Site** Tomb M21 of a high ranking official to the Qian family of the Wū-Yue state, at Banqiao in Lin'an Xian, Zhejiang province.
Contents Seventeen pieces of silver and eleven Yue ware ceramics. The silver items included four dishes, a spittoon, two boxes, two ewers, two large and one small bowl, a spoon and a pair of chopsticks.
Published *Wenwu*, 8, (1975), 66-72.

5. **Site** A hoard at Zhuta in Chun'an Xian, Zhejiang province.
Contents Twelve silver pieces: six silver cups on high footrings, two with flat

undersides, a silver cup with a pattern of woven matting, the lid for a tall ewer, a necklace.
Published *Kaogu*, 11, (1984), 979.
In the excavation report the ewer and six cups are described as a wine set. They are somewhat later than the vessels from Dingmaoqiao ("Tang Dynasty Hoards from Other Parts of China", 1) and are compared by the excavators with the contents of the Wū-Yue tombs above.

Liao Period Tombs and Hoards from Northern China

1. **Site** Tomb 1 near Jingfeng (Hexigten Banner) in Inner Mongolia.
Contents Gold jewellery and silver utensils, three cups, two bowls, a cup stand, a *hu* and a dish decorated with birds and flowers in Tang style.
Published *Neimenggu wenwu kaogu*, 3, 80-90.

2. **Site** A hoard found at Balinyouqi in the Yu Ud Meng, Inner Mongolia.
Contents The hoard contained ceramics, agate, jade, and bronze, as well as silver vessels. The silver items included an eight-sided ewer and basin, two cups with basket pattern, two lotus bowls, two flower-shaped bowls, a flat-lipped dish and some sections of tube.
Published *Wenwu*, 5, (1980), 45-51.

3. **Site** A hoard found in the suburbs of Chifeng, Inner Mongolia.
Contents Three gilt-silver vessels, two in the shape of pairs of fishes and one made like a leather bottle.
Published *Wenwu*, 2, (1985), 94-96.
The vessel imitating a leather bottle is descended from an example, decorated with a horse, found in the Hejiacun hoard ("Hoards of Gold and Silver Vessels from Sites in the Present-Day City of Xi'an in Shaanxi Province and the Surrounding Area", 1). These two silver bottles suggest that many of the Liao period ceramic bottles referred as much to silverware as to the original leather prototypes.

4. **Site** Tomb of Fuma Zeng, Prince of Wei (buried 959), found at Dayingzi in Chifeng Xian, Inner Mongolia.
Contents The tomb had five chambers with the coffin in the central room, the *muzhi ming* (epitaph tablet) in the front chamber, large sets of horse trappings in the south chamber, sets of ceramics in the north chamber, and a set of silver eating and drinking vessels behind the coffin in the rear chamber.
Rear Chamber The silver items included a dish decorated with a dragon, a pouring vessel (*yi*), a ewer, a cupstand, a pair of chop-sticks and a spoon. With these silver items were a white ceramic basin, cupstand and cup and also a green-glazed cup.

North Chamber This room contained sets of different types of ceramics. The white wares included twelve ewers of two different types, one tall jar, one small one, two flower-shaped dishes inscribed with the character *guan*, two of similar shape without inscription, two further flower-shaped dishes bound in gold, two long-necked bottles, one ewer, three large bowls. In addition, there were many green wares, some fragments of glass, a silver cup and a pair of wooden chopsticks ornamented in silver.
Published *Kaogu xuebao*, 3, (1956), 1-31.

5. **Site** A tomb at Jianping, Zhangjiayingzi in Liaoning province, early Liao period, late tenth century.
Contents Two flower-shaped silver dishes, a silver spoon, a pair of silver chopsticks, a silver headdress, an agate-handled knife, an agate bowl, a white porcelain bowl inscribed with *xin guan*, two white porcelain flower-shaped dishes, and various lead-glazed wares.
Published *Kaogu*, 2, (1960), 15-19.

6. **Site** A tomb at Jianping Zhulu in Liaoning province, early Liao period, late tenth or eleventh century.
Contents This tomb was less richly furnished than the previous one, but contained a silver spoon with various fine white wares, including a two-handled jar, two large bowls, two small bowls, one bowl marked *guan*, a tall-necked flask marked *guan*, and a ewer decorated with traces of lacquer.
Published *Kaogu*, 2, (1960), 19-21.

7. **Site** A tomb at Chaoyang Xian in Liaoning province, eleventh century.
Contents Like the tomb of Fuma Zeng (no.4 above), eating and drinking vessels were arranged near the coffin, with lead-glazed ewers placed in a side chamber. The vessels around the coffin included a faceted *yingqing*-glazed porcelain ewer and basin of silver shape. The tomb also contained a silver headdress and belt.
Published *Wenwu*, 12, (1980), 17-29.
As the *yingqing*-glazed ewer must have been made in south China it was probably a highly-prized item, perhaps as valuable as silver.

8. **Site** A tomb at Pingquan Xian in Hebei province.
Contents A silver headdress and a small silver bowl, together with a number of ceramics—a white glazed ewer and a green glazed one.
Published *Wenwu*, 7, (1982), 50-3.

9. **Site** A tomb south of Tongliao city in Inner Mongolia.
Contents In addition to a number of belt-fittings similar to belts found

further west in the USSR, part of a silver jug with repoussé decoration, also similar to vessels from southern Russia.
Published *Kaoguxue jikan*, 1, (1981), 231-43.

Tombs and Hoards of the Song Period (960-1279)

1. **Site** Foundation deposits from two pagodas in Ding Xian, Hebei province.
Contents (a) Pagoda of the Jingzhi Si, dated 977; the silverware included four gilded model pagodas, three coffins or boxes, one figure, one bowl, one deep dish, one incense burner, and many fragments; in addition to bronze, stone, wood and glass items the deposit also contained large numbers of fine white wares, many of Ding type, some inscribed with the character *guan*. Among these wares were as many as twenty bottles and kundikas and thirty boxes. Some of the pieces were bound in gold or silver.
(b) Pagoda of the Jingzhong Yuan, dated 995; the silverware included a model pagoda, a coffin or box, a bottle and some fragments. As in the previous deposit many Ding ware pieces were found, among which kundikas, bottles and boxes predominated.
Published *Wenwu*, 8, (1972), 39-51.
The pagoda deposits differ from the other finds listed and discussed in this paper in that the contents were intended for religious purposes and not secular feasts. The special interest of the deposit lies in the combination of silverwares with Ding wares.

2. **Site** Hoard found at Deyang in Sichuan province.
Contents One hundred and seventeen items including thirty-three vessels, among which were two *meiping*, three cupstands, ten wine cups, six boxes, three incense burners, a basin, a wine container (*zun*), a wine pourer (*yi*), and a ladle.
Published *Wenwu*, 11, (1961), 48-52.

3. **Site** Hoard found at Le'an Xian in Jiangxi province.
Contents Thirty-eight bowls decorated with fish, twenty high-footed cups, two dishes with engraved pictorial designs, two vessels with appliqué decoration, and one ladle, twenty-two spoons, twenty-three pairs of chopsticks, and two inscribed tablets.
Published *Wenwu ziliao congkan*, 8 (1983), 116-20.

4. **Site** Hoard found at Junan Xian, Shandong province.
Contents Twenty-two items, including a deep basin, two pouring vessels, ten petalled bowls, six lotus-shaped bowls, two plain bowls and a silver-gilt lion.
Published *Wenwu ziliao congkan*, 8, (1983), 133-5.

5. **Site** A hoard from Mianyang Xian, Sichuan province.
Contents Five lobed bowls with flat rims some decorated with scenes of birds and flowers at the centre.
Published *Wenwu*, 4, (1974), 78.

6. **Site** Tombs of Zhang Tongzhi and his wife buried between 1195 and 1199 at Huangyueling, Jiangpu in Jiangsu province.
Contents While the tomb of Zhang Tongzhi contained mainly writing implements, that of his wife revealed a number of eating and drinking vessels in silver, several decorated with prunus blossom, supplemented by four pieces of Ding ware. The silver vessels included one *meiping*, three boxes, a spittoon, two dishes, a basin, a bowl, two deep bowls, a covered jar, a high-footed cup, a spoon and a pair of chopsticks.
Published *Wenwu*, 4, (1973), 59-66.

7. **Site** Tombs of Shi Shengzu (1191-1274) and his wife at Quzhou in Zhejiang province.
Contents In addition to ceramics and hard-stone carvings, eleven gold and silver items were found, including jewellery, shoes and some vessels.
Published *Kaogu* 11, (1983), 1004-1011, 1018.

8. **Site** A Song tomb near Nanjing in Jiangsu province.
Contents Gold jewellery and a perfume container, and a silver box.
Published *Wenwu*, 3, (1982), 28-30.

9. **Site** Tomb of Huang Sheng (d.1243) in the suburbs of Fuzhou, Fujian province.
Contents The tomb contained many textiles, some lacquer containers, a few silver and gold ornaments and silver cups and containers.
Published Beijing (1982); *Wenwu*, 7, (1977), 1-17.

Bibliography

Beijing (1958) — *Wu sheng chutu zhongyao wenwu zhanlan tulu*, Wenwu chubanshe, Beijing, 1958.

Beijing (1964) — *Qian Shu Wang Jian mu fajue baogao*, Wenwu chubanshe, Beijing, 1964.

Beijing (1972) — *Wenhua da geming qijian chutu wenwu, di yi ji*, Wenwu chubanshe, Beijing, 1972.

Beijing (1973) — *Changsha Mawangdui yi hao Han mu*, vol.1, Wenwu chubanshe, Beijing, 1973.

Beijing (1980a) — *Sui Xian Zeng Hou Yi mu*, Wenwu chubanshe, Beijing, 1980.

Beijing (1980b)	*Tang Chang'an chengguo Sui Tang mu*, Wenwu chubanshe, Beijing, 1980.
Beijing (1982)	*Fuzhou Nan Song Huang Sheng mu*, Wenwu chubanshe, Beijing, 1982.
Dalton (1964)	Dalton, O.M., *The Treasure of the Oxus with Other Examples of Early Oriental Metal-Work*, 3rd edition, London, 1964.
Feng Xianming (1984)	Feng Xianming, "'Guan' he 'xin guan' zikuan ciqi zhi yanjiu" in *Zhongguo gudai yaozhi diaocha fajue baogao ji*, Wenwu chubanshe, Beijing, 1984, pp.393-407.
Li Huibing (1984)	Li Huibing, "Guan yu 'guan', 'xin guan' kuan baisi chandi wenti de tantao", *Wenwu*, 12, 1984, pp.58-90.
Matchabely (1976)	Matchabely, K., "La Toreutique de la Georgie dans l'Antiquité Tardive", Tbilisi, 1976.
Medley (1972)	Medley, M., *Metalwork and Chinese Ceramics*, Percival David Foundation Monographs 2, London, 1972.
Qian Hao (1981)	Qian Hao, *et al.*, *Out of China's Earth*, London and Beijing, 1981.
Rawson (1982)	Rawson, J., "The Ornament on Chinese Silver of the Tang Dynasty (A.D. 618-906)", *British Museum Occasional Papers*, 40, London, 1982.
Rawson (1984)	Rawson, J., *Chinese Ornament, the Lotus and the Dragon*, London, 1984.
Rawson (1985)	Rawson, J., "The Lotus and the Dragon, Sources of Chinese Design A.D. 400-1400", *Apollo*, April 1985, vol.cxxi, no.278, pp.220-27.
Shih Hsio Yen (1983)	Shih Hsio Yen, "Gold and Silver Vessels Excavated in North China: Problems of Origin", *New Asia Academic Bulletin*, Special Issue on Chinese Art, 4, 1983, pp.63-93.
So (1980)	So, J.F., "The Inlaid Bronzes of the Warring States Period" in *The Great Bronze Age of China*, Wen Fong, ed., New York, 1980, pp.303-20.
Walters (1921)	Walters, H.B., *Catalogue of the Silver Plate (Greek, Etruscan, Roman) in the British Museum*, London, 1921.
Watson (1973)	Watson, W., *The Genius of China, An Exhibition of Archaeological Finds of the People's Republic of China*, London, 1973.
Watson (1984)	Watson, W., *Tang and Liao Ceramics*, London, 1984.
Wechsler (1985)	Wechsler, H.J., *Offerings of Jade and Silk, Ritual and Symbol in the Legitimation of the T'ang Dynasty*, New Haven and London, 1985.
Zheng Dekun & Shen Weijun (1933)	Zheng Dekun and Shen Weijun, *Zhongguo mingqi*, Yenjing Journal of Chinese Studies, Monograph Series no.1, Beijing, 1933.

The Survival of Precious and Base Metal Objects from the Medieval Islamic World

J.W. ALLAN

This volume is designed to focus on the relationship between precious metal and ceramics. But in so many early or medieval cultures there is a problem of survival. What are we going to say about such a relationship if virtually no precious metal survives? How are we going to establish the possible links and influences? This question certainly arises in the medieval Islamic context, for there are probably only 75 or 80 silver vessels from the medieval Islamic world known today. The bulk of these come from two large hoards found in Iran or from finds in the Soviet Union.

The more coherent of the two hoards is that of Valgīr ibn Hārūn, an amir or officer of state who must have lived in Western Iran c.1000 A.D (**Figs.1-2**).[1] This hoard consists of the following silver items: 3 bowls, 2 saucers, a ewer, a bottle, a vase, a jar, a cup and a dish. They are decorated with an inscription giving the name and titles of the amir inlaid in niello. The second hoard was supposed to have been found in Northern Iran, and was acquired by the collector Harari (**Figs.3-4**).[2] It is now in the L.A. Mayer Memorial Institute in Jerusalem. It consists of: 7 rosewater sprinklers, 4 incense-burners with handles, 2 dish incense-burners, 3 jugs, a handled bowl, 2 caskets, and a spoon, as well as numerous harness ornaments. The objects appear to fall into two groups, one of Khurāsāni origin and late 10th century, the other North Iranian and a century or so later.

The various silver finds from the Soviet Union are undoubtedly the result of trading contacts at different periods.[3] One might cite as examples a bottle in the name of a vizir of Balkh, Abū 'Alī Aḥmad ibn Shāzān, who died c.1060 A.D.,[4] and a table-top of a Khwārazm-Shāh,[5] datable to c.1040 A.D. Both were found near Tobolsk on the east side of the Urals.

Why are we so short of precious metal objects? Religiously speaking, there

1. Wilson (1931), nos.139 A-L; Wiet (1933), 18-19 and pls.1-3; Pope (1938), pls.1345-6; Melikian-Chirvani (1968), 144, no.2; Allan (1982a), 14-15.

2. Pope (1930), 480; Wilson (1931), no.131 A-T; Pope (1938), pl.1315 and fig.828; Allan (1976), figs.63-68.

3. Smirnov (1909), pls.71-73, 79-84, 117.

4. Smirnov (1909), pls.81, 83, no.147.

5. Smirnov (1909), pl.82, no.150.

has always been tension between precious metal and faith in the Islamic world. It was because of such antipathy towards silver that according to al-Birūnī high-tin bronze, or bell metal, became so fashionable. Its silvery colour made it a good substitute. But the literary evidence shows that silver and gold objects were widely used by the wealthy in medieval Islam, at least at certain periods (see Melikian-Chirvani's paper in this volume).

A more important reason for the small number of extant pieces is obviously the remelting of precious metal for reworking or for issuing as coinage. We can gauge the fate of precious metal over a period of a few centuries by taking, as an example, the situation in the Near East in late Mamlūk and early Ottoman times. By the 1370's metal was becoming more expensive in Egypt, and so in 1374 A.D. Sulṭān al-Ashraf Sha'bān, wanting to increase his fame by initiating a building project in Cairo, wrote to Baydamur, governor of Damascus, requiring him to gather together all the fittings he could from buildings in Damascus, and send them to the Sulṭān. The gold and silver thus looted by Baydamur is reported to have weighed 2,200 kg.[6] The declining availability of silver in the next twenty years led to extreme shortages, and in the mid-15th century Maqrīzī reports that people had been digging the silver inlay out of inlaid brasses, so great was the value of the precious metal.[7] He also records how the silver shortage brought silversmiths into direct conflict with the government: in 1435 A.D., he says, the government prohibited the making of silver objects and carried off all the silver to the mint.[8] Such a shortage would have obviously meant a considerable depletion of surviving stocks of silver objects, and the manufacture of relatively few new ones.

Then in 1517 A.D. came the Ottoman conquest. "And when our Lord the Sulṭān Selim Khan went out from Egypt", writes al-Ṣīddīqī, "there were with him a thousand camels laden with gold and silver, besides what he looted, consisting of rarities, weapons, porcelain, copper vessels, encrusted things, horses, mules, camels etc."[9] And if any Mamlūk gold or silver objects actually arrived at the Ottoman treasury in Istanbul intact, their chances of survival there were remote. In 1623 A.D. Murad IV went into his treasury and found only six purses of money, a bag of coral and a chest of china![10]

Such problems are not, of course, confined to medieval Islam, but medieval Islam did suffer from a more peculiar shortage—a shortage of silver metal, which seems to have hit the whole of the Near East in the 11th and 12th centuries. The silver and gold issues up to 1350 A.D. at some of the main

6. Brinner, i, (1963), 249-50, ii, 188.

7. Maqrīzī, ii, (1854), 105.

8. Maqrīzī, iv, (1972), pt.2, 549. For further details of the situation in 15th-century Egypt see Allan (1984).

9. Allan and Raby (1982), 36, 219, n.89. The author's full name is Shams al-Dīn Abī 'Abdallāh Muḥammad ibn Aḥmad al-Bakrī al-Ṣiddāqī.

10. Allan and Raby (1982), 21.

gure 1. Hoard of silver objects inlaid with niello in the name of the Amīr Valgīr ibn Hārūn. (After Pope, 1938.)

gure 2. Hoard of silver objects inlaid with niello in the name of the Amīr Valgīr ibn Hārūn. (After Pope, 1938.)

minting centres of the Islamic world are tabulated in **Table 1**. Of particular significance here is the band across the Table showing the period in which there were virtually no silver issues. There is argument among economic historians and numismatists about the reasons for this apparent silver shortage, and its significance, but the present article will not enter into this discussion.[11] It is important to draw attention to it, however, as it must have affected the silversmithing industry, and the production of precious metal objects.

Few finds of precious metal objects, a tradition of remelting, of looting, of periodic shortages of bullion, and two centuries of widespread silver famine. The situation certainly sounds gloomy. But, it may not be as gloomy as all that. First of all, those silver objects which survive do have something to say on the question. Secondly, there is, I believe, a huge group of base metal objects which can be used in the same way as silver in any discussion of the relationships of precious metal objects and ceramics. This completely transforms the possibilities, and gives medieval Islam a very important role in relating precious metal and ceramics world-wide.

The base metal in question is either brass, high-tin bronze, or a quaternary alloy of copper, lead, zinc and tin, inlaid with silver, and sometimes with copper or gold as well. It was manufactured in an area stretching from Egypt to Pakistan from the early 12th to the early 16th century, and vast quantities have survived. The reason for its survival is not far to seek: copper is so common in the Near East, especially in Iran and Eastern Anatolia, that it would rarely be worth confiscating large numbers of copper vessels and deliberately remelting them. Of course, as Maqrīzī relates, it was sometimes worth removing the silver and gold inlays, but the vessels themselves have usually remained intact. Now in most societies base metals do not fulfill the same function as precious. They are for a less wealthy clientele, and indicate the more limited taste as well as the more limited financial resources of their patrons. Hence it is important to show why in medieval Islam inlaid metalwork can be discussed as though it were precious metal itself.

In talking about inlaid metalwork one must be careful not to lump all of it together—it was fashionable for a long period over a huge area, as I have mentioned, and situations and society differed from one time to another, and from one place to another. If, however, we take the western area of the Near East—Egypt, Syria and the Jazīra—from 1200-1400 A.D. as one group, and Khurāsān, Transoxiana and Pakistan from 1150-1250 A.D. as another, we can define general principles on which the close relationship of inlaid metalwork to silver can stand.

11. Watson (1967); Blake (1937). The problem is discussed by Melikian-Chirvani (1982), though he excludes the numismatic evidence from the argument.

gure 3. Silver gilt and nielloed objects from the Harari Hoard. (Photo: British Museum Research Laboratory.)

gure 4. Silver gilt incense-burner from the Harari Hoard. (Photo: British Museum Research Laboratory.)

1. Brass rosewater sprinkler base.

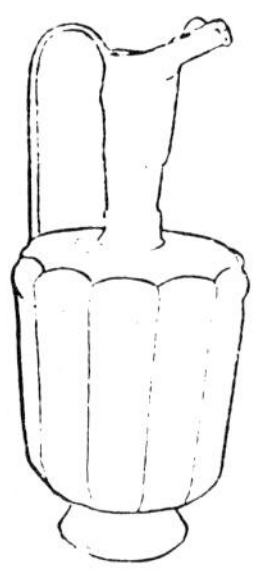

2. Brass ewer.

3. Brass ewer.

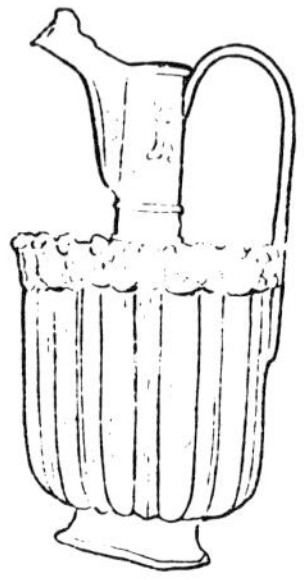

4. Brass ewer.

5. Brass candlestic

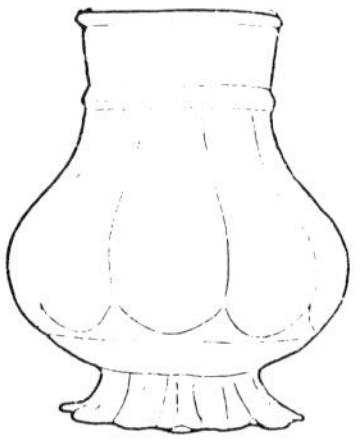

6. Brass jug.

7. Brass lid.

8. Brass table-top.

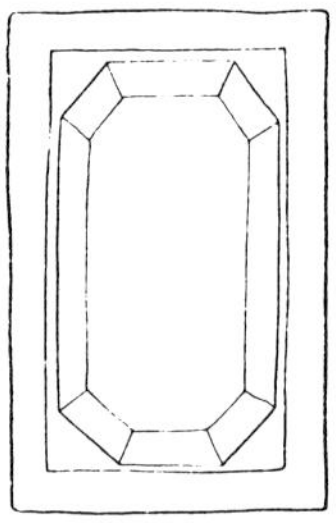

9. Brass table-top.

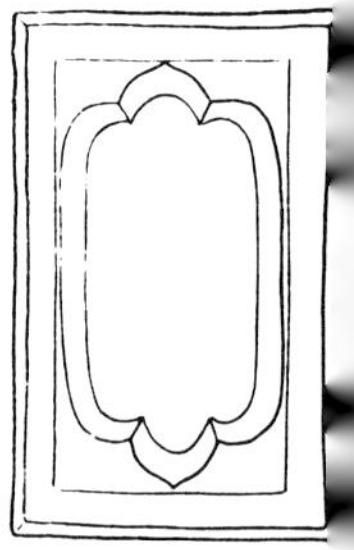

10. Brass table-top

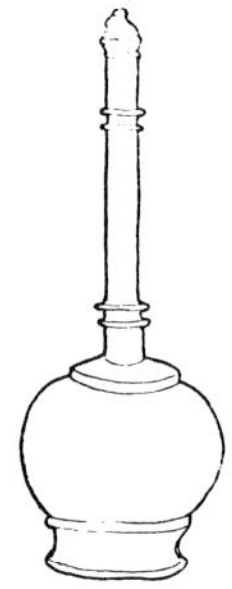

11. Silver rosewater sprinkler.

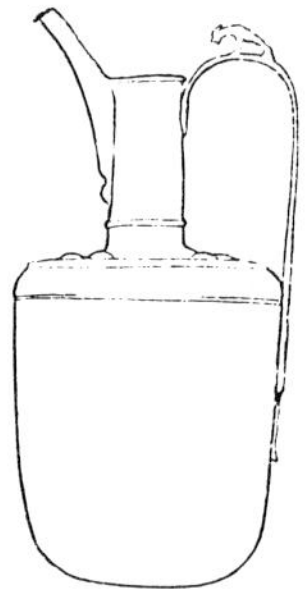

12. Silver ewer.

13. Silver table-top

Figure 5. Beaten brass shapes, nos. 1-10, Iran, c.A.D. 1200. Beaten silver shapes, nos. 11-13, Iran, 11th-12th century A.D. (After Allan, 1976.)

igure 6. Brass ewer inlaid with silver and copper, in the ame of Abū'l- Qāsim Maḥmūd ibn Sanjar Shāh. Mosul, arly 13th century. Nuhad Es-Said Collection, no.6. (After llan, 1982.)

Figure 7. Brass incense-burner inlaid with gold and silver in the name of Sulṭān al-Malik al-Nāṣir Muḥammad ibn Qalā'ūn. Nuhad Es-Said Collection no.15. (After Allan, 1982.)

Taking first the eastern group, we find inlaid metalwork which makes few pretensions to being the prerogative of kings. In fact only four objects have so far been published which indicate royal or semi-royal patrons. A pair of silver-inlaid table-tops recently came to light on the London art market bearing the name of a governor of Peshawar in the early 13th century;[12] a silver-inlaid pen-case was made in 607/1210 for Majd al-Mulk, grand vizir of the ruling Khwārazm-Shāh;[13] a silver-inlaid stem bowl is dedicated to a Khurāsāni petty prince, one Amīrānshāh.[14] An inkwell in the name of a

12. *The V & A Album*, 2, (1983), 181.
13. Herzfeld (1936).
14. Rice (1955), pl.xivb; Wiet (1965), 655-69, and pl.i.

Figure 8. Underglaze-painted ceramic jug. Jazīra, 14th century. Ashmolean Museum, Reitlinger Gift, no.1978.1658.

Figure 9. High-tin bronze jug inlaid with silver. Jazīra, 14th century. Nuhad Es-Said Collection no.10. (After Allan, 1982.)

mushrif, or court inspector, is the only other piece which could remotely rank as a court object.[15] The only other identifiable patrons are religious figures or merchants, and objects with patrons' names on them only just run into double figures, compared with a total surviving number of anonymous objects which must run into many hundreds if not thousands. How then can we relate such inlaid metal to silver? How can we suggest that the two are comparable?

The answer lies in a very striking group of common features, found both on surviving silver work and on inlaid bronzes and brasses. First of all it is noticeable that the finest beaten brass shapes follow those known from silver objects: cylindrical-bodied ewers, table-tops, and rosewater sprinklers occur in both media (**Fig.5**).

Secondly, there is a close technical relationship between early Islamic silver in Iran and inlaid brasses. Both are generally beaten metal; both have a striking emphasis on repoussé work; both have the same colour scheme. Thus gilded silver inlaid with niello, gives a golden, silver and black colour scheme. This is directly paralleled in inlaid brass, the brass giving the golden colour, the silver inlay the silver, and a cheaper bituminous substance the niello

15. Baer (1972), figs.1-5.

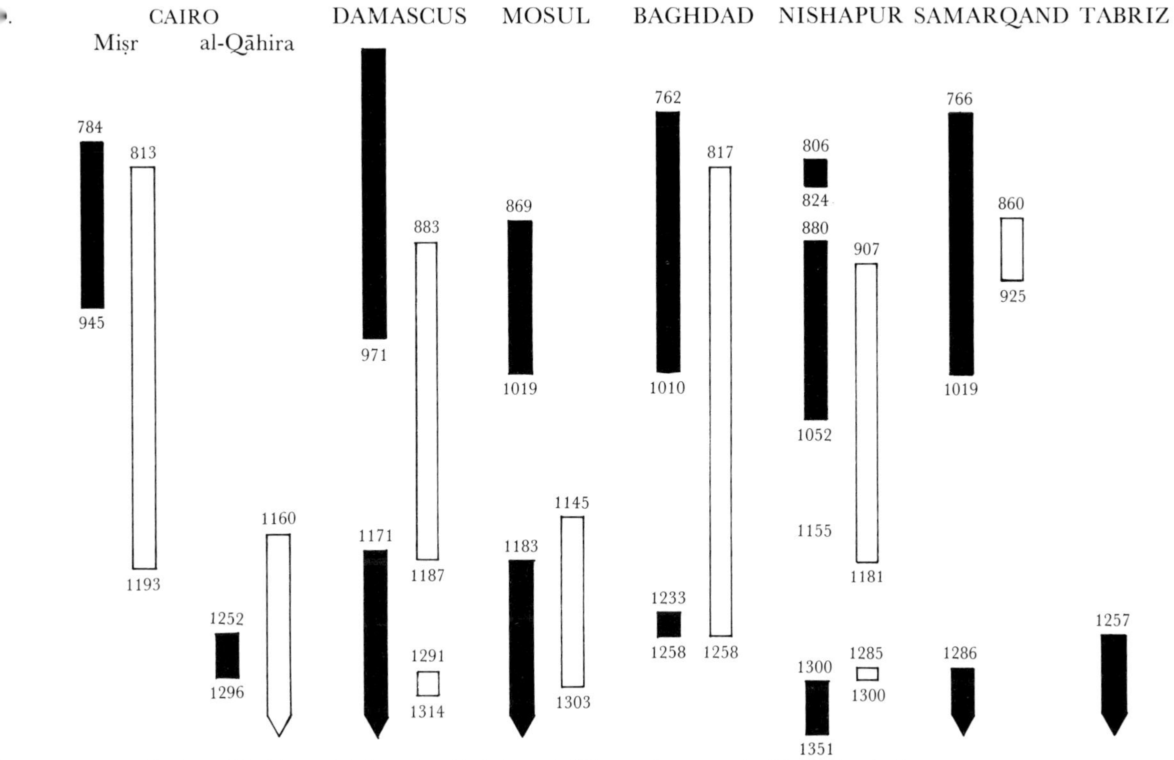

BLE ONE Select Table of Islamic Gold and Silver Issues A.D. 700-1350

black. Couple these technical parallels with the sheer technical and artistic brilliance of the finest inlaid brass pieces, and there seems little doubt that we are dealing here with an industry which was extremely closely related to the silversmithing industry. Indeed, I believe it was an industry created by silversmiths, as the supply of silver dwindled in the 11th and 12th centuries, to meet an increasing demand for luxury metalwork from middle and upper class society in Seljuq Iran.[16]

Turning now to Egypt, Syria and the Jazīra from 1200 A.D. onwards, we find a great paucity of precious metal objects. Whereas in the east there is enough surviving silver to show a direct physical relationship with inlaid metalwork, in the west there is not. No Atabeg, Ayyūbid or Mamlūk silver vessel has yet been identified, and there is therefore no possible comparison between silver and inlaid metalwork to be made.

One possible way round this is to identify the origins of some of the shapes further back in time, and this I did in a paper given at last year's Oxford conference on Islamic Art.[17] Two examples may be mentioned here. A

16. For a full discussion see Allan (1976), and for a contrary view see Melikian-Chirvani (1982).

17. Allan (1985).

Figure 10. Lustre painted ceramic dish. Kāshān, A.D.1210. Freer Gallery of Art, no.41.11. (After Atil, 1973.)

Figure 11. Brass dish inlaid with silver. Eastern Iran, early 13th century. (After Pope, 1938.)

famous Ayyūbid piece, the "Barberini Vase", made for the Ayyūbid ruler Salāḥ al-Dīn Yūsūf (1237-60 A.D.), is of a form which goes back to a Byzantine prototype in silver, exemplified by the so-called Ḥoms vase, dating from the late 6th century.[18] And a group of Jazīran 13th-century objects is represented by a stem cup now in Florence.[19] The bowl of this cup is the same shape as that of the 6th-century Riha chalice,[20] while the stem of another Jazīran cup in the Dauphin collection is like the stem of the Riha chalice.[21] Hence, there is a definite connection between earlier silver and 13th-century inlaid metalwork, even if the contemporary silver examples no longer survive.

More important, however, is the fact that inlaid metal under the Atabeg dynasties, Artuqids, Ayyūbids and Mamlūks, was royal metalwork. The geographer Ibn Sa'īd in his description of Mosul in the 13th century says: " There are many crafts in the city, especially the making of inlaid copper vessels, which are exported and presented to rulers, as are the silken garments woven there.[22] " We know from surviving objects and textual evidence that the ruler of Mosul, Badr al-Dīn Lu'lu', owned inlaid metal objects;[23] so did other rulers in the Jazīra (as the list in **Table 2** shows) (**Fig.6**); so did the

18. Paris (1971), 103-4, no.151; Coche de la Ferté (1958), 51, no.49.

19. Rice (1955), pl.xiiia.

20. Dodd (1961), 68-69, no.8.

21. Geneva (1985), no.284.

22. Rice (1957), 284.

23. Rice (1957), 284.

TABLE TWO
Inlaid Metal Objects made for 13th-Century Rulers in the Jazīra and Syria

Artuq Arslān ibn Īl-Ghāzī Artuq of Mārdīn and Mayyāfāriqīn (1200-39).
Candlestick base. (Ḥaram al-Sharīf Museum, Jerusalem; shortly to be published by Dr Marwan Abu Khalaf.)

Abū'l Qāsim Maḥmūd ibn Sanjar Shāh, atābak of Jazīra ibn 'Umar. (1208-42/1250).
Ewer. (Nuhad Es-Said Collection; Allan (1982), 54-57, no.6.)
Basin. (Sarre Collection; Sarre (1906), no.19, pl.vi.)

Badr al-Dīn Lu'lu' of Mosul (1218-59).
Box. (British Museum; Rice (1950), 628-30 and pls. 14, 16.)
Tray. (Victoria & Albert; Rice (1950), 632-34 and pl.13.)
Tray. (Munich; Sarre and van Bercham (1907).)
Tray. (Kiev; see Rice (1950), 628, notes 2-3 for bibliography.)
Candlestick. (Hermitage; Guzelian (1948).)

Shihāb al-Dīn Tughril, atābak of al-Malik al-'Azīz Ghiyāth al-Dīn Muḥammad of Aleppo.
Ewer, made in 1232. (Freer; Atil (1975), 61-63, no.26)

al-Malik al-Muẓaffar Fakhr al-Dīn Qarā Arslān ibn Īl Ghāzī of Mārdīn (1261-93).
Basin. (Melikian-Chirvani (1968), no.1, pls.xi-xii.)

TABLE THREE
Inlaid Metal Objects Made for Ayyūbid Sultans

al-Malik al-Ashraf Muẓaffar al-Dīn Mūsā of Diyārbakr and later Damascus (1210-37).
Astrolabe, made in 1227/8. (Oxford, Museum of the History of Science, Mayer, 1956, p.30.)

al-Malik al-'Azīz Ghiyāth al-Dīn Muḥammad of Aleppo (1216-37).
Box. (Naples; Scerrato (1967), no.7.)

al-Malik al-Mu'aẓẓam Sharaf al-Dīn 'Īsā, governor of Damascus (1201-18), Ayyūbid ruler of Damascus (1218-27).
Astrolabe, made in Damascus in 1217-18. (Istanbul, Deniz Müzesi; Brieux Maddison, forthcoming.)

al-Malik al-Kāmil I Nāṣir al-Dīn Muḥammad of Egypt and Damascus (1218-38).
Ewer. (Istanbul; Aga-Oglu (1930), 27 and pl.B.)
Globe. (Naples; Scerrato (1967), no.38 and figs.19-20)
Dish. (Ex Goupil Collection; Lavoix (1878), p.785.)

al-Malik al-Nāṣir Ṣalāḥ al-Dīn Yūsuf of Aleppo and Damascus (1236-60).
Ewer, made in Damascus 1258. (Louvre; Paris (1971), 104, no.152)
Vase. (Louvre; Paris (1971), 103-4, no.151.)
Basin. (Montreal; Salam-Liebich (1976), fig.5)

al-Malik al-'Ādil II Sayf al-Dīn Abū Bakr of Egypt and Damascus (1238-40).
Incense-burner. (Keir Collection; Fehérvári (1968).)
Basin. (Louvre; Paris (1971), 103, no.150.)
Box. (Victoria & Albert; Lane-Poole (1886), pl.80.)

al-Malik al-Ṣāliḥ Najm al-Dīn Ayyūb of Egypt and Damascus (1240-49).
Basin. (Freer; Atil (1975), 64-68, no.27.)
Platter. (Louvre; Paris (1971), 104-5, no.153.)
Basin. (Cairo; 'Izzi (1965).)
Bowl. (Kelsey Museum; Grabar (1961), 360-66.)

Ayyūbids of Syria (see **Table 3**). Under the Mamlūks there are abundant inlaid brass objects made for ruling Sulṭāns, and literally hundreds bearing the names and titles of officers of state—so many that to list them would be a considerable task. One may simply cite here some examples of metalwork which belonged to the most powerful and wealthy of all the Mamlūk Sulṭāns, Muḥammad ibn Qalā'ūn (1294-1340 A.D.)—the Nuhad Es-Said incense-burner (**Fig.7**) and incense-box, or the great basin in the British Museum.[24] Such was the recognized quality of these objects that contemporary rulers of the Yemen, the Rasūlid Sulṭāns, ordered them for their own personal use.[25]

An interesting passage from Maqrīzī, with a parallel in another historical source, shows the relationship of precious and inlaid metal under one of the early Mamlūk rulers, Khalīl (1290-94 A.D.). In 1291-93 A.D. he is recorded as having ordered from Damascus 100 copper candlesticks bearing the titles of the Sulṭān, and 100 other candlesticks, 50 of gold and 50 of silver.[26] In other words, he was a patron of both precious and inlaid metal (for the copper ones from surviving examples undoubtedly were inlaid), and it was presumably the price which dictated the relative quantities he ordered of the different types.

Thus it is clear that in medieval Islamic culture there is a quite remarkable opportunity for relating precious metal to other media, including ceramics. This may be illustrated by reference to two examples. A ceramic jug made in Syria or the Jazīra in the 14th century copies in its shape, in its flattened handle form, in its torus moulding and in the vertical emphasis of its neck decoration, a form of inlaid metal jug common in the region at this period (**Figs.8-9**). Another ceramic object, this time a dish from Kāshān dated 607/1210, copies a common Persian type of inlaid metal dish of the same period (**Figs.10-11**). These are but two examples among many. All the more is it apparent that the inlaid metalwork that survives in such huge quantities was either designed to stand side by side with silver, or even to be the prized luxury possession of some of the wealthiest rulers of the age.

24. Allan (1982), nos.14-15; Barrett (1949), pl.28.

25. Dimand (1931).

26. Maqrīzī, ii, (1854), 112.

Bibliography

Aga-Oglu (1930)	Aga-Oglu, M., "Two Thirteenth-Century Bronze Ewers", *Burlington Magazine*, 57, 1930, pp.27-28.
Allan (1976)	Allan, J.W., "Silver: the Key to Bronze in Early Islamic Iran", *Kunst des Orients*, 2, 1976-7, pp.5-21.
Allan (1982)	Allan, J.W., *Islamic Metalwork: Nuhad Es-Said Collection*, London, 1982.
Allan (1982a)	Allan, J.W., *Nishapur: Metalwork of the Early Islamic Period, Metropolitan Museum of Art*, New York, 1982.

Allan & Raby (1982)	Allan, J.W., and Raby, J.A.J., "Metalwork" in *Tulips, Arabesques and Turbans*, ed. Y Petsopoulos, London, 1982, pp.17-72.
Allan (1984)	Allan, J.W., "Sha'bān, Barqūq and the Decline of the Mamlūk Metalworking Industry", *Muqarnas*, 2, 1984, pp.85-94.
Atil (1975)	Atil, E., *Art of the Arab World*, Washington, 1975.
Baer (1972)	Baer, E., "An Islamic Inkwell in the Metropolitan Museum of Art", in *Islamic Art in the Metropolitan Museum of Art*, ed. R. Ettinghausen, New York, 1972, pp.199-211.
Barrett (1949)	Barrett, D., *Islamic Metalwork in the British Museum*, London, 1949.
Blake (1937)	Blake, R.P., "The Circulation of Silver in the Moslem East down to the Mongol Epoch", *Harvard Journal of Asiatic Studies*, 2, 1937, pp.291-328.
Brieux & Maddison (forthcoming)	Brieux, A., and Maddison, F., *Répertoire des Facteurs d'Astrolabes et de leurs Oeuvres, Prèmier Partie: Islam, Byzance, Arménie, Géogie et Inde Hindoue*, Paris, C.N.R.S., forthcoming.
Brinner (1963)	Brinner, W.M., *A Chronicle of Damascus 1389-1397*, Berkeley, California, 1963.
Coche de la Ferté (1958)	Coche de la Ferté, E., *L'Antiquité Chrétienne au Musée du Louvre*, Paris, 1958.
Dimand (1931)	Dimand, M.S., "Unpublished Metalwork of the Rasulid Sultans of Yemen", *Metropolitan Museum Studies*, 3, 1931, pp.229-37.
Dodd (1961)	Dodd, E.C., *Byzantine Silver Stamps*, Dumbarton Oaks, 1961.
Ettinghausen (1957)	Ettinghausen, R., "The 'Wade Cup' in the Cleveland Museum of Art, its Origin and Decoration", *Ars Orientalis*, 2, 1957, pp.327-66.
Fehérvári (1968)	Fehérvári, G., "Ein Ayyūbidisches Räuchergefäss mit dem Namen des Sultan al-Malik al-'Ādil II", *Kunst des Orients*, 5, 1968, Part 1, pp.37-54.
Fehérvári (1976)	Fehérvári, G., *Islamic Metalwork of the Eighth to the Fifteenth Century in the Keir Collection*, London 1976.
Geneva (1985)	*Treasures of Islam*, Musée d'Art et d'Histoire, ed. T. Falk, Geneva, 1985.
Grabar (1961)	Grabar, O., "Two Pieces of Islamic Metalwork in the University of Michigan", *Ars Orientalis*, 4, 1961, pp.360-68.
Guzelian (1948)	Guzelian, L.T., "Nadpis imenem Badr al-dīna Lūlū na bronzovom podsvetchnike Gosudarstvennovo Ermitazha", *Epigrafika Vostoka*, 2, 1948, pp.76-82.
Herzfeld (1936)	Herzfeld, E., "A Bronze Pen-Case", *Ars Islamica*, 3, 1936, pp.35-43.
'Izzi (1965)	'Izzi, W., "An Ayyūbid Basin of al-Ṣāliḥ Najm al-Dīn", *Studies in Islamic Art and Architecture in Honour of Professor K.A.C. Creswell*, Cairo, 1965, pp.253-59.
Lane-Poole (1886)	Lane-Poole, S., *The Art of the Saracens in Egypt*, London, 1886.
Lavoix (1878)	Lavoix, H., "Le Galerie Oriental du Trocadéro", *Gazette des Beaux-Arts*, 2nd period, vol.xviii, 1978, pp.769-91.
Maqrīzī (1854)	al-Maqrīzī, *al-Mawā'iz wa'l-I'tibar bi Dhikr al-Khiṭaṭ wa'l-Āthār*, Bulaq, 1854.

Maqrīzī (1972)	al-Maqrīzī, *Kitāb al-Sulūk li Maʿrifat Duwal al-Mulūk*, ed. S. Ashūr, Cairo, 1972.
Mayer (1956)	Mayer, L.A., *Islamic Astrolabists and Their Works*, Geneva, 1956.
Melikian-Chirvani (1968)	Melikian-Chirvani, A.S., "Le Bassin du Sultan Qarā Arslān ibn Īl-Ġāzī", *Revue des Études Islamiques*, 36, 1968, pp.263-78.
Melikian-Chirvani (1968)	Melikian-Chirvani, A.S., "La Coupe d'Abu Sahl-e Farhad-Jerdi", *Gazette des Beaux-Arts*, 6ème période, 71, 1968, pp.129-46.
Melikian-Chirvani (1982)	Melikian-Chirvani, A.S., "Argenterie et Féodalité dans l'Iran Médiéval", *Art et Société dans le Monde iranien*, Paris, 1982, pp.143-75.
Melikian-Chirvani (1982a)	Melikian-Chirvani, A.S., *Islamic Metalwork from the Iranian World, 8th-18th Centuries*, Victoria and Albert Museum Catalogue, London 1982.
Paris (1971)	*Arts de l'Islam des Origines à 1700*, Paris, 1971.
Pope (1930)	Pope, A.U., "Treasures Found in an Earthenware Jar: Fine Seljuk Silver", *Illustrated London News*, September 20, 1930, pp.480-82.
Pope (1938)	*A Survey of Persian Art*, ed. A.U. Pope, Oxford, 1938-39.
Pope (1960)	Pope, A.U., *Masterpieces of Persian Art*, London, 1960.
Rice (1950)	Rice, D.S., "The Brasses of Badr al-Dīn Lu'lu'", *Bulletin of the School of Oriental and African Studies*, 13, no.3, 1950, pp.627-34.
Rice (1955)	Rice, D.S., *The Wade Cup in the Cleveland Museum of Art*, Paris, 1955.
Rice (1957)	Rice, D.S., "Inlaid Brasses from the Workshop of Ahmad al-Dhaki al-Mawsili", *Ars Orientalis*, 2, 1957, pp.283-326.
Salam-Liebich (1976)	Salam-Liebich, H., "A Little Known Collection of Islamic Art", *Apollo*, May 1976, pp.35-39.
Sarre (1906)	Sarre, F., *Sammlung F. Sarre. Erzeugnissen islamischer Kunst. Teil 1: Metal*, Berlin, 1906.
Sarre & van Berchem (1907)	Sarre, F., and van Berchem, M., "Das Metallbeken des Atabeks Lu'lu' von Mossul", *Münchener Jahrbuch der bildenden Kunst*, 1, 1907, pp.18-37.
Sarre & Martin (1912)	Sarre, F., and Martin, F.R., *Die Ausstellung von Meisterwerken muhammedanischer Kunst in München 1910*, Munich, 1912.
Scerrato (1967)	Scerrato, U., *Arte Islamica a Napoli*, Naples, 1967.
Smirnov (1909)	Smirnov, Y.I., *Argenterie Orientale*, St Petersburg, 1909.
The Victoria & Albert Album (1983)	*The Victoria & Albert Album*, 2, London, 1983.
Watson (1967)	Watson, A.M., "Back to Gold—and Silver", *Economic History Review*, 2nd series, 22, no.1, 1967, pp.1-34.
Wiet (1933)	Wiet, G., *L'Exposition Persane de 1931*, Cairo, 1933.
Wiet (1965)	Wiet, G., "Deux Objets d'Art Retrouvés" in *Arabic and Islamic Studies in Honor of H.A.R. Gibb*, ed. G. Makdisi, Leiden, 1965, pp.655-61.
Wilson (1931)	*Catalogue of the International Exhibition of Persian Art, Royal Academy of Arts, London, 7th January to 28th February 1931*, ed. A.T. Wilson, London, 1931.

Temple Inventories in Ancient Greece

D.M. LEWIS

The task I have been given is to introduce you to some of the textual evidence for Greek metal-work. It is extremely copious and, particularly when it deals with gold and silver objects, it goes some way to making up for the loss of whole categories of objects which do not normally survive. With isolated exceptions, it has been neglected; my impression is that it has not really been explored by those interested in the development of metal-work, and that much remains to be done in correlating with real objects or representations of them.

My brief is to talk about inventories, that is, comprehensive documents drawn up by the responsible officials to list and publish the articles in their care. But, long before any text of this kind survives or is likely to have existed, one does get the odd text where individual donors commemorated their dedication with a separate inscription on stone or bronze. The practice is slightly different from writing the dedication on the object itself or, in the case, for example, of a statue, on its base. As the sixth century B.C. goes on, the text can become fairly explicit. The stele from Sigeion in the British Museum records the gift by Phanodikos of Prokonnesos to the citizens of Sigeion for use in the prytaneion, that is, for public entertainments, of a mixing-bowl, a stand and a strainer; the material is not specified. It has recently been suggested that the gift was thought so magnificent that Phanodikos was given the more than human status of a hero.[1] Towards the end of the century, in Samos, two citizens of distant Perinthos dedicated to Hera as a tithe a gold Gorgon, a silver Siren, a silver phiale and a bronze lamp-stand, and added that the whole dedication, including the setting up of the stone, had cost them 212 Samian staters.[2]

Inventories as such start in the fifth century and are surely to be connected, like many other kinds of publication which start then, with a spread of democratic institutions and the concept that officials were responsible to the people. I would not like to say precisely when and where this starts, but the main story begins for us in 433 in Athens, and the motive is

1. Richter (1961), no.53; Jeffery (1984), 53-4.
2. Klaffenbach (1953).

more than purely administrative; it is financial. Pericles saw the gold and silver objects in Athenian temples and shrines as part of the city's reserve capital; even the gold which went into Pheidias' chryselephantine statue of Athena was of known weight and made to be removable, though it survived many financial crises before being melted into coin at the beginning of the third century. It was with the intention of putting Athens' financial machinery in order to face the coming Peloponnesian War that the treasurers of Athena were ordered to prepare regular annual inventories of what was in their charge, distinguishing gold and silver, weighing and counting the existing stock and any new dedications of the year, and these were checked as they left office.[3]

These inventories were published on stone, and, considering the hazards of time, we have a remarkably complete collection of them covering the next hundred and thirty years. Patterns of display changed. For the first forty years or so there were separate stelai for each of the three main relevant rooms of what we call the Parthenon, but later they were consolidated into mammoth texts. By the 360s the annual stelai were 2 metres high, 1.10 metres across and a quarter of a metre thick, and could run to four hundred lines of text in letters 5 millimetres high. This could hardly go on; there was some attempt to reduce the amount of material which had to go on stone each year, and the letters get smaller and smaller.

Points of detail remain obscure, but we have a fairish picture of the vicissitudes of Athena's treasures over those hundred and thirty years. As the Peloponnesian War drew to a close, the lists became shorter and shorter as familiar objects disappeared into the melting-pot for Athens' first gold coinage. In the fourth century there is again a steady accretion of objects commissioned for public cult, dedications by officials and private individuals and crowns received from foreign states wishing to honour Athens and Athena. From time to time, we see traces of systematic operations to melt down damaged or small objects and replace them by larger ones. The biggest of these was under Lycurgus in the 330s, who revived Periclean policies and increased the stock of the jewellery and equipment of the basket-carriers of the Panathenaic procession from thirty sets to a hundred. But magnificence could not last, and the last of all the lists, from a troubled year round 300, certainly appears to list all the stock and then to end: "these we did not hand over to our successors".[4]

At this point, the continuous Athenian information breaks off and is only patchily supplied by the occasional account of the remodelling of the offerings of individual shrines; one of these I shall come back to. Its place is supplied for the next hundred and fifty years or so principally by Delos. Inventory-making

3. Meiggs and Lewis (1969), no.58 (cf. no.76); Fornara (1983), no.119 (cf. no.143).

4. Koumanoudes and Miller (1971).

had started there in the fourth century while it was under Athenian administration. It continued during Delian independence and produced texts far longer than anything we have from Athens. I confess that I do not know my way about these texts very well and they are even less exploited than the Athenian texts, except by one devoted researcher who pursues all their references to different types of coinage. The task of tackling them is not made easier by the fact that they still lack any kind of published index.

It should be clear that there is potentially a good deal of information of all kinds to be got out of these texts. I do not ask this audience to share my enthusiasm for the minutiae of Athenian administration or finance or for the sometimes invaluable diplomatic information provided by the crowns from foreign states. There is, however, religious information, not only about the type of offering thought appropriate to each god, but about the gods themselves. Such controversial importations as Bendis or Ammon get at any rate *termini ante quem* from the inventories.

There are weights. The convention was to weigh silver objects to the nearest half-obol, a bit over a third of a gram, gold objects to the nearest quarter-obol, half that. An unpublished Oxford dissertation[5] has argued that this was collective delusion and that no contemporary weighing technique was capable of anything like that accuracy, but the Athenians were evidently happy with it. It is clear that there were standard weights for various objects. Silver hydriae aspired to a weight of 1,000 drachmae (435 grams), silver phialae to one of 100 drachmae. Silver oenochoae were in the 400-600 drachmae range, drinking cups (*poteria*) 25 to 40. I have made no attempt to calculate standard dimensions. Other silver objects observed less of a standard. Around 370 B.C., for example, Athena possessed three platters (*pinakes*), one described as large at 2027 1/2 drachmae and two others at 1,028 1/8 and 719 1/2, and two lavers (*chernibeia*), at 1,040 and 940 drachmae

Gold objects, at first sight, present an extraordinary variety of weights. The explanation is to be found in the fact that the Athenians thought in terms of a silver standard. When, as they frequently did, they ordered that someone be honoured with a gold crown for 500 drachmae, they did not mean that the gold crown itself would weigh 500 drachmae, though the mistake has been made by very eminent archaeologists, but that its cost would be 500 silver drachmae, a very different matter. Attention to the likely cost of gold objects is therefore not unprofitable, and I have in my time produced a tentative sketch, on the basis of the inventories, of the ups and downs of the gold-silver ratio between the relatively fixed points of 14:1 in the 430s and 10:1 in the 330s.[6]

That the inventories and their accessions can be chronologically ordered is

5. Grayson (1975).

6. Lewis (1968).

clearly of importance, and it should on occasion be possible to determine at least when some names and descriptions come into use or are first reported. I have mentioned some names already, many of them pot-shapes as well, and you will be eager to know what I can do for you by way of descriptions. To me they only rarely seem exciting, and the fullest and most valuable of all the descriptions which the treasurers of Athena have left us is not of a separate object at all, but of the doors of the Hekatompedon, i.e. the Parthenon, where some of the metalwork had broken away and lost some bosses by the 340s. The description is sufficient to allow us to recognize the false stone door of a Macedonian tomb in Istanbul as a direct copy of the original doors.[7]

Fifth-century descriptions are rarely very full, and perhaps the general picture is more interesting. In 433 the Pronaos of the Parthenon held "the gold phiale from which they make the libations", 104 silver phialai, three silver horns (*kerata*), three silver cups (*poteria*), and a silver lamp. Virtually all its accessions for the next twenty-five years fall into these categories, though one new cup in 427/6 is specifically described as Chalcidian, whether that be an ethnic adjective or a type, and there is a growing number of *argyrides*, a very enigmatic word—(their weights vary from 60 to over 200 drachmae).

The inner room, the Hekatompedon, had much more gold. In 433 it held a gold kore on a stele, unweighed, and a silver sprinkler, also unweighed, and two gold phialai weighing 1,344 drachmae between them, to which in that year another was added, weighing 1,200 drachmae by itself. If you work that amount out in silver, you find that it would have kept a trireme at sea for three months. In subsequent years, the prevailing accessions are gold crowns, one specifically for the Nike on the hand of Pheidias' statue, but there is a little silver, particularly a heavy incense-box (*thymiaterion*, 1,000 drachmae); the *argyrides* of the Pronaos are matched, at more or less the same dates, by *chrysides* here.

What the Athenians called the Parthenon, one of the rooms at the back, is much more fun. There were some straight gold pieces in 433, a crown and some phialai, and there were silver phialai as well, but otherwise it is a strange miscellany, of no great intrinsic value. Most of it survived for the next seventy or eighty years. There was a gold *carchesion*, said to be a cup with a waist, with a silver bottom; this belonged to an out-of-town shrine of Herakles. There are two silver-gilt nails (as they weighed 800 grams between them, I cannot imagine what they were for), a silver-gilt mask and various other plated objects. The nicest of these was an imitation corn-field with twelve shoots. There were famous parallels to this at Delphi, and there are surviving

7. *Inscriptiones Graecae*, II^2, 1455.36-49, 1457.9-20, (the missing word in these texts must be *pompholugon*); Michaelis (1871), 316; Mendel (1912), no.138.

examples.[8] Some of the contents lie right outside our subject, various bits of armour and furniture and some lyres. The fifth-century accessions also tend to be miscellaneous, except for some gold crowns. The suppression of the revolt of Mytilene in 427 leaves some trace, not only in the spoil, a shield, a bronze Illyrian helmet and three silver cups (*kotylai*), but in a strange present from loyal Methymna, a gilt ivory flute-case (*sybene*). Some quite full descriptions come in. I pick out a pair of accessions datable to within a year or so of 408, two gold necklaces adorned with stones, each with twenty roses. One had a ram's head and weighed 30 drachmae, the other is described as smaller, and was evidently slightly different.

In all these rooms, practically everything meltable went in the last years of the war, together with seven of the eight golden Nikai.[9] The Pronaos in particular was emptied, with only a solitary gold crown left.

The first substantial accession of the post-war period came in 402/1 when twenty silver hydriai were made, almost certainly the processional vessels (*pompeia*), which we know to have been made from the confiscated property of the Thirty Tyrants.[10] This is a new shape for silver; Athena had possessed none before. It became a fairly regular one; by 370 thirty are listed for Athena Polias. I have already said that there was evidence that Lycurgus raised the number of basket-carriers from thirty to a hundred; perhaps in 370 there were thirty hydria-carriers as well. It is in any case likely that these silver hydriai are replacing pottery ones; hydriai are carried on the North Frieze of the Parthenon.[11] The switch from pottery to silver evidently spread to other cults. By 370 Athena Nike has four, Artemis Brauronia seven, the Dioskouroi three, Demeter and Kore five, and Aphrodite one.

I doubt if further investigation of chronological developments would be helpful within this short paper, and it would be better to pick out some fourth-century objects.

Some large objects with gold and silver on wooden frames had evidently survived the war. One gold basket adorned with ivory animals weighed over 2,000 drachmae, and there was a similar censer. In the early fourth century the Athenians went over to a bronze core for such objects. Very close to 400 we get two pairs: baskets, gold over bronze, one adorned with a Zeus, the other with an Apollo, weighing over 3,500 drachmae apiece; censers, gold over bronze, weighing nearly 3,000 drachmae, distinguished only by the leaves on one being straight, on the other curved. Where precisely the fullest

8. Plut. *Mor.*401F; one was sold at Sotheby's some time ago, but I cannot remember the metal.

9. These, the grandest of all the offerings, had two talents' weight of gold apiece; see Woodward (1937), Thompson (1944).

10. Walbank (1982), 97-8.

11. It is a well-known problem that the frieze depicts men, while the literary evidence speaks of women (Simon (1983), 60, 63-5); the silver hydriai weighed well over 4 kilos apiece, but girls should have continued to manage that.

description fits in, I don't know. This was a censer, silver over wood, weighing 1,448 drachmae and adorned with a Nike. It had a separate silver cover, weighing 58 drachmae

For the next topic, I would like to reverse the procedure and start, more or less, from some objects. One shape where the original relationship of pot and metal has always been clear is the phiale. Richter and Milne[12] take as their type phiale a pot in Boston of which they reasonably say that its ribbing imitates metalwork. Gold and silver phialai are common in literature, turning up even in private houses, and, as we have seen, they existed in quantity on the fifth-century Acropolis. There were possibilities for the shape in metalwork which did not exist in pottery, and there are traces of specialized descriptions even in the fifth century.[13] In the fourth century, the picture is a good deal richer. As far as real objects are concerned, my prime concern is with two gold phialai; there is other related material. One will be familiar from its appearance at the British Museum in 1976. It is from the Panagyurishte Treasure.[14] Its base has three rows of negroes' heads, with an inner row of acorns. The other is in New York;[15] it has three rows of acorns and an inner row of nuts. It has no known provenance, but, besides a Greek graffito, it has a weight inscription in Punic, which no-one has done very well at reading; it is the lighter of the two, weighing 747 grams

Bulgarian scholars have claimed the Panagyurishte phiale for Lampsakos, and have repeated this as a matter of fact in various places. There is nothing whatever to this ascription, which rests on a false interpretation of the weight inscriptions. It has two of these: one of them just says Η (100), the other ΗꟼΔΔΔΔΓ⊢Τ or something very like it), 196 drachmae and a quarter-obol. It actually weighs 845.7 grams. Venedikov argued at a very early stage that the aim of the inscription was to distinguish between a weight in staters and a weight in drachmae.[16] He even thought that the weight in drachmae was really appropriate to silver and anomalous for gold. Assuming that the "100" inscription proved a stater of 8.457 grams, he looked no further than Lampsakos. The truth is much simpler. The "100" represents darics, as Kahn[17] correctly saw, though without citing the clear fourth-century evidence for objects being weighed in darics.[18] It has always been pretty clear that the other weight inscription, besides being Attic in appearance, made perfect sense as an Attic weight, with a drachma of 4.313 grams.

The general view is that this phiale is late fourth century. I am not in a

12. Richter and Milne (1935), fig.181.

13. There was already a silver phiale with a gold boss or navel at Eleusis around 420; *Inscriptiones Graecae*, I³, 385.1-2)

14. Venedikov and Gerassimov (1975), figs.131-2; British Museum (1976), no.361.

15. Von Bothmer (1962-3); Strong (1966), 97-8, with pl.23A.

16. Venedikov (1958), 82-6.

17. H.A. Cahn in Simon (1960), 26-8.

18. Dittenberger (1915), nos.168, 276, the second even by Athenian colonists on Samos; Bourguet, iii/5, (1932), 61, ii, A.1-8.

position to dispute it, but the motif is certainly older. You will not find the phrase *phiale Aithiopis* in Liddell and Scott or its supplement, but it occurs. Kontoleon pointed out that Athena possessed in the 370s four gold *phialai Aithiopides* weighing 805 1/2 drachmae as a group, very similar in weight to the Panagyurishte piece.[19] I am beginning to suspect that the similarity is due to their also having been made to a hundred daric standard; the hypothesis explains some peculiar Athenian weights. It may be argued that the standard counts against their Athenian origin, but there is no other reason to suppose that the group was not made at Athens around 380; there is no indication of a foreign dedicator. I am far from sure that the Panagyurishte phiale was not made in Athens. According to Pausanias (I 33.3), Pheidias' statue of Nemesis had long before carried a phiale with Ethiopians.

What about the Metropolitan piece with its acorns and nuts? Liddell and Scott does have the phrase *phiale balanote*, but only from a fragmentary statement in Athenaeus (502B). There we are told that it was so called because there were gold knuckle-bones (if there is what *astragaloi* means here) on its base. He goes on to quote Semos as saying that in Delos there was a golden palm-tree, dedicated by the Naxians, and gold *phialai karyotai* (with nuts). Delos does indeed provide us with some firmly dated evidence. In a text of 364/3 under Athenian control (*Inscriptions de Délos*, 104) we find six *phialai chrysai balanotai* weighing 1,190 1/3 drachmae, seven *phialai chrysai leiai* (smooth), weighing 983 3/4 drachmae (much lighter), two *aktinotai* (with rays), weight lost, and one *karyote* (with nuts), dedicated by the Naxians, weighing 195 drachmae. The *balanotai* and the *karyote* fit into the weight range we have seen at Panagyurishte and Athens, and indeed the Delians were not very good at distinguishing acorns from other nuts, these *phialai balanotai* appear in later inventories as *karyotai*. Again, only the Naxian dedication takes us outside Athens or Athenian-controlled Delos, but the weight of the New York piece and its Punic inscription suggest that it comes from rather further afield, though it may have been made by a Greek whose name began with Pausi-.

We do not know how long the *phialai balanotoi* had been at Delos in 364/3 and there is some evidence for a longish history for the type. It has been claimed[20] that the Erechtheum caryatids are carrying such phialai, and they may go further back. A fragment of the comic poet Cratinus, whose last play was produced in 423, refers to *phialai balaneiomphaloi* (F54 Kassel-Austin). Hellenistic scholars explained this by saying that the boss looked like the hearth of a bath-house, but, as Cratinus' latest editors remark, without knowing much of the evidence, acorns are more likely to be relevant than

19. Kondoleon (1962), with slight inaccuracies. There was another group along with them, six *phialai ptilotai* (with wings), weighing 1,036 drachmae, a good deal lighter.

20. Strong (1966), 81.

bath-houses. We have no actual acorn-shaped bosses as yet.[21] We can perhaps look forward to them, we can certainly hope for wings and rays. Contrariwise, we might eventually learn the name of the phiale from Kul Oba in the Hermitage with bearded heads, gorgons, panthers and dolphins.[22]

As the world expanded, more exotic objects will have come to swell Athena's store. There had long been one or two pieces of Persian spoil, not fully described. It is a great pity that the full description has not survived of a series of presents made by Alexander's Queen, the Bactrian Roxana; we can only distinguish a golden rhyton, a term making its first appearance in the inventories, and a gold neckpiece; more was said about them, but it is off the stone. Similarly, I have spent endless hours trying to decipher just what it was with ivory feet and bronze supports which was dedicated by Euthydike, the Athenian descendant of Miltiades the victor of Marathon, mistress of Demetrios Poliorcetes and wife of a dynast of Cyrene, forerunner of a long series of great Hellenistic ladies.

In the later lists, for almost the first time, we start getting a few names of craftsmen, but there is not much to say about them. At least one, Nikokrates of Kolonos, was an Athenian citizen; others, Kittos, Herakleiodoros and Platon, were probably not. Some of the names are presumably hereditary. In the 330s there is one with the unattractive name of Mys. He will have been named after the craftsman who made the shield of Pheidias' Athena Promachos to Parrhasios' design.

More light on fourth-century metal workers comes from Delphi, and goes some way to demonstrating the importance of Athens in the craft. In the 330s Delphi faced the task of replacing the major offerings melted into coin by the sacrilegious Phocians, notably the great gold and silver bowls dedicated by Croesus. Apparently all the possible contractors were selected from Athens, six of uncertain origin, though one of them may be the same Nikokrates, two certain Athenian citizens and four Corinthians.[23] They stayed for twelve days to survey the problems and make their bids, receiving a ration allowance while on site.[24] Whether we are seeing the actual craftsmen rather than

21. That acorn bosses existed is suggested by another group of *phialai* which came into the inventories around the middle of the century, (*Inscriptiones Graecae*, II[2], 1443.143-153; see Lehner (1890), 113-4). The metal is not certain: the weights are enormous, apparently 1,200-1,400 drachmae. Three appear to be described as having the little sphinx on *the* acorn, three as having the little sphinx on *the* nut, one as having the little sphinx on *the* apple, one as having the palladion on something slightly different, perhaps a knuckle-bone. These would clearly make better sense as referring to the shape of a central boss rather than to numerous articles arranged in rows. The *phiale balanote* is not only a gold shape; there is a bronze one, (*Inscriptiones Graecae*, II[2], 1425.357).

22. See New York 1973-74, no.83 with pl.20; the weight of this piece is 698.55 grams; Paris (1975), no.94.

23. There is a problem about one of these, Theomnestos, later (see n.25) referred to as a Sicyonian.

24. Bourguet, iii/5, (1932), 48.23-41.

contractors is perhaps doubtful. The sums involved were very substantial, nearly 5 talents for replacing the silver bowl which held 600 amphorae, and the money was paid over only by instalments.[25]

In this case, of course, they had to find the metal as well. Most of our Athenian evidence relates to remaking from metal objects provided for the purpose. For the fourth century we are more or less confined to some rather fragmentary accounts which only cover losses in melting. In one such case the goldsmith was given 2,950 drachmae weight of gold objects. 14 per cent. of this was lost in the melting, leaving 2,531 drachmae of pure gold, but a rake through the ashes produced another 116 drachmae, reducing the loss to 10 per cent. I am sure that there is more to be found, but I think that we have to wait for the end of the third century in Athens for a really detailed account to give the workman's pay (*Inscriptiones Graecae*, II[2], 839.80-88). This is one of the remelting operations I referred to earlier. In the shrine of the Hero Physician there were thirty-three small dedications of models of various parts of the body; eyes and thighs are specified. These weighed 116 drachmae, but there was also a phiale weighing 100 drachmae and 18 drachmae in cash. The five citizens and the public slave who supervised the operation reported that, as instructed, they had spent 15 drachmae on a sacrifice to appease the Hero. The melting of the 216 drachmae of objects produced a 6 per cent. loss. 8 1/2 drachmae were reserved for putting up the stele with the accounts. The workman of the new oenochoe got 12 drachmae. They were left with an oenochoe weighing 183 1/2 drachmae and 2 drachmae over. With this they promised to make another model. Whether a making charge of 7 per cent. was anything like standard, I cannot tell,[26] and I would not like to venture a cost of living figure for the late third century. What is perhaps significant is that the craftsman is not named. We should not exaggerate the social importance of routine metal work.

25. Bourguet, iii/5, (1932), 62.5-9.

26. But see my article (n.6), 108, where I calculated a 6 2/3 per cent. making charge for a phiale in 434.

Bibliography

SOURCES. The fifth-century Athenian texts have had a recent edition in *Inscriptiones Graecae*, I[3], (1981), nos.292-362, with summaries on pp.305-6, 318, 331-2; the fourth-century texts are in *Inscriptiones Graecae*[2], II.1 (1927), nos. 1370-1496, with important addenda in II.2 (1931), pp. 797-810, but much has been changed since then, not all of which is published, and I have been sparing in annotation.

Von Bothmer (1962-3) Von Bothmer, D., "A Gold Libation Bowl", *Bulletin of the Metropolitan Museum, New York*, 21, 1962-3, pp.154-66.

Bourguet (1932) Bourguet, E., ed., *Fouilles de Delphes*, iii, vol.5, *Les comptes du iv e siècle*, 1932.

British Museum (1976)	*Thracian Treasures from Bulgaria*, British Museum, London, 1976.
Dittenberger (1915)	Dittenberger, W., ed., *Sylloge Inscriptionum Graecarum*, 3rd edn., Leipzig, 1915.
Fornara (1983)	Fornara, C.W., *Archaic Times to the End of the Peloponnesian War: Translated Documents of Greece and Rome*, 1, 2nd edn., Cambridge, 1983.
Grayson (1975)	Grayson, C.H., *Weighing in Ancient Greece*, Oxford D.Phil. thesis, 1975.
Jeffery (1984)	Jeffery, L.H., "Lordly Tombs: an Epigraphic Sidelight on Archaic Attic Society", *Proceedings of the Eighth International Congress of Greek and Latin Epigraphy*, 1, 1984, pp.52-4.
Kirchner (1927)	Kirchner, J., ed., *Inscriptiones Graecae*, II, 2nd edn., 1, Berlin, 1927.
Kirchner (1931)	Kirchner, J., ed., *Inscriptiones Graecae*, II², Berlin, 1931.
Klaffenbach (1953)	Klaffenbach, G., "Archaische Weihinschrift aus Samos", *Mitteilungen des Deutschen Archäologischen Instituts*, 6, 1953, pp.15-20.
Kontoleon (1962)	Kontoleon, N., "The gold treasure of Panagurischte", *Balkan Studies*, 3, 1962, pp.185-200.
Koumanoudes & Miller (1971)	Koumanoudes, S.N. and Miller, S.G., "*Inscriptiones Graecae*, II², 1477 and 3046 rediscovered", *Hesperia*, 40, 1971, pp.448-57.
Lehner (1890)	Lehner, H., *Ueber die athenischen Schatzverzeichnisse des vierten Jahrhunderts*, Diss. Strassburg, 1890.
Lewis (1968)	Lewis, D.M., "New Evidence for the Gold-Silver Ratio", in C.M. Kraay and G.K. Jenkins, *Essays in Greek Coinage presented to Stanley Robinson*, Oxford, 1968, pp.105-110.
Lewis (1981)	Lewis, D.M., ed., *Inscriptiones Graecae*, I, 3rd edn., Berlin, 1981.
Meiggs & Lewis (1969)	Meiggs, R. and Lewis, D., *A Selection of Greek Historical Inscriptions to the End of the Fifth Century B.C.*, Oxford, 1969.
Mendel (1912)	Mendel, G., *Musées Impériaux Ottomans: Catalogue des Ssculptures Grecques, Romaines et Byzantines*, 1, Constantinople, 1912.
Michaelis (1871)	Michaelis, A., *Der Parthenon*, Leipzig, 1871.
New York (1973-74)	"From the Lands of the Scythians", *Bulletin of the Metropolitan Museum, New York*, 32/5, 1973-74.
Paris (1975)	*Or des Scythes, Trésors des Musées Soviétiques*, Paris, 1975.
Richter and Milne (1935)	Richter, G.M.A. and Milne, M.J., *Shapes and Names of Athenian Vases*, New York, 1935.
Richter (1961)	Richter, G.M.A., *The Archaic Gravestones of Attica*, London, 1961.
Simon (1960)	Simon, E., "Der Goldschatz von Panagjuriste—eine Schöpfung der Alexanderzeit", *Antike Kunst*, 3, 1960, pp. 3-29.
Simon (1983)	Simon, E., *Festivals of Attica: an Archaeological Commentary*, Madison, Wisconsin, 1983.
Strong (1966)	Strong, D.E., *Greek and Roman Gold and Silver Plate*, London, 1966.
Thompson (1944)	Thompson, D.B., "The Golden Nikai Reconsidered", *Hesperia*, 13, 1944, pp.173-209.
Venedikov (1958)	Venedikov, I., "Sur la Date et l'Origine du Trésor de Panaguristé", *Acta Antiqua*, 6, 1958, pp.67-86.
Venedikov & Gerassimov (1975)	Venedikov, I. and Gerassimov, T., *Thracian Art Treasures*, Sofia, 1975.

Walbank (1982)	Walbank, M.B., "The Confiscation and Sale of the Poletai in 402/1B.C. of the Property of the Thirty Tyrants", *Hesperia*, 51, 1982, pp.74-98.
Woodward (1937)	Woodward, A.M., "The Golden Nikai of Athena", *Archaiologike Ephemeris*, 1, 1937, pp.159-70.

Some Literary Evidence for Gold and Silver Vessels in the Ming Period (1368-1644)

CRAIG CLUNAS

In the China of the 14th, 15th, 16th and 17th centuries gold and silver tableware was ubiquitous in the homes of the wealthy. Gold was more highly thought of as a luxury item than silver. The luxurious nature of vessels in precious metals, accepted by almost all contemporary commentators, brought them within the scope of Ming sumptuary laws, laws which were however frequently broken. Over-indulgence in gold and silver vessels was, in some circles at least, viewed as vulgar ostentation, and they were avoided for certain types of function, such as religious and funerary offerings. Despite the millions of vessels in circulation, the loss of which radically distorts our picture of the Ming applied arts, the actual craft of silversmithing stood low in the esteem of the élite.

It is remarkable in fact how few names of silversmiths survive, either on objects or in written sources. A brief list is given by the mid-14th-century author Tao Zongyi who comments:
" There is but a short count of those among the silversmiths of Zhexi whose workmanship is skilled and who are known of by name.[1] " He names four contemporaries, two of whom are probably father and son, and the most renowned of whom is Zhu Bisham, maker of the famous silver "raft cups".[2] Another author, writing about 1600, is able only to repeat Tao's list, showing that no further nameable silversmiths had registered on educated consciousness in the intervening two centuries.[3] Only two more names are known, one being that of the early 17th-century Lu Guohua, whose vessels for wine were "number one in the empire", and one named Guang Fangzhou, whose appearance in a late 16th-century source has nothing to do with his art and everything to do with his dramatic escape from gaol when under sentence of death.[4]

The near-total anonymity of workers in precious metal places the craft

1. Tao (1980), 372-373.
2. Chen (1936), 4, 12b.
3. Zhen (1984), 52-57.
4. Xie, i, (1980), 211; Shen Defu, ii, (1980), 481.

mid-way in a hierarchy of élite values. At the top are crafts like bamboo-carving, which partake of some of the status of fine art, many of whose practitioners are mentioned by name. In the middle, but still above silver, are those crafts with several recorded names, and one classic "core" craftsman (often active in the late 16th century) like the jade-carver Lu Zigang and the bronze-caster Hu Wenming. At the bottom of the hierarchy of crafts are those, such as furniture making and weaving, whose workers are all anonymous. This was not a matter of "importance": fine clothes were highly important yet we do not have the name of a single tailor. Silver and gold are in something of the same situation, with only Zuh Bishan as the "big name" to whom objects could be attributed. Here is one connoisseur writing in about 1600:
" I managed to see at Song Yan's house a figure of (Wang) Zhaojun on horseback with her lute. Her eyebrows, hair and clothing were all finely patterned, and the hairs on the mane were exquisitely detailed. On the horse's belly was a hole no bigger than a bean, the inside being hollow. It weighed 2 *qian*, 7 *fen*, and the two characters *Bishan* were incised on the lute.[5] " Derek Gillman has shown how at least one object carrying the Zhu Bishan signature is unlikely to have been made before about 1580, suggesting that his name retained its appeal throughout the Ming.[6] With the exception of objects attributed to Zhu Bishan there is no connoisseurship of silver and no interest in old silver visible in Ming texts.

Yet archaeological and literary evidence combine to prove the overwhelming predominance of silver and to a lesser extent gold utensils on the dining tables of the wealthy. The tomb of Tang He (d.1390), found unrobbed in central Anhui in 1973, contains the complete table service of an early Ming magnate, one of the original adherents of the Ming founder.[7] Here silver utensils outnumber those of bronze or porcelain, while gold is confined to hair ornaments. Leaving out ornaments, spoons and chop-sticks, nine different vessel shapes are represented, from plain bowls and stemcups with well-known parallels in porcelain, to an incense-burner of a type also imitated in *jun* and Longquan ceramics.

But much more surprising is the literary evidence for the property of Yan Song at his death (1480-1565). Yan, a Grand Secretary from 1542 to 1562, was the most powerful politician of the mid-16th century, whose purging in 1562 left historians free to vilify him as corrupt, factious and above all rapaciously greedy. It is hard, given the nature of the evidence, to disentangle just from unjust accusations. What concerns us here is the inventory of his property taken at his fall from power on its forfeiture to the state, a uniquely detailed document which to an extent rare in China parallels the Ottoman *muhallefat* records.

5. Chen (1936), 4, 12b.

6. Gillman (1984), 15.

7. Fengbu (1977), 35-39.

In 1562, in a variety of properties in the capital and elsewhere, Yan Song owned 3,185 pure gold vessels, with a total weight of 11,033.31 *liang*. He owned 367 gold vessels studded with gems, weighing 1,827.72 *liang*. In addition to vast quantities of jewellery, he possessed 1,649 silver vessels, weighing 13,357.35 *liang*.[8] All these vessels are individually itemized as to weight and decoration, and some pieces were of very large size. One gold ewer and dish set weighed 24 *liang*, that is 900 gm. of metal.[9] One silver incense-burner alone is registered as weighing 572 *liang*, or 21,450 gm., over 756 oz. of silver.[10] This is not, it should be pointed out, unbelievably large. The largest piece of English silver, a wine cooler of Queen Anne date at Burghley House, weighs 3,400 oz.

By way of comparison, Yan Song owned a mere 857 jade vessels, though he did have 15,000 un-itemized porcelain bowls.[11] Yan Song was very, very rich but his tastes were not freakish. Zhang Juzheng, one of his successors as Grand Secretary, owned when purged in 1582 a total of 617 gold vessels (3,711 *liang*), and 986 silver ones, (5,240 *liang*).[12]

Nor were Yan's great incense-burners unique. One set of reminiscences of late 16th-century Nanjing recalls a vast silver incense-burner of 30 feet in circumference, once the property of the semi-legendary plutocrat Shen Wansan, in the household of one Zhang Jiangling. Both of these owners came to bad ends, and no wonder, comments the author, given the massive profligacy implied by such an object.[13] For at least in some circles gold and silver was viewed with suspicion as a material for everyday life. Ming sumptuary law assumes that anyone who can afford it will use it in preference to porcelain or lacquer, and attempts to restrict its use in ritual contexts to the cult of the imperial family.[14] Silver was suitable in some contexts and not in others.

It *was* suitable for gifts to the imperial household. Throughout the Yongle reign (1403-1424) Korean diplomatic missions ten times presented gold and silver vessels, while gold winepots, dishes, and religious utensils were sent to the Japanese court and to Tibet from China at the same time.[15] The alchemist Duan Chaoyong tried to establish his *bona fides* at court by, in 1540, presenting "several dozen" gold and silver vessels to the emperor.[16]

Yet, we know that in the 1580s the banquets served to successful examination candidates and to their examiners, quite senior members of the bureaucracy, in Peking were eaten off porcelain only.[17] Perhaps here a more

8. Zhou Shilin (1727), 18a, 21b and 71a.
9. Zhou Shilin (1727), 3a.
10. Zhou Shilin (1727), 62a.
11. Zhou Shilin (1727), 85a.
12. Zhou Shilin (1727), *fulu*, 1a.
13. Zhou Hui, i, (1955), 203.
14. Pope (1956), 37, translates the relevant sections of *Da Ming hui dian*, (1511), *juan*, 42-105.
15. Osumi (1984), 14-34.
16. Lui (1976), 1267.
17. Shen Bang (1980), 157 and 159.

austere ambience was deemed appropriate. We do know also that some arbiters of taste condemned the flaunting of wealth through precious tablewares. The highly fastidious He Liangjun (1506-1573) writes:
" I once visited a friend in Jiaxing, and noted that when entertaining guests the household used silver braziers and golden spittoons. Every guest had a set of golden dish and dish-stand, and a great golden cup with a pair of *chi* dragons. Each set contained about 15 or 16 *liang*. I passed the night there, and the next morning washed my face in a silver basin chased with plum blossom. The hangings, curtains and bed clothes were all of brocaded gauze, and my sight was assaulted to the point where I could not close my eyes all night. I have heard that the family even has incense- burners of gold, making them the richest family in Jiangnan, and at the same time the acme of common vulgarity incapable of being outdone.[18] "

Not everyone was so squeamish. The famous collector Xiang Yuanbian had several pieces of display silver in archaic shapes, which excited the admiration of a visitor in 1595, who described his Shang-style vessels as "extraordinary objects".[19] And the merely rich had no inhibitions, as can be seen by opening Ming fiction almost at random. It is a novel, *Jin ping mei*, "The Golden Lotus", which incidentally confirms another parallel between silversmithing and lowly crafts such as cabinet-making, in that there the craftsmen are summoned to work in the customer's home. In *Jin ping mei* 25, they are sent for in order to make a set of four silver figures, and two golden winepots.[20] Significantly, these are a birthday gift for an influential figure in the capital. Silver in Ming China played the same role as it did in Pepys' England, suitable as a gift, bribe or sweetener. A rather pathetic testimony of this is the Tongdao hoard, excavated in south-west Hunan in 1982.[21] Twenty-eight vessels, mostly in the form of wine cups and saucers but including some archaic vessel forms, a total of 2,728.6 gm., represent the silver of one Dang Zhe, an official of the remnant southern Ming killed in 1647 by the Manchus. The objects, mostly inscribed as birthday gifts, were presumably buried by his fleeing family. They show a struggle to maintain the cultural patterns of earlier, more prosperous times, even though by now no sets can be assembled, nothing matches anything else, and thirty-nine subordinates were forced to club together to buy Dang Zhe one small saucer. The falling off from the glories of Yan Song's mansions is striking, but striking too is the continued centrality of precious metal vessels as an index of prosperity. If we allow the scarcity of surviving pieces to push this to the backs of our minds, we cannot but continue to have an unbalanced picture of the material culture of Ming China.

18. He (1983), 314.
19. Chen (1936), 1, 6a.
20. *Jin ping mei* (1963), 25, 12a.
21. Huaihua (1984), 88-93.

Bibliography

Chen (1936)	Chen Jiru, *Ni gu lu*, Meishu congshu, Shanghai, 1936.
Fengbu (1977)	Fengbu shi bowu zhanlanguan, "Ming Tang He mu qingli jian bao", *Wenwu*, 2, 1977, pp.35-39.
Gillman (1984)	Gillman, D. "A source of Rhinoceros Horn Cups in the Late Ming Dynasty", *Orientations*, December , 1984, pp.10-17.
He (1983)	He Liangjun, *Si you zhai cong shuo*, Yuan Ming shiliao biji congkan, Peking, 1983.
Huaihua (1984)	Huaihua diqu wenwu gongzuodui and Tongdao xian wenhua ju, "Hunan Tongdao faxian nan Ming yao zang yin qi", *Wenwu*, 2, 1984, pp.88-93.
Jin ping mei (1963)	*Jin ping mei ci hua*, Tokyo, 1963.
Liu (1976)	Liu Ts'un-yen, "T'ao Chung-wen", *Dictionary of Ming Biography*, New York and London, 1976.
Ōsumi (1984)	Ōsumi Akiko, "Mindai Eiraku-ki okeru chōkō ni tsuite", *Museum*, 398, 1984, pp.14-34.
Pope (1956)	Pope, J.A. *Chinese Porcelain from the Ardebil Shrine*, Washington, 1956.
Shen Bang (1980)	Shen Bang, *Wan shu za ji*, Peking, 1980.
Shen Defu (1980)	Shen Defu, *Wanli ye huo bian*, Yuan Ming shiliao biji congkan, Peking, 1980.
Tao (1980)	Tao Zongyi, *Nancun zhuo geng lu*, Yuan Ming shiliao biji congkan, Peking, 1980.
Xie (1980)	Xie Gozhen, *Mingdai shehui jingji shiliao xuanbian*, Fuzhou, 1980.
Zheng (1984)	Zheng Minzhong, "Guanyu Zhu Bishan yin cha de bian wei wenti", *Gugong Bowuyuan yuankan*, 3, 1984, pp.52-57.
Zhou Hui (1955)	Zhou Hui, *Jinling suo shi*, Peking, 1955.
Zhou Shilin (1727)	Zhou Shilin, *Tian shui bing shan lu*, Zhi bu zu zhai congshu, pp.108-122.

Silver in Islamic Iran: The Evidence from Literature and Epigraphy

ASSADULLAH SOUREN MELIKIAN-CHIRVANI

Silver and gold loomed large in Iranian culture from pre-Achaemenid times down to the 19th century. In the Islamic period, references to silver and gold plate abound at all times in every form of literature, historical, geographical, technical or poetical.[1]

Yet, because so little has survived, it has been assumed in the recent past that the production of silver plate had stopped by the 12th century as a result of a "silver famine".[2] A theory was put forward that the raising technique associated with silver had been transferred to bronze-making by goldsmiths anxious to apply their skill to whatever medium might be available.[3] A somewhat different picture emerges from written sources. They point to the constant use of silver plate at court and in the upper strata of the military aristocracy in early times, but also in the 12th, 13th and 14th centuries, when it was supposed to have died out. They show that silver plate was a status symbol of that aristocracy as it had been in Sasanian times, and thus bear out the evidence of the surviving pieces. Furthermore, they suggest an explanation for the present scarcity of surviving silver and gold plate, used as a currency reserve every time a financial crisis occurred.

So important was silver as a symbol of royal splendour that it was lavishly used in religious shrines, from the Ka'ba in Mecca and the Dome of the Rock in Jerusalem, to the mausoleums of the Mongol Īl-Khāns of Iran. The architectural use of silver is the least known aspect of Islamic culture, and demonstrates that opposition to the use of silver can never have been very strong, even in religious circles.

1. Melikian-Chirvani (1982b).

2. Allan (1982), 16, quoting A.M. Watson, who based his theory of a "savage silver famine" on numismatics. Since 1967, numerous discoveries have led to a different understanding of monetary trends.

3. Allan (1982), particularly 11, 13 and 16—"many silversmiths must have given up working in precious metals and begun working in sheet bronze or brass instead".

Gold and Silver in Religious Shrines

The earliest text providing detailed information on shrines is the travel account, or *Safar-Nāme*, written in 1045 A.D. by Nāṣer Khosrow. This Iranian poet and philosopher travelled down the Syrian coast—including the Lebanon and Palestine, reckoned part of Syria. About a mausoleum in Tyre (Sūr), he writes:[4]

و بر در شهر مشهدی راست کرده‌اند و آنجا بسیار فرش و طرح و قنادیل و چراغدانهای زرین و نقرگین نهاده.

" They have erected a mausoleum by the city gate in which they have laid out a quantity of rugs and patterned hangings, gold and silver mosque lamps, *qanādī*, and oil lamps on stands, *cherāghdānhā*.[5] " In Jerusalem, Nāṣer Khosrow describes a crypt mosque, apparently the Holy Sepulchre. After mentioning the existence of two *miḥrābs*: "the *miḥrāb* of Mary", and "the *miḥrāb* of Zacharias", inscribed with the *sūras* relating to Mary and Zacharias, the traveller writes:

این مسجد معروفست بمهد عیسی علیه السّلام، و قندیلهای بسیار بر نجین و نقرگین آویخته چنانکه همه شبها سوزد.

" This mosque is known as the Sepulchre of Jesus, peace on him. They have hung many bronze and silver mosque lamps that burn every night.[6] " Yet more important is his account of the Dome of the Rock, the third holiest shrine to Muslims after the Ka'ba and Madīna:

و از میان خانه بر سر صخره قندیلی نقره بر آویخته‌است بسلسلهٔ نقرگین. و در این خانه بسیار قنادیل نقره است بر هر یکی نوشته که وزن آن چند است، و آن قندیلها سلطان مصر ساخته‌است چنانچه حساب میگرفتم یکهزار من نقره آلات در آنجا بود.

" A silver lamp hangs over the Rock from a silver chain coming down from the centre of the structure. There are many silver mosque lamps. Each one is inscribed with its weight and the name of the Sulṭān of Egypt who commissioned it (literally, "made it"). According to my calculation the silver utensils there weighed a total of 1,000 *man*.[7] " Impressive as the display of silver in the Dome of the Rock must have been, it pales into insignificance, compared with the architectural silver fittings inside and outside the Ka'ba. The two-leaf entrance door, made of teakwood and inscribed at the top with the Koranic verse III; 96, had two sets of silver door rings, and a silver lock which Nāṣer Khosrow describes as follows:

4. Nāṣer Khosrow (1341/1922), 21.

5. Melikian-Chirvani (1982a), 384, example illustrated in fig. 71.

6. Nāṣer Khosrow (1341/1922), 35.

7. *op. cit*, 42. One *man* would approximate 1 kilogram plus or minus 20 per cent. See Hinz (1970), 17.

gure 1. Silver bowl raised and beaten, to the name of Badr al-Dīn Qaragöz. The detail shows the titles *[amīr] al-arā ulugh homāyūn ākhurbeg Qaragöz zahīr amīr [al-mu'minīn]*. Western Iran, between 1198 and 1219. (Photo Melikian-ırvani.)

دو حلقهٔ نقرگین بزرگ که از غزنین فرستاده‌اند بر دو مصراع در زده چنانکه دست هر کس که خواهد بدان نرسد، و دو حلقهٔ دیگر نقرگین خردتر از آن هم بر دو مصراع در زده چنانکه دست هر کس که خواهد بدان رسد، و قفل بزرگ از نقره بر این دو حلقهٔ زیرین بگذرانیده که بستن در بآن باشد و تا آن قفل بر نگیرند در گشوده نشود.

" Two large silver door rings which were sent from Ghazneyn have been fixed on the two leaves so that the hands of those who might want to do so cannot get at them. The smaller silver rings have been fixed on the two leaves so that the hands of anyone wanting to do so can reach them. A big lock made of silver is laid across the two lower rings allowing the door to be locked. Until the lock is removed, the door won't open.[8] " These doors were seen by Khosrow shortly after 442/1050-51.[9] We learn *en passant* that Ghazni, the new capital of the Eastern Iranian world, was an important metalworking centre, in addition to being a literary capital.

Inside the Ka'ba, silver was put to even more spectacular use:

دیوار خانه همه تختهای رخام پوشیده‌است از الوان، و بر جانب غربی شش محراب است از نقره ساخته و بمیخ بر دیوار دوخته هر یکی بالای مردی بتکلّف بسیار از زرکاری و سوادسیم سوخته.

" The walls of the house are entirely covered with marble slabs of different colours. Six *miḥrābs* made of silver are nailed to the western wall, each one the size of a man. They are richly decorated with goldwork and black niello.[10] " To the right of the entrance door was a cell with a flight of stairs leading up to the roof terrace:

دری نقرگین بیك طبقه بر آنجا نهاده و آنرا باب الرّحمة خوانند و قفل نقرگین بر او نهاده باشد، و چون بر بام شدی دری دیگر است افکنده همچون در بامی، هر دو روی آن نقره گرفته.

" It has been fitted with a silver door made from a single plate. They call it the Door of Compassion, *Bāb al-Raḥma*. It is fitted with a silver lock. As one reaches the terrace, there is another door exactly like the door leading to the terrace. Both sides are plated with silver.[11] " Sulṭāns appear to have been eager to advertise their gifts of silver and gold fittings to the Ka'ba. Nāṣer Khosrow notes further on:

بر دیوار پیش خانه از بالای چوبها کتابه ایست زرّین بر دیوار آن دوخته و نام سلطان مصر بر آنجا نوشته که مکّه گرفته و از دست خلفای بنی عبّاس بیرون برده و آن العزیز لدین الله بوده‌است. و چهار تختهٔ نقرگین بزرگ دیگریست برابر یکدیگر هم بر دیوار خانه دوخته بمسمارهای نقرگین و بر هر

8. Nāṣer Khosrow (1341/1922), 107-8.

9. *op. cit*, 93 and 116.

10. *op. cit*, 108-9.

11. *op. cit*, 109.

Figure 2. Ottoman silver mug, cast, with carved and engraved details. Probably first half of 16th century. (Photo Sotheby's.)

يك نام سلطانى از سلاطين مصر نوشته كه هر يك از ايشان بروزگار خود آن تختها فرستاده‌اند، و اندر ميان ستونها سه قنديل نقره آويخته‌است.

" On the front wall of the building, over the rafters [?], a gold inscription is nailed to the wall. It carries the name of the Sulṭān of Egypt who wrested Mecca from the 'Abbāsid Caliphs. This was al-'Azīz li-Dīn Allāh. There are four other large silver plaques facing one another. They too are attached to the walls with silver nails. Each one is inscribed with the name of the Egyptian Sulṭān who sent it in his time And between the pillars three silver mosque lamps are hanging.[12] " I hope to comment elsewhere on Nāṣer Khosrow's account of the shrine, which deserves to be translated in full, in view of its importance for the history of Mecca, and architectural decoration in early Islamic times. Its precision is a sign of the interest taken by the cultivated élite in architectural fittings and religious vessels—the lamps—including the materials of which they were made. The tradition of silver architectural fittings is echoed several times in Persian literature, where it is associated with royal palaces. Asadī Ṭūsī, describing the palace of the "Shāh of Rūm" writes in 458/1065:

درش بر شبه درّ و بيجاده بود　　زمينش همه مرمر ساده بود

دو صد خانه هم زين نشان در سراى　　سراسر بسيمين ستونها بپاى

12. *op. cit*, 109.

Its doors had simulated pearls and garnets
Its floor was entirely covered with monochrome marble
Two hundred pavilions showed the same features in the palace
All were supported by silver pillars[13]

That Asadī Ṭūsī's description is not mere fiction, but reflects some architectural reality, is supported by an account of the Golden Horde's royal camp, given some three centuries later. The Moroccan traveller Ibn Baṭṭūṭa, visiting the Crimea in May 1334, witnessed the celebrations that took place on the occasion of the *'īd al-fiṭr*.[14] He describes the *bārgāh*[15] or royal tent erected in the royal camp, *wiṭāq*:

وقد نصبت هناك باركة (بارگاه) عظيمة، والباركة عندهم بيت كبير له أربعة أعمدة من الخشب مكسوّة بصفآئح الفضة المموَّهة بالذهب وفي أعلى كلّ عمود جامور من الفضة المذهبة له بريق وشُعاع.

" They set up a big *bārgah*. Their *bārgah* is a big house, *bayt*, with four pillars made of wood covered with gilded silver *plates*. Each pillar is topped by a capital made of gilded silver which glitters.[16] " Silver architectural fittings and furnishings thus appear to have been associated with royalty in the Iranian world and its Turkish sphere of influence.

Further evidence of this is to be found in the abundance of silver and gold mosque lamps that hung in the mausoleum of Ghāzān Khān, who died in 703/1304. Khwāndamīr notes in the *Ḥabīb al-Siyar*:

در تاريخ وصّاف مسطور گشته كه هشتاد عدد قنديل زرين و سيمين كه وزن هر يك از آنها پا نزده‌بود از آن مقبرهٔ منوّره آويخته‌بود.

" It is recorded in *Vaṣṣāf's Chronicle*, that eighty gold and silver (mosque) lamps each weighing fifteen *man* had been hung in that illuminated mausoleum.[17] " At this stage, one feels tempted to speculate that the royal connotation of silver in architectural fittings may have inspired their use in the shrines at Mecca and Jerusalem as an allusion to God's world kingship and, concerning the *Qubbat al-Ṣakhra*, to the Prophet as the "Prince of Prophets", *sayyid al-anbiyā'*. While this must remain a tentative suggestion as long as direct textual evidence does not come to light, it is possible to be more assertive about the use of silver vessels at all times.

13. Asadī Ṭūsī (1317/1938), 323.

14. Defrèmery and Sanguinetti in Ibn Baṭṭūṭa, ii, (1979), "Avertissement", XI.

15. Noted by Ibn Baṭṭūṭa in the "lighter" form *bārgāh* with the *gāf* normally rendered by a *kāf* in Arabic.

16. Ibn Baṭṭūṭa, ii, (1979), 405-6.

17. Khwāndamīr, iii, (1333/1954), 187-8. One *man* in this context was probably still the equivalent of 833 grams, Hinz (1970), 18.

Silver and Gold Plate in the Bazm Ceremony

Silver wine services, or *majles khāne*, to give them their Persian name, which dates from the 12th century, were an indispensable feature of the Iranian ceremony known as *bazm*. In the *Farrokh-Nāme*, completed in 580/1184-5, Yazdī defines it as:

بزم: مجلس می خوردن و شادی کردن بود.

"*Bazm*: a gathering, *majles*, for wine drinking and merry-making.'[18] The *bazm* was a long and elaborate feast in which banqueting was followed by music, poetry, and chanting, with wine being passed around. Silver plate was kept in the treasury and considered part of the most precious crown belongings. This is evident from many verses of the *Shāh-Nāme*. When Bahman, for example, angered by the behaviour of Zāl, has him seized by his guards and lets his army loot his palace, they remove gold coins, gems, thrones, carpets, gold plate, *zarrīne*, gold crowns, silver plate, *sīmīne*, ear-rings and belts—in that order.[19]

In any financial emergency, gold and silver plate served as a currency reserve. The *Tārīkh-e Sīstān* describes how two secretaries to the treasury, *vakīl*, struck coins from the gold and silver plate they melted. This took place in Ramadan 282, i.e. about December 895:

و اندر خزینه مال نماند از زر و سیم که همه بکار برده و داده شد و دست فرا کردن اندر اوانی فروختن و زرینه و سیمینه درم و دینار زدن.

" No gold or silver was left in the treasury. It had all been used or given away. They began to sell off vessels, and to strike dirhams and dinars from the gold plate, *zarrīne*, and silver plate, *sīmīne*.[20] " Gold and silver plate had the same treatment from private individuals of the upper classes. A dramatic story about, Shams al-Dīn Juwaynī, who was *ṣāḥib dīwān*, a ministerial function of the utmost importance under Abaqā Khān (663-80/1265-81)—is told by his brother, the historian 'Alā al-Dīn 'Aṭā Malek Juwaynī. It occurs in the *Tasliyat al-Ikhwān*, an autobiographical work as yet unpublished. The minister, who was repeatedly accused by envious enemies of embezzling state funds, was, at one point, forced to raise a large sum instantly:

باوّل هر چه در خانهٔ او و فرزندان او بود از اوانی زر و نقره و جواهر بیرون آورد

" First he gathered all the gold and silver plate and the jewellery that could be found in his house and that of his children.[21] " This method of raising money was not confined to Iran. In neighbouring Anatolia, where Iranian

18. Jamālī Yazdī (1346/1967), 322.
19. Ferdowsī, v, (1838-1878), 10.
20. Anon, *Tārīkh-e Sīstān* (1314/1935), 280.
21. 'Aṭā Malik Juwaynī, i, (1912-1937), Persian introduction, pages *mū-maz*.

usage prevailed, Ibn Bībī reports that when the *amīr* Ẓahīr al-Dīn had to send 400,000 dirhams to al-Malik al-Ṣāliḥ in 634/1237:

كافهٔ امرارا حاضر کردند و هر یکی از نقرینه و زرینه آنچه داشت در میان آورد

" They summoned all the *amīrs*, and everyone produced whatever silver plate and gold plate he had.[22] " This happened shortly after Ghiyāth al-Dīn Kay-Khusraw ibn Kay-Qubādh succeeded his father, who died on 4 Shawwāl 634, that is Monday 31 May 1237.[23]

The use of silver and gold plate as a currency reserve was naturally fatal to its survival as plate. A remarkable parcel-gilt bowl, sold several years ago at Sotheby's, where it was acquired by Edmund de Unger, provides us with a rare piece of evidence for the destructive process (**Fig. 1**). When first published in 1976, it was described as Syrian, because of the misreading of a name, and the omission of some titles typical of Iranian protocol.[24] It bears the honorific name, *laqab*, name, *ism*, and full titles of an *amīr*, the "great *iṣfahsālār*", "King of *amīrs*", and equerry, *ākhurbeg*, Badr al-Din Qaragöz.[25] His career in the Hamadan area can be followed through the *Ẕeyl-e Saljūq-nāme* by Abū Ḥāmid, the *Rāḥat al-Ṣudūr* by Rāvandī, and the *Jāmiʿ al-Tawārīkh* by Rashīd al-Dīn, who incorporates Rāvandī's information. The bowl illustrates an otherwise unknown style.[26] It had been broken up into many large fragments, clearly not the result of accidental damage. The most plausible interpretation seems to be that it was hurriedly broken in order to mint coins, probably at the time of the Mongol invasion.[27]

In short, early Iranian silver and, indeed, later silver too, went the same way as 17th-century French silver, which was melted, virtually in its entirety, to finance the wars waged by Louis XIV. Silver and gold vessels of the Ṣafavid age fared no better than their predecessors.

Yet historical literature and poetry suggest that gold and silver plate was invariably displayed at parties of the *bazm* type—later *majles-e bazm*, or simply

22. Ibn Bībī (1350/1971), 225.

23. *op. cit*, 207.

24. Fehérvári (1976), 102-3, no.127, details pl.42a-d; no general view is given.

25. Melikian-Chirvani (1982b), 150. The inscriptions omitted in Fehérvári's publication can be read 145-6, in figs.59 and 60, *humāyūn āḥurbeg Qaragöz ẓahīr amīr al-mu'minīn*.

26. It bears no relationship to two bowls attributed to Cilicia, (Little Armenia) by Marshak (1982), 173, pl.9 and 175, pl.17. 1. It has no bas relief motifs. 2. It is engraved with an epigraphic frieze. 3. The construction of the shape, typically Iranian, Melikian-Chirvani (1982), 145-7, differs widely from that of the two bowls. 4. The career of Badr al-Dīn Qaragöz, whose name it carries, was entirely in Western Iran going by what sources tell us. Marshak's tentative attribution of this bowl to "Asia Minor" merely echoes Fehérvári's, which was based on a misreading of the inscription.

27. As far as the eye can tell, the breaks are ancient. When silver objects are broken up by peasants in accidental finds, the fragments are naturally shared and dispersed. When this object came up for auction, it was still in fragments, obviously found together, with no trace of glueing.

majles—as a symbol of royal or aristocratic magnificence. Gold and silver were royal presents *par excellence*, given at the end of a royal party. Niẓām al-Mulk tells a revealing story about a party given in Bukhārā by the Sāmānid Naṣr ibn Aḥmad, who died on 13 Shawwāl 287/11 October 900. As Naṣr is about to set off, he tells his companion:

بمجلس شراب رویم و هر یك چهار پیاله بخوریم و زرینه و سیمینه با فرش و آلت بجمله بزرگان لشکر پخش کنیم.

" Let us go to the wine-party. Each of us will have three or four cups of wine. Then let us give the gold plate and the silver plate, along with the rugs and vessels, to all the great army chiefs.[28] "

More than a century later, Gardīzī, who completed the chronicle entitled *Zayn al-Akhbār* around 440/1048, described the *bazm* party given by Maḥmūd, the Ghaznavid, to honour, and above all to impress, Qadar Khān, the ruler of Māvarā an-nahr, whom he had come to meet:

چون از خوان فارغ شدند بمجلس طرب آمدند و مجلس آراسته بود سخت بدیع از سپر غمهای غریب و میوه‌های لذیذ و جواهر گرانمایه و مجلس جامها زرین و بلور و آئینهای بدیع و نوادر چنانچه قدر خان اندر آن خیره ماند و زامانی نشستند و قدر خان شراب نخورد از آنچه ملوك ماوراء النهررا رسم نیست شراب خوردن خاصه آن ملکان ترکان ایشان [کذا] و زمانی سماع شنیدند و بر خاستند پس امیر محمود رحمة الله بفرمود تا نثاری که بایست حاضر کردند از اداتها زرین و سیمین و گوهرهای گرانمایه و طرایفهای بغدادی و جامهای نیکو (. . .) و مر قدر خان‌را باعزاز و اکرام باز گردانید.

" When they rose from the table, (literally, "circular tray" laid on a trestle) they proceeded to the party. It had been splendidly laid out, with extraordinary sweet-smelling flowers, delicious fruits, gems, a dinner service of gold and silver, crystal ware, mirrors and other rare things. Qadar Khān stared at it all. They sat together for a while. Qadar Khān did not have wine: it is not customary for the Kings of Māvarā an-nahr to have wine, particularly not the King of the Turks among them. They listened to music for some time, and stood up. Then Prince Maḥmūd, may God grant him compassion, ordered a gift to be prepared of gold and silver utensils, costly gems, Baghdad filigree, fine fabrics. . .to be given to Qadar Khān as a mark of honour and generosity.[29] "
Further down, Gardīzī mentions silver bridles, *setāmhā*, and moon discs as part of camel trappings. The silver bowls and trappings, together with the commissioning of the Ka'ba door rings in Ghazni, as mentioned above, confirm the existence of an active royal goldsmiths' atelier in Ghazni.

28. Niẓām al-Mulk, ed. M. Qazvīnī, revised by M. Modarresī, 2537sh./1978, 240-41.

29. Gardīzī, (1928), 83.

A bowl in the Hermitage gives us some idea of what the court style or styles may have been in late 11th-century Iran.[30] At the centre, a mythical being with the body of a bird and the bust of a woman is a distant reflection of the mythical being—however different in its three-dimensional rendering—represented by a green-glazed pottery vessel in the Mūzīm-i Mellī at Kabul.[31] On the underside of the bowl is an Arabic inscription *li-Khumārtigīn al-khāzin*, "belonging to Khumārtigīn the Treasurer". Several Khumārtigīns are recorded in history, none of whom is called a "treasurer".[32] One of the two mentioned by Bayhaqī would seem to be more likely than the much earlier Khumārtigīn, a military commander under Isma'īl ibn Aḥmad.[33]

Under the Seljuqs, silver plate was equally prominent, and similarly associated with wine drinking. When describing a reception given by Malik Shāh, in his treatise on warfare, Fakhr-e Modabber dwells on the wine drinking that followed the meal:

مجلس خانه آراسته بودند در بارگاه و از زرینه و سیمینه و شفّافینه و آوندهای زرکوفت چنانکه بابت پادشاهان باشد. . . .

" A wine service, *majles-khāne*, had been displayed in the royal tent, *bārgah*: gold plate, silver plate, transparent ware, (i.e. crystal and glass), gold-inlaid vessels, as befits kings. . .[34] "

Rashīd al-Dīn, describing a reception given by Arghūn in the Spring of 1256, again notes the wine service which had been carried into the royal tent, *bārgāh*:

مجلس خانهٔ ملایم آن از اوانی زر و نقرهٔ مرصّع بجواهر نفیس. . . .

'A wine service, *majles-khāne*, consisting of gold and silver vessels encrusted with costly gems. . .'[35]

Iranian usage adopted by the Mongols was carried into the Crimean cities of the Golden Horde. Ibn Baṭṭūṭa tells us about the gold and silver vessels, which were plentiful. When taken into the presence of the Sulṭān's spouse, the traveller saw "about fifty girls" washing cherries in "gold and silver basins", *ṭayāfīr al-dhahab wa'l fiḍḍa*.[36] A gold tray, for which Ibn Baṭṭūṭa uses a Persian word in Arabized form, *ṣīniya*, was laid in front of the princess, *khātūn*.[37] When

30. Darkevich (1976), pl.29, 1-5, described 29-30, attributed to Māvarā an-nahr, following B. Marshak.

31. Rowland (1966), 40, pl.28, briefly described 52. The rhyton is obviously a Buddhist vessel, and belongs to the art of Iranian Buddhism, not Alexandria, as I shall explain elsewhere.

32. e.g. Ibn al-Athīr, ix, 91—Khumārtigīn al-Ḥafsī, and ix, 648, x, 176,—Khumārtigīn al-Tughrā'ī, *shaḥna* of Baghdad.

33. Favoured by B. Marshak in his 1973 doctoral thesis, according to Darkevich, see note 30.

34. Fakhr-e Modabber, 155, Melikian-Chirvani (1982b), 167.

35. Rashīd al-Dīn (1836), 158-60.

36. Ibn Baṭṭūṭa, ii, (1979), 391.

37. On the *ṣīnī*-type, see Melikian-Chirvani (1982a), 308-9.

describing the *'īd al-fiṭr* celebrations in the Crimea, Ibn Baṭṭūṭa says that food is laid on "gold and silver tables", *mawā'id al-dhahab wa'l fiḍḍa*, and wine served after the meal in gold and silver vessels.[38]

Iranian usage, likewise, spread through Anatolia, as far as the Aegean shores. In Izmir, Ibn Baṭṭūṭa saw a *faqīh*, or doctor in Islamic Law, presenting a *shaykh* with 'a big silver vessel, *'inā' fiḍḍa kabīra*, which they call *mashraba*, filled with silver coins".[39] *Mashraba*, although formed from an Arabic root, was used in Persian only with the meaning, "drinking vessel".[40] The silver example reproduced here illustrates the later Ottoman type in the 16th century (**Fig. 2**).[41] Not a single 14th-century example has been recorded so far.

Scanty as it may be, the evidence of what little silver plate has survived in Iran fully bears out what the chroniclers say about royal parties and royal gifts to the military aristocracy. The majority of recorded silver vessels carry the names of high-ranking military chiefs. A wine service in the Mūze-ye Īrān Bāstān which has not yet been recognized for what it is—a *majles khāne*, consisting of two bowls, two decanters, differing in size, two small jugs, and a tray—is inscribed in the name of an *amīr* Abū'l 'Abbās Valgīn ibn Harūn. He is called *mawla amīr al-mu'minīn*, "liege of the Prince of Believers".[42] It is probably to be dated to the first half of the 11th century. At that period, such a title is borne by provincial governors—for example, the governor of Sīstān appointed by Sulṭān Maḥmūd in *Muharram* 421/January 1030,[43] or the "ruler", *pādishāh*, of Āzabāyjān mentioned by Nāṣer Khosrow in *Ṣafar* 438/August 1046.[44]

Part of another early *majles khāne* has survived in the form of a pitcher and an octagonal tray, clearly made to match, by the same hand.[45] The pitcher again has an inscription including the title *mawla amīr al-mu'minīn*:

لابي صعيد عرّاق بن [ا]لحسين مولا امير المؤمنين.

'Belonging to Abū Sa'īd 'Arrāq ibn [a]l-Ḥusayn, liege of the Prince of Believers.'[46]

A shallow bowl with traces of parcel gilding in the Freer Gallery of Art,

38. Ibn Baṭṭūṭa, ii, (1979), 407 and 408.

39. *op. cit*, ii, 311.

40. On the identification of the *mashraba*, Melikian-Chirvani (1982a), 394. Illustrated examples 249, pl.109, 256, pl.114, 258, pl.116.

41. Sotheby's (1985), no.126.

42. *A Survey of Persian Art*, (1965), pls.1345-1346.

43. *Tārīkh-e Sīstān*, (1314/1935), 362

44. See Nāṣer Khosrow (1341/1922), 8. For additional examples, Melikian-Chirvani (1982b), 159, note 71.

45. Smirnoff (1909), pl.lxxi, no.127; Darkevich (1976), pl.28.

46. Darkevich (1976) reproduces Smirnoff's line drawing pl.28.4. The *li-abī* is not perfectly reproduced in the drawing. Further comments on the epigraphy in Melikian-Chirvani (1982b), 159.

probably made in the 11th century, is inscribed in the name of an *iṣfahsālār*, or commander-in-chief.[47]

A rectangular tray with the name of an unidentified king is preserved in the Hermitage. It is inscribed in elegant slender Kufic, with the words *al-malik al-ʿādil*, and the regional title (or name?) Khwārazmshāh.[48]

Of special interest is a circular tray of the *ṣīnī* type which has been known since the turn of the century. The inscription was not fully read by the Swiss scholar Max Van Berchem, who missed the first part of the name Sharaf al-Nisā', and read "Onor" instead of "Atsiz".[49] Apparently of Turkish stock, she is of princely rank:

الخاتون الاجلّ السيّدة / شرف النّساء بنت عزّ الدين / آتسز ادام الله عصمتها. و.

" The most glorious *khātūn*, the *sayyida* Sharaf al-Nisā', daughter of 'Izz al-Dīn/Atsiz [?], may God perpetuate her purity. W. " Such pieces, to which a few more might be added, including the bowl made in the 13th century for Badr al-Dīn Qaragöz, demonstrate the accuracy of the literary evidence: silver plate was to a large extent a status symbol in court circles and among the military aristocracy. This merely continued the tradition of pre-Islamic Iran, when kings had silver bowls with bas-relief scenes depicting them generally as hunters, or in a *bazm* scene.[50] Similarly, provincial governors, or rulers from Georgia, in the Caucasus, to Ṭabaristān, owned silver bowls inscribed with their names and titles on the underside.[51]

In short the chronicles and the literary evidence indicate a fair abundance of silver plate at all times, and emphasize its royal and aristocratic connection fully borne out by those few pieces that have escaped destruction. Supply problems do not appear to have hampered production.

Silver, Religion and Tradition

This should cause no surprise. Several sources tell us that silver ore was being extracted from a large number of small mines, in the very period which has been described as one of "silver famine". Abū'l Qāsim al-Qāshānī, the

47. Melikian-Chirvani (1968), 131.

48. Latest discussion in Melikian-Chirvani (1982b), 161-3, with publication of inscription, until then read with minor mistakes.

49. Van Berchem (1909), 410-11, reproduced by Darkevich (1976), 20; Melikian-Chirvani (1982b), 63.

50. Harper (1978), 39, fig.6, 40, fig.7, 59, fig.17b, which should be dated to the late 7th or 8th rather than 5th to 7th century. See 74, fig.25 for a *bazm* scene with court entertainment.

51. Gignoux (1984), correcting several earlier readings and completing others, e.g. 24, no.7, the famous Hermitage dish bearing the name of the Sepahbad Dād-Burz-Mihr, and 28, the bowl from Armasiskhevi in Georgia, with the name of a *bidakhsh*, or governor.

well-known historian, who also wrote a technical treatise on metals, minerals and gems around 1300, says that in so many words:
" Mines are to be found in many places, going east and west. Among those seen by the writer in the districts of Rūm, are the Lu'lu'a mine, the Isbihr mine, and the Gümüsh Bāzār mine. In Rūm, they occur in as many as thirty different locations.[52] " The anonymous geographical compendium *Haft Keshvar*, also called *Ṣuwar al-Aqālīm*, indicates in 748/1347-8 that "silver, mercury, diamonds, malachite and tin are plentiful in Cyprus, *Qubruṣ*".[53]

Another indication of the abundance of silver is the use of silver ingots as a gift, to a shrine or to a departing traveller. In 718/1318, two Mongol soldiers committed acts of vandalism in the famous Ṣūfī complex that encloses the mausoleum of Pīr Ḥusayn, in Arrān, some 30 miles west of Bākū. The Mongol prince Owrang, who was a Muslim, was outraged by the desecration. He had one of the looters executed and:

اورنگ خان به ساکنان بقعه پنجاه عدد شفشفهٔ نقره که آنرا «سوم» خوانند و هر سومی معادل بیست دینار رایج است انعام داد.

" ...donated to the dwellers in the enclosure fifty silver ingots, *shafshafe-ye noqre*, which they call *sūm*. Each *sūm* being equivalent to twenty currency dinars.[54] " Sixteen years later, as Ibn Baṭṭūṭa was preparing to leave the Caspian Sea port of Ḥāj Tarkhān, (Hazhtarkhān, in Persian and Turkish, Astrakhan, in Russianized form), each Mongol princess (*khātūn*) presented him with a silver ingot, *ṣawm*, which he spells with a *ṣād*.[55] Further on, Ibn Baṭṭūṭa specifies that *ṣawms*, as he explicitly vocalizes the word, are imported from the mountains of the Rūs, "where they serve as a normal means of payment".[56]

Last, but not least, there is the evidence of poetry, in which references to silver plate are common at all times. Two instances out of hundreds may be quoted here. They are from two poets who were born in North-Western Iran—Shirvān and Āzarbāyjān respectively—from which no silver plate has survived. Both tend to draw their images and comparisons from observation of real life. Mujīr al-Dīn Bilaqānī wrote in the second half of the 12th century, (metre *mojtaṣṣ*):

عروس سبزه چو در جلوه به مجلس گل   ز سیم خام طبقها شکوفه کرد نثار

As the bride of the greenery proceeded to the party, of the flowers,
The blossom scattered trays made from pure silver[57]

52. al-Qāshānī (1345/1966), 224.
53. *Haft Keshvar* (1353/1974), 94. *Dahnaj*, translated by Steingass as "a gem resembling emerald", means malachite, according to the Islamic science historian Ž. Vessel (private communication).
54. Vaṣṣāf (1346/1967), 365.
55. Ibn Baṭṭūṭa, ii, (1979), 412.
56. *op. cit*, ii, 414.
57. Mujīr al-Dīn Bilaqānī (1979), 99.

The expression "pure silver", *sīm-e khām*, following the mention of the trays (*ṭabaqhā*), leaves little doubt about the real object behind the image, associated as it is with the party, *majles*, that includes wine-drinking.

'Abdī Beg Shīrāzī writes more prosaically in his *masnavī* romance dealing with Bahrām Gūr, the *Haft Akhtar*, "The Seven Planets", (metre *khafīf*):

خادمان سفرها در آوردند کاسه از نقره و زر آوردند

The servants brought out the table cloths,
They brought out bowls made of silver and gold[58]

"The Seven Planets" was written in 946/1539-40, a period from which not one silver piece has survived.[59]

Attempts were made at different times by puritans to forbid the use of silver plate. They invariably failed. I drew attention to the ban on silver imposed in Iran by al-Ḥajjāj in the late 7th century, when I identified the alloy called in Persian *safīdrūy*, literally "white bronze", after an analysis of various unpublished groups of 8th to 11th-century vessels.[60] Al-Bīrūnī reports that when the Arab proconsul ordered gold and silver vessels to be broken in Iraq and Fārs, an Iranian named Fīrūz, who disliked drinking out of glass, had his vessels made from a mixture of silver and copper.[61] Later, silver was replaced by tin, giving birth to *isbidrūy*—the word used in Arabic by al-Bīrūnī when referring to *safīdrūy*. He makes it clear that the ban on silver and gold was primarily caused, not by dislike of the metal, but by disapproval of its link with wine drinking in Iranian usage:

الحجّاج لما كسر اواني الذهب والفضة بارض العراق وفارس وشدّد في خطر الشرب الخ.

" When al-Ḥajjāj ordered gold and silver vessels to be broken in Iraq, (i.e. *'Irāq-e 'Ajam*, "Iranian Iraq", the vast area from Rayy to Iṣfahān and Fārs), and emphasized the danger of wine drinking, etc. " In later times, new arguments were put forward, influenced by ascetic circles. One of the most interesting examples occurs in the anonymous *Baḥr al-Favāyed*, an encyclopaedia written in Persian for a high-ranking Turkish chief in Syria called Alp Qutlugh Chibughā. He is given the Turkish titles *ulugh aṭābeg*, "great *aṭābeg*", followed by the Arabic titles *ẓahīr amīr al-mu'minīn*.[62] Interestingly, these are the titles inscribed on the bowl made for Badr al-Dīn Qaraqöz, mentioned above. In a chapter entitled "The Book of Permitted and Forbidden Things", the section "On the Interdiction of Gold and Silver Vessels" contains the following paragraph:

" Vessels for liquid substances. Bowls containing food and beverages. If made of gold or silver, its use is forbidden to men and women. It is improper to use

58. 'Abdī Beg Shīrāzī (1974), 205.

59. *op. cit*, Persian preface, 21.

60. Melikian-Chirvani (1974), 123-51.

61. al-Bīrūnī (1937), 264.

62. *Baḥr al-Favāyed* (1966), 4.

it for drinking or eating, for the Prophet, may God's grace descend upon him, has said: 'Verily, he who drinks out of gold or silver vessels is like a man in whose stomach the fire of Hell would be burning...'[63] " The same applies to rosewater sprinklers and incense-burners. Having invoked the Prophet's authority, the anonymous author then adds three arguments of his own:

" Consorting with someone who uses gold and silver vessels is forbidden because gold and silver were created to define the price of wares and the going rates of merchandise. When vessels are made from them, locked up in a prison, and deposited in a treasury, they can no longer perform their role in arbitrating, *qāżī'ī*, and maintaining public order, *moqavvemī*, life becomes difficult, and God's precepts are broken. " Secondly,

" To use it (gold and silver plate), is to imitate tyrants and oppressors, *dar este'māl-e ān tashabboh ast-be jabbārān va gardankeshān.* " Here again is confirmation that gold and silver plate was a prerogative of the court circles and military chiefs. Thirdly,

" It drives the poor to despair. When they consider the luxury of the rich, they get desperate at the thought that these have gold and silver plate when they cannot even get earthenware. It has, therefore, been banned, so that the poor should not grow desperate. " However, even the most pious characters among the ruling classes appear to have ignored such condemnations of silver and gold plate.

Rāvāndī describes the ceremonies that followed the burial of Sulṭān Arslān ibn Ṭughril's mother, a deeply religious woman, much admired for her exemplary life, and of *aṭābeg* Īldegiz.[64] In December 1175, their sarcophagi were carried to Hamadan.

" Countless invitations were sent out. The *imāms* of the city came. All kinds of delicacies and sweetmeats were brought, and a table was laid with silver bowls, *va khwānī*, (circular tray on trestle), *nahādand az kāsehā-ye sīmīn.* " Indeed, even doctors in Islamic law were divided on the subject. Ibn Baṭṭūṭa, describing a reception given by Sulṭān Muḥammad Uzbak at Ḥāj Tarkhān, writes that a big tent had been set up for the religious dignitaries, the *qāḍī*, the preacher, the descendants of 'Alī, *shurafā'*, the doctors in Islamic law, *fuqahā'*, and the spiritual leaders, *mashā'ikh*. Ibn Baṭṭūṭa, as a foreign traveller and guest of honour, had been seated among them. The Sulṭān ordered gold and silver tables to be brought to them by high-ranking Turkish officers. Watching the *fuqahā'*, Ibn Baṭṭūṭa notes: "among them, some ate their meal, others refrained from eating food laid on silver and gold tables".

The ascetic objections against silver, which had no basis in Koranic teaching, were weaker than the power of Iranian tradition. The *bazm* ceremony was deeply rooted in the Sasanian past.[65] It goes back several

63. *Baḥr al-Favāyed* (1966), 205-6.

64. Rāvāndī (1921), 300.

65. MacKenzie (1971), 18.

centuries before Achaemenid times. The use of silver and gold was inseparable from wine drinking—for reasons of religious symbolism, as I will show elsewhere. The symbolism, modified by Islam, remained. As late as the 15th century, the Ṣūfī poet Ahlī Shīrāzī wrote in an ode entitled "In praise of the King's bowl", (metre *ramal*):

اینچه روح افزا شراب و اینچه سیمین ساغرست چشمه خضرست یا آیینهٔ اسکندرست

جوهر روح است یا گیتی نما بگداختند   شیره جان است دروی یامی جان پرورست

. . .   .

گرچه جام می نماید در کف شاه از صفا   گر بمعنی بنگری جام شراب کوثرست

> What soul-expanding wine is this? What silver vessel is that?
> Is it the Fountain of Kheżr, or is it the mirror of Alexander?
> Is it the substance of the soul, or did they melt the World Revealing [mirror]?
> Is the nectar of the loved one in it, or the wine that nourished the soul?
> Although it appears as a bowl of wine in the hand of the Shāh,
> If you consider its meaning, the bowl of wine is the Kowṣar[66]

66. Ahlī Shīrāzī (1344/1965), 450.

Bibliography

'Abdī Beg Shīrāzī (1974)	'Abdī Beg Shīrāzī, *Haft Akhtar*, ed. A. Hashimoghli Rahimov, Moscow, 1974.
Abū Ḥāmid (1953)	Abū Ḥāmid, Moḥammad ibn Ibrahīm, *Ẓayl-e Saljūq-Nāme*, continuing Ẓahīr al-Dīn Nayshābūrī's *Saljūq-Nāme*, Tehran, 1332/1953.
Ahlī Shīrāzī (1965)	Ahlī Shīrāzī, *Kolliyāt*, ed. H. Rabbānī, Tehran, 1344/1965.
Allan (1982)	Allan, J., "Silver: the Key to Bronze in Early Islamic Iran", *Kunst des Orients*, 11, 1/2, 1982, pp.6-21.
Anon (1935)	*Tārīkh-e Sīstān*, ed. Malek osh-Sho'arā Bahār, Tehran, 1314/1935.
Anon (1966)	*Baḥr ol-Favāyad*, ed. M.T. Dāneshpazhūh, Tehran, 1345/1966.
Anon (1974)	*Haft Keshvar yā Ṣovar al-Aqālīm*, ed. M. Sotūde, Tehran, 1353/1974.
Asadī Ṭūsī (1938)	Asadī Ṭūsī, *Garshāsp-Nāme*, ed. Ḥ. Yaghmā'ī, Tehran, 1317/1938, reprint 1354/1975.
'Aṭā Malik Juwaynī (1912-37)	'Aṭā Malik Juwaynī, *Tārīkh-e Jahāngoshā*, ed. Mīrzā Moḥammad (Qazvīnī), London, 1912-37.
van Berchem (1909)	van Berchem, M., "Inscriptions mobilières arabes en Russie", *Journal Asiatique*, X, 4, 1909, pp.401-13.

Bilaqānī (1979)	Bilaqānī, Mujīr al-Dīn, *Dīvān*, ed. Dr. M. Ābādī, Tabrīz, 1358/1979.
al-Bīrūnī (1937)	al-Bīrūnī, Abū Rayḥān Muḥammad ibn Aḥmad, *Kitāb al-Jamāhir fī Ma'rifat al-Jawāhir*, Ḥaydarābād, 1355/1937.
Darkevich, (1976)	Darkevich, V.P., *Khudozhestvennij Metall Vostoka*, Moscow, 1976.
Fakhr-e Modabber (1967)	Fakhr-e Modabber, *Ādāb al-Ḥarb va'sh-shojā'at*, ed. A. Sohaylī Khwānsārī, Tehran, 1346/1967.
Fehérvári (1976)	Fehérvári, G., *Islamic Metalwork of the Eighth to the Fifteenth Century in the Keir Collection*, London, 1976.
Ferdowsi (1838-78)	Ferdowsi, *Shāh-Nāme, Le Livre des Rois*, ed. J. Mohl, Paris, 1838-78, 7 vols.
Gardīzī (1928)	Gardīzī, Abū Sa'īd 'Abd al-Ḥayy ibn aẓ-Ẓaḥḥāk, *Ketāb-e Zayn ol-Akhbār*, ed. M. Nazim, Berlin, 1928.
Gignoux (1984)	Gignoux, P.,"Eléments de Prosopographie II. Les Possesseurs de Coupes Sassanides", *Studia Iranica*, 13/1, 1984, pp.19-40.
Harper (1978)	Harper, P.O., *The Royal Hunter*, New York, 1978.
Hinz (1970)	Hinz, W., *Islamische Masse und Gewichte*, Leiden, 1970.
Ibn Baṭṭūṭa (1979)	Ibn Baṭṭūṭa, *Voyages d'Ibn Battûta*, ed. and tr. C. Defrèmery and B.R. Sanguinetti; preface and notes by V. Monteil, Paris, 1979, 4 vols.
Ibn Bībī (1350/1971)	Ibn Bībī, *Mokhtaṣar-e Saljūq-Nāme*, ed. M.H. Houtsma, Leyden, 1902. Reprint with important historical introduction in Dr. J. Mashkūr, *Akhbār-e Salājege-ye Rūm*, Tehran, 1350/1971.
Jamālī Yazdī (1967)	Jamālī Yazdī, Abū Bakr Moṭṭahar, *Farrokh-Nāme*, ed. I. Afshār, Tehran, 1346/1967.
Khwāndamīr (1954)	Khwāndamīr, Ghiyāṣ al-Dīn ibn Homām al-Dīn al-Ḥosayni, *Tārīkh-e Ḥabīb os-Siyar*, Tehran, 1333/1954, 4 vols.
Kramarovskij (1980)	Kramarovskij, M., "Klad serebrianikh platezhnikh slitkov iz starovo Krima, Zoloto-Ordinskie sumi" *Soobshcheniya Gosudarstvennovo Ermitazha*, Leningrad, xlv, 1980, pp.68-72, 4 figs.
MacKenzie (1971)	MacKenzie, D.N., *A Concise Pahlavi Dictionary*, London, 1971.
Melikian-Chirvani (1968)	Melikian-Chirvani, A.S., "La Coupe d'Abu Sahl-e Farhad-Jerdi", *Gazette des Beaux-Arts*, vie période, Tome lxxi, no.1190, March, 1968, pp.129-46.
Melikian-Chirvani (1982a)	Melikian-Chirvani, A.S., *Islamic Metalwork from the Iranian World, 8th-18th century*, London, 1982.
Melikian-Chirvani (1982b)	Melikian-Chirvani, A.S., "Essais sur la Sociologie de l'Art Islamique —I, Argenterie et Féodalité dans l'Iran Médiéval", *Art et Société dans le Monde Iranien*, Paris, i, 1982, pp.143-75.
Nāṣer Khosrow (1922)	Nāṣer Khosrow, *Safar-Nāme*, ed. M. Ghanīzāde, Berlin, 1341/1922. Tehran reprint issued by the Masjed-e Solṭānī.
Niẓām al-Mulk (1978)	Niẓām al-Mulk, *Siyāsat-Nāme*, ed. M. Qazvīnī, revised reprint of C. Schefer's 1891 edition, 295 pages, Tehran, 2537sh./1978.
Pope & Ackerman (1939)	Pope, A.U., and Ackerman P., eds. *A Survey of Persian Art*, London and New York, 1939, 6 vols.
al-Qāshānī (1966)	al-Qāshānī, Abū'l Qāsim 'Abdallah ibn 'Alī, *'Arāyes ol-Javāher va Nafāyes ol-Aṭāyeb*, ed. I. Afshār, Tehran, 1345/1966.

Rashīd al-Dīn (1836)	Rashīd al-Dīn, *Jāme' ot-Tavārīkh*, ed. M. Quatremère, Paris, 1836, 2 vols.
Rāvāndī (1921)	Rāvāndī, Muḥammad ibn 'Alī, *Rāḥat oṣ-Ṣodūr va Āyat os-Sorūr*, ed. M. Iqbāl, London, 1921.
Rowland (1966)	Rowland, B., *Ancient Art from Afghanistan*, New York, 1966.
Smirnoff (1909)	Smirnoff, Y.I., *Argenterie Orientale / Vostochnoye Serebro*, St Petersburg, 1909.
Sotheby's (1985)	Sotheby's, *Islamic Works of Art, Carpets and Textiles*, London, 16 April, 1985.
Vaṣṣāf (1967)	Vaṣṣāf, *Taḥrir-e Tārīkh-e Vaṣṣāf*, ed. 'A. Āyatī, Tehran, 1346/1967.

The Attitude towards Gold and Silver in Early Islam

G.H.A. JUYNBOLL

In the early seventh century A.D., when the Prophet Muḥammad started to preach a new religion in the city of his ancestors Mecca,[1] gold and silver were both available in the Arabian peninsula, though not on a large scale. Gold as well as silver was mined, as the Arabic term *rikāz* seems to suggest.[2] But later both metals were mainly imported,[3] when they had become the basis of the official Muslim coinage instituted by 'Abd al-Malik towards the end of the seventh century A.D.[4]

If we assume (but see note 1 below) that the oldest manifestation of Islam extant today is the Qur'ān, we must look there first for Islam's earliest reactions to the two metals. Gold and silver receive little attention in the Book. There are various references to the denizens of paradise making use of cups made of silver or gold,[5] and only one clear reference to the metals in the hands of mortal man—that is IX, 34:
" Those who hoard gold and silver and do not spend it in the path of the Lord (i.e., in Holy War against the infidels), tell them about a painful punishment. " This says nothing about the use of implements made of gold and silver, but simply forbids the amassing thereof. When asked what one was permitted to amass instead, the Prophet is alleged to have answered: "A tongue mentioning (God), a grateful heart and a spouse who supports her husband in his faith".[6] An analysis of the *isnād*s points to Manṣūr ibn

1. For the sake of argument I adhere to the chronology of early Islam as established in early Muslim sources and accepted by the majority of western scholars. The "revisionist" ideas, as propounded of late by, for instance, Suliman Bashear (1984), which suggest a chronology significantly different from the one given here, will not occupy us here, no matter how fascinating these ideas may appear.

2. *Rikāz* is a plural connoting pieces of gold or silver extracted from the ground or from a mine, cf. *Lisān al-'Arab*, s.v. One fifth of all gold or silver found in the earth has to be submitted to the treasury, according to a maxim for the circulation of which, and of a few others, Ibn Shihāb al-Zuhrī (d.124/742) may be assumed to have been responsible, cf. Muslim, iii, (1955-6), 1334-5.

3. For an extensive list of gold and silver mines in the peninsula and elsewhere in the Islamic world, see Dunlop (1974).

4. See *EI*, 2, s.v. *dhahab*, *dīnār*, *fiḍḍa*, Ehrenkreutz and Cahen.

5. For an assessment of these verses and the similarities they bear to early poetic images, see Wendell (1974).

6. Ṭabarī, xiv, (1374), 220-2, nos.16661, 16662, 16663 and 16666; Tirmidhī, v, (1937-65), 277; Ibn Māja, i, (1952-3), 596; Ibn Ḥanbal, v, (1313), 278, 282 and 366.

al-Mu'tamir (d.132/750) as the originator of this saying.[7]

When the Muslims embarked upon the conquest of the lands outside the peninsula, they acquired large masses of booty. Although the historicity of the earliest reports describing these scenes is hard to establish, a source such as the *Annales* of Ṭabarī (d.310/923) can lay claim to our credence, because of a peculiarity in many of its chains of transmitters, *isnāds*, which are meant to authenticate the historical reports. Unlike most other collections of early Muslim historical data, Ṭabarī's has preserved for posterity a large number of reports collected by Sayf ibn 'Umar (d.c.180/796), who is virtually the only known collector who frequently gives separate *isnād*s going back to different eye-witnesses, all apparently describing the same historical event. To call the similarities, or sometimes the partial over-lap, in the separate accounts of the same event "mere coincidence" is, in my view, tantamount to rejecting the only historical material deserving of our cautious trust.

It is in a few separate Sayf ibn 'Umar reports that we find multiple references to what are obviously the same Persian artifacts turning up in the plunder after the conquest of al-Madā'in (Ctesiphon) in the year 16/637. Thus, the Muslim warriors came upon vessels of gold and silver,[8] and Kisrā's crown so heavy that it was held aloft on two jewel-encrusted props;[9] a golden figure of a horse, with a silver saddle, its crupper and breast girth studded with rubies and emeralds set in silver, and a silver figure of a she-camel, with saddlecloth, halter and bridle of gold, complete with figures of riders, were alleged to have been attached to the two props of Kisrā's crown.[10] In the royal palace of al-Madā'in it is reported that there were statues, which nobody thought of moving when the Muslims assembled to perform their prayer rituals, an indication that the well-known Islamic *Bilderverbot*, the prohibition against making images of living things, had not yet been formulated.[11]

References to similar golden and silver artifacts as well as vessels are numerous and, eventually, it became imperative that the attitude of the religion towards these precious objects be formulated. We do not know exactly what happened in the course of that first/seventh century. As we have seen, the Qur'ān did not contain definite clues and it became, therefore, the concern of Islam's second holiest literature, the tradition or *Ḥadīth* literature—allegedly comprising the sayings of the Prophet Muḥammad, but in all likelihood containing solutions to problems formulated by others—to determine the position of Islam in this matter.[12]

7. What *isnād* analysis entails is hinted at below.

8. Ṭabarī, i, (1897-1901), 2445.

9. Ṭabarī, i, (1897-1901), 2446.

10. Ṭabarī, i, (1897-1901), 2448.

11. Ṭabarī, i, (1897-1901), 2443 and 2451.

12. In the following, use will be made of sunnite *Ḥadīth* literature only, shī'ite *Ḥadīth*, as far as could be ascertained, not offering on this subject anything basically different from its sunnite counterpart.

Now, the *Ḥadīth* literature took some time to develop. Six of its major collections became in the end canonical. Whereas Muslim consensus holds that the attribution of the various sayings in those collections to Muḥammad is, on the whole, beyond question and that, therefore, the chronology of Islam's second most important source of Law overlaps with that of the Qur'ān, most western scholars are of the opinion, especially since the findings of Goldziher[13] and Schacht,[14] that the true originators of the sayings must be sought in later generations. Neither of these two scholars developed a method to determine the identity of these originators, however, and until today most western scholars have believed that the bulk of "prophetic" *Ḥadīth* is "late", at least second/eighth century.

In 1983 I published a study[15] in which I tested the efficacy of one of Schacht's major theses, the so-called common link theory. Although Schacht originated this theory, he himself rarely used it. But my tests may have established the usefulness of this theory, and in the following study I shall make frequent use of it. The particulars of my analytical method have, however, no place here, and that is why I refer readers interested in them to work of mine published elsewhere. The outcome of my analysis, which is mainly restricted to *isnāds*, is not without interest, I believe, and contains sometimes unmistakable pointers to the originators of certain classical Islamic values, which in the opinion of the world of Islam were formulated by the Prophet himself.

Returning now to Islam's point of view concerning gold and silver as expressed in its *Ḥadīth* literature, we find a great many references to the metals, which can be listed under the following rubrics:

1. The use of gold and silver vessels.
2. Gold and silver (signet) rings.
3. Gold and silver jewellery.
4. Gold and silver used for other purposes.

1. The first rubric contains perhaps the *oldest* tradition of Islam's stance concerning these metals in all its literature. The tradition is *not yet* moulded into a legal prescript, maxim or slogan, which is the form legal issues generally take in later traditions, but is *still* embedded in an account of an "historical" event, from which the reader/listener is expected to distill religious learning. I deliberately italicized the words "oldest", "not yet" and "still", because what these traditions tell us about the chronology and development of legal themes and issues concerning gold and silver matches the chronology and development of traditions dealing with other legal matters. Or conversely, the evolution in legal parlance apparent in traditions treating of certain other

13. cf. Goldziher (1890).

14. cf. Schacht (1950).

15. Juynboll (1983).

legal issues finds also expression in the evolution of those dealing with gold and silver.

The oldest tradition, then, tells the story of how an important Companion of the Prophet, in recently-conquered Iraq, asked for a drink of water and was offered water in a silver vessel by a local Persian nobleman. In disgust the Companion, Ḥudhayfa ibn al-Yamān, threw the vessel down, saying, "The Messenger of God has forbidden me to drink from a vessel made of gold or silver".[16] The common link of its *isnād*, and the man who is in all probability responsible for having first told the story, is Mujāhid ibn Jabr, a *mawlā* of the Meccan Makhzūm clan, who died between 100/718 and 103/721. Although he is alleged to have been active in the Ḥijāz, the majority of his *Ḥadīth* pupils, who are supposed to have heard traditions from him, were from Iraq. To assume that all those Iraqi, mainly Kūfan, pupils learned his traditions in Mecca, for example while on pilgrimage, is less easy than to surmise that Mujāhid, (although this is not borne out by the scanty information about him in the biographical literature), spent some time in Kūfa where he spread, among other traditions, this one about the inadmissibility of gold and silver drinking vessels, claiming that he himself had heard it from the Kūfan legal expert 'Abd al-Raḥmān ibn Abī Laylā (d.82/701).

Another well-known, slightly later, tradition in this vein is the slogan: "He who drinks from a silver vessel will have Hellfire gurgling in his belly". The common link/originator of this text is the famous *mawlā* of Ibn 'Umar, Nāfi' (d.117-20/735-8). After him it spread via Baṣra and Egypt to other parts of the Muslim empire. Nāfi''s reputation as a jurisconsult may have helped to make this slogan famous.

2. The second rubric contains references to gold and silver rings. One of the oldest is a saying probably brought into circulation by one Ash'ath ibn Abī Sha'thā' Sulaym from Kūfa, who is said to have died in 125/743.[17] His true identity is doubtful, because he often seems to have been confused with namesakes who lived more or less during the same period.[18] The prohibition against wearing a golden signet ring is mentioned as one of seven prohibitions instituted by Islam. In these seven we see distinctly the earliest customs of the conquered territories to be imitated by the conquerors, against which Islam had to take a definite stance: lamenting the dead, dyeing the hair and other cosmetic practices, making images of living things, and wearing golden

16. Embellished with various sequels, this tradition is found in Bukhārī, iii, (1862-1908), 503, iv, 38 and 83-4; Muslim, iii, (1955-6), 1637-8: Tirmidhī, iv, (1937-65), 299; Abū Dāwūd, iii, (1935), 337; Ibn Māja, ii, (1952-3), 1130; Nasā'ī, viii, (1348), 198; Ṭayālisī (1321), no.429; Ḥumaydī, i, (1380-2), 209; Dārimī (1293), 272, and Ibn Ḥanbal, v, (1313), 396-8 and 400.

17. cf. Mizzī, i, (1965-82), 63-5.

18. cf. Juynboll (1983), 50, and Ibn Ḥajar, i, (1325-7), nos.639, 640, 641, 643, 645, 647, 648 and 652.

jewellery and silk. Later it became permissible to wear a silver signet ring.[19] Women wore only plain rings, on which they were expected to pay alms tax, according to a tradition initiated by Ibn Jurayj (d.150/767).[20]

3. As for the third rubric, gold jewellery, that was on the whole frowned upon. Yaḥyā ibn Abī Kathīr (d.129-32/747-50) is a transmitter who, on the basis of scanty information about him in the biographical lexica,[21] can be assumed to have gathered *Ḥadīth* in Medina—he was accustomed to claim that he had received his material from Medinan masters—and who later disseminated his traditions in Baṣra, after which he settled in Yamāma. He can be credited with the following story:

" A woman came to Fāṭima, the Prophet's daughter, to complain about Muḥammad's having expressed his displeasure at her wearing a golden ring. Then Fāṭima took off a golden necklace, which was given to her by her husband 'Alī, and had it sold in the market. With the money it fetched she bought a slave, whom she then set free. When Muḥammad heard this story, he exclaimed: 'Praise be to God who has delivered Fāṭima from Hellfire'.[22] "

All jewellery made of gold was defined by the Prophet as being made of Hellfire, according to a report probably brought into circulation by Muṭarrif ibn Ṭarīf from Kūfa, who died in 141-3/758-60.[23] "But", Muḥammad added, "why do you women not take for yourselves bracelets, earrings, necklaces etc. made of silver, which you may then afterwards paint golden with saffron?"[24]

Eventually, the prohibition against wearing gold in any form, as well as the ban on wearing silk was restricted to men,[25] women being excluded from this ban as long as they decked and beautified themselves only in the seclusion of their homes in order to please their husbands. Later men were permitted to use gold in their clothing, but on a very limited scale, for which the Arabic term used is *muqaṭṭaʿan*.[26] Furthermore, they were allowed to have the hilts of

19. One very late tradition has the Prophet forbid the wearing of iron rings, because they become rusty and apparently thus cause festering, cf. Haythamī, v, (1352-3), 151.

20. cf. Mizzī, v, (1965-82), 5-6.

21. Ibn Ḥajar, xi, (1325-7), no.539; Ibn Abī Ḥātim, iv, (1952-3), 2, no.599, and Ibn Saʿd, v, (1905-17), 404.

22. Nasā'ī, viii, (1348), 158, and Ibn Ḥanbal, v, (1313), 278-80.

23. Nasā'ī, viii, (1348), 159, and Ibn Ḥanbal, ii, (1313), 440.

24. In Arabic *zaʿfarān*; another colouring agent suggested is *ʿabīr*, cf. Lane (1863-93), s.v.

25. cf. Mizzī, vi, (1965-82), 415-6; the probable originator of the tradition listed here is 'Ubayd Allāh ibn 'Umar (d.147/764), one of Medina's seven foremost jurisconsults. Another, probably later author of a similar prohibition is al-Layth ibn Saʿd (d.175/791). cf. Mizzī vii, (1965-82), 407-8. Men suffering from lice were allowed to wear silk, though, cf. Mizzī, i, (1965-82), 357-8; the man who probably brought this so-called *rukhṣa* tradition (i.e., one that declares something hitherto prohibited to be permissible) into circulation was Hammām ibn Yaḥyā al-Muḥallimī (d.163-780) from Baṣra.

26. cf. the *rukhṣa* traditions listed in Mizzī, viii, (1965-82), 453, 435 and 442.

their swords made of silver. The person who spread the presumably very early saying permitting this was Qatāda ibn Di'āma from Baṣra, who died in 117/735.[27] Another, probably later, attempt to allow hilts of swords to be made of silver *and* gold apparently never caught on: the saying is thought to be doubtful and the culprit responsible for it is identified as one Ṭālib ibn Ḥujayr, who flourished in the early third/ninth century.[28] As all this seems to indicate, gold and silver gradually became used for decorative purposes. A statement ascribed to Mālik ibn Anas (d.179/795) may contain a hint that, in his days, even Qur'āns were decorated with gold. It says:

" When a copy of the Qur'ān, *muṣḥaf*, a sword or a ring is sold in which there is gold or silver, these may change hands, if the value of the precious metal(s) does not exceed one third of the overall value of the object.[29] "

4. One more rubric of traditions contains indications of special uses made of these metals in early Islamic society. Thus people were allowed to cap their teeth with gold. According to Tirmidhī, the permission is based on the story of a man who had lost his nose in a skirmish and had made for himself one of silver.[30] When this started to fester, it is reported that he was ordered by the Prophet to make for himself a nose of gold. The person who brought this story into circulation was probably one Abū'l Ashhab Ja'far ibn Ḥayyān from Baṣra, who is said to have died in 165/782. This man seems to have had a namesake, Abū'l Ashhab Ja'far ibn al-Ḥārith, with whom he was commonly confused.[31]

Cracked drinking vessels could be repaired with little plates made of silver, *ḍabba*. It is difficult to determine who may have been responsible for this rule, but a likely candidate seems to be Sharīk ibn 'Abd Allāh from Kūfa (d.177/793).[32]

This concludes the survey of *Ḥadīth* dealing with gold and silver in early Islam. There is one more type of Islamic literature, also occasionally referring to gold and silver, which deserves to be studied, a literature squarely based on *Ḥadīth* literature, namely *fiqh*, jurisprudence. Here we find various traditions already mentioned set in their legal contexts.

Thus we read how the literalist legal school of Dāwūd al-Ẓāhirī (d.270/884) declares *eating* from gold or silver vessels to be allowed, since the prohibition ascribed to the Prophet speaks only of *drinking*.[33] Furthermore,

27. cf. the traditions enumerated in Mizzī, i, (1965-82), 301. In Ibn Rajab (1396), 436, we read that Qatāda's pupil Jarīr ibn Ḥāzim was commonly held responsible for having spread this story.

28. cf. Mizzī, viii, (1965-82), 375; cf. also Ibn Ḥajar, v, (1325-7), 8.

29. Mālik ibn Anas, ii, (1951), 635-6.

30. cf. Tirmidhī, iv, (1937-65), 240-1; Abū Dāwūd, iv, (1935), 92; Nasā'ī, viii, (1348), 163-4, and Mizzī, vii, (1965-82), 291.

31. Ibn Ḥajar, ii, (1325-7), nos.135 and 136.

32. cf. Ibn Ḥanbal, iii, (1313), 139, 155 and 259.

33. cf. Goldziher (1971), 42.

the question arose whether a ritual ablution with water from a gold or silver vessel is valid. One opinion says that it is valid, comparing it with the validity of a ritual ablution performed in a house which is illegally appropriated, *maghṣub*. Another opinion denies the validity, arguing that the performance of a prayer ritual in an illegally appropriated house is not valid either.[34]

Likewise, the manufacturing of gold and silver vessels has been a matter of disagreement. Thus the school of Shāfiʿī (d.204/820) permits it, arguing that manufacturing something and using it are two different things; one is after all also allowed to sew a blouse of silk. But the school of Aḥmad ibn Muḥammad ibn Ḥanbal (d.241/855) declares the manufacturing forbidden, *simply because* the use is prohibited.[35] They argue that, although women are allowed to adorn themselves with gold and silver jewellery, this is only permissible in front of their husbands inside their houses, while the possession of gold and silver vessels may lead to intemperance.[36]

The obligation to pay alms tax imposed on vessels made of precious metals has also given rise to a certain amount of casuistry. Although these vessels are forbidden, one is obliged to pay alms tax on them, if they exceed the legal minimum value, the *niṣāb*. If the vessel is said to be worth more than the intrinsic value of the gold and/or silver that went into the making of it, then that does not count and is of no consequence, since the manufacturing of the vessel is forbidden in the first place. Anyone owning gold and/or silver vessels is obliged to pay one fortieth of the value of the precious metal(s) in alms tax; if he wants, he may do so in unmoulded gold or silver. And if he does not have any to spend in this way, he may smash or break the vessel(s) and pay one fortieth in fragments.[37]

Also gold and silver ornaments on saddles, stirrups, bridles etc., carry alms tax to the value of one fortieth. But it is recommended that the ornaments, for instance those on the harness of a horse donated to fight in the path of the Lord, i.e., in the Holy War, be removed and be sold, and that the proceeds be made into a separate endowment, for example to feed the horse. Thus lamps ornamented with gold and silver, donated to a mosque, have to be smashed and the gold and silver must be spent on repair work in the mosque. If a drinking vessel with a hole or a crack is repaired with a small plate of silver, a *ḍabba*, the drinker should make sure that his mouth never touches it.[38] Ceilings with gold or silver coatings may be left alone, if it is thought that the coating is not durable, but if it is thought to be durable, the coating has to be removed.[39]

34. al-Khiraqī/Ibn Qudāma, i, (1367), 76.

35. In Arabic this is argued with the words: *al-ittikhādh ʿalā hayʾāt al-istiʿmāl.*

36. al-Khiraqī/Ibn Qudāma, i, (1367), 76-7.

37. al-Khiraqī/Ibn Qudāma, iii, (1367), 16.

38. al-Khiraqī/Ibn Qudāma, viii, (1367), 322.

39. al-Khiraqī/Ibn Qudāma, iii, (1367), 16-7.

The attitude of Islam towards gold and silver in their various uses in society is eloquently summed up in an adage one comes across time and again in a major Ḥanbalite work on *fiqh* which says:
" All ornamentations in, or amassing of, gold and/or silver may lead to excess and arrogance, and may subsequently break the hearts of the poor.[40] "

40. al-Khiraqī/Ibn Qudāma, iii, (1367), 16.

Bibliography

Abū Dāwūd (1935)	Abū Dāwūd, *Sunan*, ed. Muḥammad Muḥyī al-Dīn 'Abd al-Ḥamīd, Cairo, 1935, 4 vols.
Bashear (1984)	Bashear, Suliman, *An Introduction to the Other History. Towards a New Reading of Islamic Tradition*, in Arabic, Jerusalem, 1984.
Bukhārī (1862-1908)	Bukhārī, *Ṣaḥīḥ*, ed. L. Krehl and Th. W. Juynboll, Leiden, 1862-1908, 4 vols.
Dārimī (1293)	Dārimī, *Sunan*, lithograph, Cawnpore, 1293.
Dunlop (1974)	Dunlop, D.M., "Sources of Gold and Silver in Islam According to al-Hamdānī (10th century A.D.)", *Studia Islamica*, 2, 1974, pp.29-49.
EI, 2 (1960-)	*Encyclopaedia of Islam*, new edition, Leiden, 1960-.
Goldziher (1890)	Goldziher, I., *Muhammedanische Studien*, Halle, ii, 1890.
Goldziher (1971)	Goldziher, I., *The Ẓāhirīs, their Doctrine and their History*, tr. Wolfgang H. Behn, Leiden, 1971.
Haythamī (1352-3)	Haythamī, *Majma' al-Ẓawā'id*, Cairo, 1352-3, 10 vols.
Ḥumaydī (1380-2)	Ḥumaydī, *Musnad*, ed. Ḥabīb al-Raḥmān al-A'ẓamī, Beirut/Cairo, 1380-2, 2 vols.
Ibn Abī Ḥātim (1952-3)	Ibn Abī Ḥātim, *Kitāb al-Jarḥ wa'l-Ta'dīl*, Hyderabad, 1952-3, 8 vols.
Ibn Ḥajar (1325-7)	Ibn Ḥajar, *Tahdhīb al-Tahdhīb*, Hyderabad, 1325-7, 12 vols.
Ibn Ḥanbal (1313)	Ibn Ḥanbal, *Musnad*, Cairo, 1313, 6 vols.
Ibn Māja (1952-3)	Ibn Māja, *Sunan*, ed. Muḥammad Fu'ād 'Abd al-Bāqī, Cairo, 1952-3, 2 vols.
Ibn Rajab (1396)	Ibn Rajab, *Sharḥ 'Ilal al-Tirmidhī*, ed. al-Sayyid Ṣubḥī Jāsir al-Ḥumaydī, Baghdad, 1396.
Ibn Sa'd (1905-17)	Ibn Sa'd, *Kitāb al-Ṭabaqāt al-Kabīr*, ed. E. Sachau, Leiden, 1905-17, 9 vols.
Juynboll (1983)	Juynboll, G.H.A., *Muslim Tradition. Studies in Chronology, Provenance and Authorship of Early "Ḥadīth"*, Cambridge, 1983.
al-Khiraqī/Ibn Qudāma (1367)	al-Khiraqī/Ibn Qudāma, *al-Mughnī*, ed. Muḥammad Rashīd Riḍā, Cairo, 1367, 9 vols.
Lane (1863-93)	Lane, E.W., *Arabic-English Lexicon*, London/Edinburgh, 1863-93, 8 vols.
Lisān al-'Arab (1300-7)	Ibn Manẓūr, *Lisān al-'Arab*, Būlāq, 1300-7, 20 vols.

Mālik ibn Anas (1951)	Mālik ibn Anas, *al-Muwaṭṭa'*, ed. Muḥammad Fu'ād 'Abd al-Bāqī, Cairo, 1951, 2 vols.
Mizzī (1965-82)	Mizzī, *Tuḥfat al-Ashrāf bi-Ma'rifat al-Aṭrāf*, ed. 'Abd al-Ṣamad Sharaf al-Dīn, Bhiwandi, 1965-82, 14 vols.
Muslim (1955-6)	Muslim, *Ṣaḥīḥ*, ed. Muḥammad Fu'ād 'Abd al-Bāqī, Cairo, 1955-6, 5 vols.
Nasā'ī (1348)	Nasā'ī, *Sunan bi-Sharḥ al-Suyūṭī*, Cairo, 1348, 8 vols.
Schacht (1950)	Schacht, J., *The Origins of Muhammadan Jurisprudence*, Oxford, 1950.
Ṭabarī (1879-1901)	Ṭabarī, *Annales*, ed. M.J. de Goeje *et al* Leiden, 1879-1901, 15 vols.
Ṭabarī (1374)	Ṭabarī, *Jāmi' al-Bayān 'an Ta'wīl āy al-Qur'ān*, ed. M.M. and A.M. Shākir, Cairo, 1374.
Ṭayālisī (1321)	Ṭayālisī *Musnad*, Hyderabad, 1321.
Tirmidhī (1937-65)	Tirmidhī, *al-Jāmi' al-Ṣaḥīḥ*, ed. A.M. Shākir and others, 5 vols.
Wendell (1974)	Wendell, C., "The Denizens of Paradise", *Humaniora Islamica*, 2, 1974, pp.29-59.

Plate and its Substitutes in Ottoman Inventories

MICHAEL ROGERS

Ottoman attitudes to gold and silver vessels in the 16th and 17th centuries were complex and doubtless somewhat inconsistent. The force of the traditional disapproval of display in the works of the *muḥaddithīn* must not be discounted and study of the fetvas of lawyers like Ebü's-Sü'ûd[1] will certainly throw light on how the authorities and the Court reacted to Orthodox pronouncements. On the other hand, the requirements of Court ceremonial, and the lack of standard regalia in the European sense,[2] led the Sultans not only to display plate prominently at Court banquets but also to commission grand display pieces, like the jewelled gold water-jug (*matara*) which Filiz Çağman has convincingly attributed to Selim II.[3] This, as miniatures from 1566-1590 show, was carried, along with weapons and other more traditional appurtenances of Islamic kingship, by one of the chamberlains at audiences and feasts. Nor does the Ottoman custom of the later 16th century of eating off porcelain[4] necessarily represent an attempt to follow the precepts of the *muḥaddithīn*. Firstly, it was costly, highly esteemed and, for most of the 16th century, confined to the Palace Treasury. Secondly, celadons especially were believed to detect poison. Thirdly, exactly as in contemporary Western Europe, its value and appearance were customarily enhanced by elaborated gold, silver or silver-gilt mounts, often encrusted with jewels or worked with enamels or niello.[5] If to forswear plate was a condition of religious orthodoxy,

1. Düzdağ (1972), 187-78 The fetvas cited mostly relate to dress, but a pronouncement that *tombak* vessels were licit shows that even gilt-copper must have aroused the conscience of the scrupulous.

2. The principal exception seems to be the "sword of 'Osman" with which the Sultans came to be girded on their accession. The relics in the Hırka-i Saadet Dairesi, which had mostly come into Ottoman hands after Selim I's conquest of the Hijaz, were not generally displayed, but, as Filiz Çağman (1984), 51-87, has shown, piety led Murad III to commission masterpieces of jewelled goldsmith's work for some of the principal relics in the late 16th century. It is unclear whether the Christian relics collected by Mehmed II, and mostly dispersed among the Christian rulers of Europe under Bayazid II, Babinger (1956), 17-28, were ever the object of Ottoman goldsmith's work.

3. *Anatolian Civilizations* (1983), E 206.

4. First recorded by Menavino (1551), 135-6.

5. Ünal (1963), 673-714. Spallanzani concludes (1978), 126, that though in contemporary Florentine inventories porcelains in price ranked second only to plate, "la porcellana puo rientrare nel settore dei prodotti di qualità, anche se non

therefore, the Sultans's use of porcelain at table was scarcely the observance even of the letter of the law.

Nevertheless, this period shows repeated edicts against the use of gold and silver. It is interesting that although, for example in the later 17th and 18th centuries, edicts forbidding the manufacture of metal thread (*sırma*) or deliberately debasing its quality are certainly a response to silver shortages,[6] for much of the 16th century purely economic considerations appear to have been given rather low priority. This was partly because the importance of textiles richly brocaded with large amounts of gold and silver thread in the Ottoman honours system obliged the authorities to encourage the luxury industries. Accordingly, the Bursa *kanunname-i ihtisab*[7] promulgated in the reign of Bayazid II, as well as later edicts relating to the weight and quality of gold leaf used for the manufacture of gold thread, actually lay down *minimum* standards. Economic considerations affecting the consumption of precious metals came into play, however, at the fiscal level: this must be the explanation of, for example, a late 16th-century edict[8] that all silver sold in the Bedesten in Istanbul is to be taken for assay and stamping to the office of the Court jeweller (*kuyumcubaşı*) Mehmed. How far other prohibitions were

è assolutamente in grado di reggere confronte con i veri articoli di lusso che caratterizzavano la Firenze di Lorenzo il Magnifico. In un mondo dominato da argenti e gioelli, legni intagliati e codici miniati, tappete e stoffe preziose, dipinte e sculture antiche la porcellana si colloca inequivocabilmente agli ultimi posti". Although he finds it difficult to admire the mounts made to raise the importance of porcelains in the eyes of Medici connoisseurs, he observes the curious coincidence of the taste in their decoration in late Gothic and Renaissance and Mannerist Europe. And in Ottoman Turkey too, one might add.

6. Refik (1935b), 54-6, no.79, where the explicit grounds for the prohibition are the shortage of silver at the Mint, mid-Receb 1128/early July 1716.

7. Barkan (1942), 15-40; Refik (1935a), 135-6, no.59; Rogers, (forthcoming, b).

8. Refik (1935a), 136, no.60, dated Cumada I 1000/March-April 1592. Dalsar (1960), 344-6, observes that the stamping of silk fabrics was already an established practice by the reign of Bayazid II, but that it was purely fiscal and that the possibilities of controlling the quality of the silks manufactured were ignored. The late 16th-century edict specifically forbids the manufacture of silver vessels from debased metal, but this could simply be a response to widespread fraudulent practices. The actual meaning of the stamps on silver vessels of the early 16th century is so far unknown, but that could easily have been largely for fiscal purposes too. Early 16th-century *kanunnames*, Anhegger and Inalcık (1956), with regulations regarding the mining of gold and silver show that, as early as the reign of Mehmed II, the authorities regarded precious metals, not just for the coinage but also for goldsmith's work, as a State monopoly.

sumptuary[9] is difficult to say, but their motivation is rarely entirely economic, and it generally covers moral moderation and a degree of social repression as well as economic restraint.

Like the laws of Cosimo de Medici of 1546, 1562 and 1568 on Florentine dress, which are characterized (though with numerous exceptions) by rigid social distinctions—married ladies; unmarried ladies; married and unmarried women and girls; children up to the age of puberty; harlots, etc.—Ottoman sumptuary edicts are often an incidental way of putting certain classes in their place (Christians or women or Jews). The harlots, both Ottoman and Florentine, are presumably included, not because an overdressed harlot was thought to be even more immoral but because they had been dressing like ladies; whereas, for tax-purposes if for no other reason they had to be immediately recognizable. Whereas the costumes in Cesare Vecellio's noted work[10] are presented in a rigid social hierarchy, Cosimo's sumptuary legislation probably took that for granted, but was directed to the restriction of consumption, though probably not equally. Such was also the case in Ottoman Istanbul, and with gold and silver, not just clothing.

The most comprehensive list of Ottoman plate which has come to my attention is an inventory of 1505[11] purporting to be from the Treasury (*hazine-i 'Amma-i Enderun*) of Bayazid II. The vessels include wine-bowls (*badiye*), flasks (*sürahi*), jugs (*maşraba*, possibly a back-formation from Florentine *mesciroba*), cups (*kadeh*), pitchers (*desti*, modern Turkish, *teste*), ladles and strainers (*kepçe* and *kefgir*), dishes (*sahan*) and, though these are out of series, plates (*tabak*). There are also salts (*tuzlu*) and *nefs* or *navicelle* (*gemi*): late Gothic salts were often boat-shaped anyway.[12] Not all the descriptions are easy to interpret[13] (for *Evrenusi* see below), but many were gilt (*mutalla*,

9. Bonito Fanelli (1980), 407-26. It may, of course, well be that the motives for sumptuary legislation differ from society to society. The view in Florence that over-dressing in men was effeminate, like the occasional exploitation of sexuality in Italian fashion, was probably not shared by the Ottomans, though Counter-Reformation morality, with its encouragement of sober dress and sombre colours, had much the same effect as the Ottoman Sultan's view that bright clothes were for young princes. Süleyman the Magnificent, for example, is always portrayed in grey, beige or white, plain or moiré. This was presumably inculcated by the *muḥaddithīn*, for whom over-dressing was just as immoral as for the Counter-Reformation.

10. Vecellio (1590).

11. Rogers (forthcoming, a), reproduced in facsimile in *Topkapı Sarayı Müzesi arşivi kılavuzu*, Istanbul, 1938.

12. These were principally table-ornaments, the *nefs* generally containing the prince's napkin, his cutlery and his assay, that is, one or more *Natternzunge* (fossil sharks' teeth, which were believed to sweat in the presence of poison), Lightbown (1978), 30-1. The Bayazid inventory interestingly lists *adları nama'lum dişler* (various teeth, the names of which are unknown). These were very probably *Natternzunge*, which may have come with one of the *nefs*. Their description in the inventory suggests that their designation was also unknown.

13. For example, a *sahan*, described as NWRGI. Should this be read *Tūrkī*?

altınlu or *memzuc*). The principal sense of this last is "blended", which implies an alloy, so that perhaps the other two refer to parcel-gilt pieces. That silver is involved and not an alloy of base metal is shown by a list of the official presents to the ambassador of the Mamlūk Sultan, Kansuh al-Ğavri to the Ottoman Court in Cumada I 909/November 1503,[14] which include silver cups and trays (*tepsi 'an nükre*) and four *maşraba-i memzuc*: there is plenty of evidence for the primacy of silver in exchanges of diplomatic gifts.

There are further signs that the Bayazid inventory, though not invariably expert, was carefully drawn up by well-informed officials. Types of vessels—with handles (*saplu*), footed (*diplü*), or with covers (*kapaklu*)—are indicated, as well as their proximate provenance—Üngürüs (Hungarian, or possibly Transylvanian); Trabzon (which before its capture by the Ottomans on 1461 had occupied a strategic position as the port for the silver mined at Byzantine Argyropolis, not too far from the modern Gümüşhane); Lazi (from the Eastern Pontus: possibly to be read *Lari*, hence a reference to the Persian silver coin of which it had been fashioned); or Firengi (in practice, not Frankish, but *Italian*). An interesting term is *gebr*, which describes cups and a flask. Barkan has observed that *gebr* in the Süleymaniye accounts[15] is used neither in its original sense, an abusive term for fire-worshippers, nor in the sense of modern Turkish *gâvur*, an abusive term for non-Muslim non-Turks, nor for the non-Muslim skilled labour force, but for the convicts or foreign prisoners of war employed on the works. Some could have been prisoners from Süleyman's Eastern campaigns; but it is far more likely that they were Europeans. Assuming that "heathen" is a good enough translation of its force, what is the point of describing silver as *gebr*? Other objects in the Bayazid inventory similarly stigmatised are pictures (*g. tasvirleri*), playing cards (*g. gencifesi*), bows (*g. yayı*, listed together with a *zemberek* or spring-bow, so presumably some rather new-fangled cross-bow) and an illustrated book (*g. musavver kitabı*).

Cross-bows had continued to arouse moral disapproval in Western Europe well into the Renaissance, and it seems highly likely that the Ottomans, like the Mamlūks before them, would have had similar moral worries, at least as long as they felt themselves to be on the target end. The rest of the *gebr* objects seem most probably to have been *illustrated*: the playing cards would have been Italian *tarocchi* and, like the card stuck into Hazine Album 2153[16] in the Topkapı Sarayı Library, would have had figured court cards or *trionfi*. They did not acquire their occult significance in Europe till much later,[17] though in the eyes of the *'ulamā'* all card-games were games of chance and therefore

14. Barkan (1979), 181, 193.
15. Barkan, 1, (1972-9), 133-7.
16. Hind (1933), 279-96; Raby (1984), 42-9.
17. Dummett (1973), 1-6; Malaguzzi Valeri (1917), 64-8; Dummett and Mann (1980), 102-63.

proscribed: *gebr*, indicating some extra disapproval, must therefore be an allusion to their figural elements.[18] In the case of the silver it is certainly relevant that so much of it is described as *Firengi* and that terms like *tuzlu* and *gemi* are calques, the objects to which they refer being grand imported Western European salts and *navi* (or *navicelle*). These may well have been not heirlooms but diplomatic gifts of outmoded plate,[19] for Lightbown remarks that by 1500 *navi* were no longer in fashion as table-ornaments in Italy. By 1500, moreover, Northern Italian silver was turning towards the profusion characteristic of High Renaissance figural decoration in which, doubtless, conceits of varying propriety played an increasingly important part.[20]

The Bayazid inventory is incomplete, and I have suggested elsewhere that it is in fact a list of objects either to furnish Bayazid's own mosque in Istanbul, which was inaugurated only a few weeks after it was drawn up, or to be sold for the benefit of its endowments.[21] This would explain, *inter alia*, why practically nothing in the list can be now identified in the collections of the Topkapı Sarayı. The silver must thus have been unwanted; as for the *gebr* pieces, like the *gebr tasvirleri*, which cannot have been at all suitable for the mosque, they must have been disposed of elsewhere.[22] Lightbown has well

18. Though Kreiser (1978), 549-56, on balance concludes that Ottoman iconoclasm was never a powerful force, 16th-century European travellers in Turkey and the Ottoman provinces are unanimous that the Ottomans would not tolerate images. Conclusive proof that they were not entirely mistaken are the documents regarding designs for clocks to be made for Sokollu Mehmed Paşa in the Vienna archives recently published by Günther Mraz, *Österreich* (1983), nos.97 and 100.

19. Lightbown (1978), 43.

20. Malaguzzi Valeri (1917), 350-6.

21. Rogers (forthcoming, a). Dr Julian Raby kindly informs me that in a Palace inventory of 1513, exactly the same porcelains are listed as in the 1505 Bayazid inventory. These at least plainly cannot have been disposed of. But even if, as I have argued, they were for the Imperial apartments in the mosque of Bayazid they could have remained within the Treasury: the document purports to be an "inventory", not a "*waqfiyya*", which would have recorded their alienation. And even if, as the *gebr* objects suggest, the list was of objects to be disposed of, Bayazid II, or one of his officials, could easily have had second thoughts about some of them. But the checking of the whole of the 1513 inventory against that of 1505 is necessary before any further conclusions can be drawn.

22. There is a story, frequently retailed but generally rejected as a fabrication, of the Venetian merchant, Angiolello, that Bayazid II disposed of his father Mehmed II's collection of European paintings in the Bazar after he succeeded to the throne. The actual text, misattributed to Donado da Lezze, is in Angiolello's *Historia Turchesca*, Ursu (1909), 120-1, "Fu dal detto Gentil, (*sc.* Gentile Bellini), fatto diversi belli quadri, et massime di cose di lussuria in alcune cose belle in modo che ne haveva nel serraglio gran quantità, et all'intrar che fece il figluolo Baiasit Signor li fece vendere tutto in Bazzaro, et per nostri mercanti ne furono comprati assai...". The motive generally attributed to Bayazid has generally been disapproval of painting, or European painting, or of indecent pictures (though there is no need to take *cose di lussuria* quite literally). Since Bayazid was a noted patron of the arts and, moreover, is not known to have disapproved of painting at all, it has been easy to dismiss the account as sheer European invention. However, the *gebr tasvirleri* in the 1505 inventory must have been among the things which were not

shown how extremely vulnerable European secular plate was to changes in fashion: indeed, only the Church regularly preserved objects in antiquated styles, as much because it could not afford to replace them as out of piety to the memory of benefactors.[23] What was true of 14th and 15th-century France can have been no less true of the Court of Bayazid II, all the more so in that silver or silver-gilt vessels were brought by every incoming embassy and thus remarkably rapidly reflected the vagaries of Italian, Ragusan or Transylvanian fashion.

It is therefore practically impossible to determine what the Bayazid silver, either Turkish or Western European, actually looked liked, partly also because so much must subsequently have been melted down for the Mint or accidentally destroyed in the periodic fires in the Palace. Practically the only object which is at least chronologically appropriate to the date of the inventory (1505) is a "nussschalenformiges Kristallgefäss" in the Hazine with a silver mount decorated with stars in blue enamel, which might well be late 15th-century Venetian work.[24] But the forms and decoration of Florentine and Venetian secular silver of this date also have to be reconstructed largely from liturgical vessels,[25] which, not unnaturally, give little idea of how secular vessels evolved in shape and principally give an idea of technique, not of the motifs or decorative programmes used.[26] The contemporary use of the term "secondo costume d'alemagna" to describe them, however, suggests that up to 1500 Venetian silver was highly conservative and strongly indebted to Northern European models.

For shapes or vessel types household inventories of the period, like the Fieschi inventory of 1532,[27] are also of some use: this lists a *stagnara* (jug, ewer) of silver with relief decoration; a basin; a covered salt; an *overa* (egg-cup); a lemon-squeezer; four candlesticks, plain and decorated; and two *confetere lavorate a la barceloneiza* (sweetmeat containers, the Barcelona-work possibly being an allusion to glass, with silver mounts). Earlier inventories are, however, eclipsed by the magnificence of the plate of Florimond Robertet, minister of Francis I of France.[28] This included: three basins, two with roundels showing the triumph of Neptune and Amphitrite, and one with

required for the mosque of Bayazid and would therefore have been sold on the market. The reason must have been a (temporary) shortage of funds. If Bayazid had disapproved so much of his father's taste he would surely have disposed of the pictures much earlier; and if he had disposed of them earlier there would have been no *gebr tasvirleri* to arouse his clerk's disapproval. It looks, therefore, as though these were Mehmed's pictures, and that Angiolello was right.

23. Lightbown (1978), 43.

24. Steingräber (1961-3), 147-92.

25. *ibid*; *Oreficeria* (1977), *passim*.

26. Steingräber (1961-3), identifies two *nefs* in the Treasury of Toledo Cathedral as Venetian work of 1430-70, one being the so-called "Reliquary of St. Leocadia", but both originally secular in purpose. A covered cup with animal decoration in the same Treasury may, he suggests, also be Venetian, circa 1425-50.

27. Manno (1874), 751-2.

28. Grésy (1868), 30-5.

figures of the Nile, the Jordan, the Euphrates, the Danube and the Rhine, with Neptune in a nautilus chariot at the centre drawn by three sea horses; three swelling vases on foliate feet with Bacchantes, twisted serpent handles and mouths of roaring lions; three covered ewers or jugs with handles like ibex-horns and historiated shoulders; three cups, one with vine-scrolls and birds, one with Ceres and wheatsheaves, and one with a fiery furnace and laurel wreaths; three vinaigrettes in the form of eagles grasping a tortoise; three sugar containers; a table fountain with all sorts of novelties, animals, genii, florets and cornucopias; a large kettle or cauldron with a tap below and two lug handles; and candlesticks, lamps and a *torchère* in the form of a silver globe with a crown of prongs.[29] For this sort of thing *gebr* seems rather a mild term.

This list doubtless represents the acquisition of several decades, so, apart from the extravagance of the figural scenes, little or none of it need have looked High Renaissance or Manneristic. The table-fountain, for example, would not have been wholly out of place in the inventory of Charles V of France, who died in 1380.[30] This, of course, is not to claim that any of the plate actually was so old, but the decoration of European silver is often conservative because, being as much for display as for actual use, it demonstrates its owner's pretensions, to antiquity or nobility of lineage: too much novelty, and the display would become parvenu vulgarity. Styles, moreover, transcended frontiers and decades, and it is probably relevant to cite in this context a Habsburg present of silver to Murad III:[31] two silver-gilt *Bannen* (read *Kannen*?); two large flasks with chased foliate decoration or fretwork (*Laubwerck*); two *Wasserkessel* (cauldrons); two large enamelled dressers (*Credenz*); *Stessbeck* and candlesticks, all gilt. The Paşas received proportionately less, though Lala Mustafa Paşa's present included a *Schiff*, that is, a *nef* or *nave*. Though Schweigger follows his European contemporaries in asserting that this silver was sent straight off to the Mint to be melted down, there is no reason to believe that the Sultan's and his viziers' admiration of it was not genuine. It is quite probable, therefore, that some of the silver from such presents did survive and is to be identified with the silver objects in

29. Robertet also owned forty-two pieces of porcelain, which his widow describes as "des premières qui soient venues en France depuis que les européens vont en Chine", evidently acquired via the Portuguese trade and very probably Jiajing in period, therefore.

30. Associated with Charles V is a famous, ruined Late Gothic table-fountain of Franco-Burgundian workmanship, now in the Cleveland Museum of Art (24.859), allegedly from Istanbul, cf. Lightbown (1978), 43-6; *Fastes* (1981), no.191. Assuming that it really did reach Istanbul it could have been a present from the Burgundian court to one of the last Byzantine emperors; or part of the European tribute to the Ottomans after the Battle of Nicopolis in 1396; or a gift, much later, to Mehmed II or even to Bayazid II. Later table-fountains show many similarities: cf. Miller (1977), nos.8, 11 and 12.

31. Schweigger (1964), 61.

inventories of the imperial box (*mahfil-i latif*) of the mosque of Sultan Ahmed—lanterns, fretwork (*müşebbek*) lamps, drinking vessels with floral (*şükûfeli*) ornament, and all sorts of globes (*top*) or hanging ornaments, gilt or jewelled.

The presents of *Credenz* (that is, dressers, but probably bearing a service of plate) to Murad III continue a custom of considerable antiquity in Western Europe, that of exhibiting the monarch's plate at Court banquets on a stand (*dressoir*). This was still the custom in 16th-17th-century Muscovy,[32] as well as in Mamlūk Cairo, for Maqrīzī's *Khiṭaṭ* describes dressers (*dikka*) of silver and other vessels, formerly ordered for the trousseaux of daughters of emirs, viziers and high bureaucrates.[33] Since the Ottomans fully shared this view of plate as being for display, it is more than likely that some of the *Credenz* presented to them were used. This may possibly explain the obvious lack of resemblance between the Habsburg offerings and such goldsmiths' work as the Sultans ordered the Court craftsmen to make for them.[34] The only surviving table vessels of the earlier 16th century, which are also attested in the 1505 Bayazid inventory, are, however, of zinc (*ruh-i tutiya*), though with elaborate gold tracery encrusted with turquoises and balas rubies which made them somewhat unsuitable for everyday use.[35] Flasks and cups of this type appear in the early portrait albums of the reign of Shāh Tahmasp, but Filiz Çağman has identified some of the zinc vessels in the Hazine, encrusted with rubies, turquoises and emeralds, as 16th-century Ottoman work,[36] and they very probably appear in a painting of the banquet given by Lala Mustafa Paşa to his generals at Izmit in the 992/1584 copy of the *Nüsretname* of Gelibolulu Mustafa 'Alī.[37] The vessels shown there are dishes, some of them footed, but the closed shapes follow the shapes of base metal in Tīmūrid and early Ṣafavid

32. Smith and Christian (1984), 112-3.

33. The well known passage is part of his lament on the decay of the Sūq al-Kuftiyyīn in Cairo and, in addition to presenting various cruces, may well be a considerable exaggeration on Maqrīzī's part. The dressers (*dikka*) were, he says, showy pieces of furniture, of wood inlaid with ebony and ivory or else of wood, polished or varnished (*madhūn*), which bore services (*dast ṭāsāt*) of seven dishes of diminishing sizes. Grand brides were given seven such dressers—of silver, inlaid brass, tin-bronze (*nuḥās abyaḍ*), polished or varnished wood, *ṣīnī* (Chinese blue and white or possibly celadon), *billūrī* (more probably Venetian *cristallo* glass than rock-crystal) and *kadāhī*, which Maqrīzī glosses as "lacquered and polished cardboard from China". cf. Raymond and Wiet (1979), 203-4.

34. Çağman (1984), 51-87.

35. Ivanov, Lukonin and Smesova (1984), 27, pl.64, basin, inventory no.VZ 285. Filiz Çağman kindly informs me that vessels of this type are indeed made of zinc: the conjecture of Allan and Raby (1980), 17-48, that the group is really of tarnished silver is thus to be rejected.

36. *Anatolian Civilizations* (1983), E 95-6, E 215.

37. Topkapı Sarayı Library, H.1365, fol.34b.

Iran, notably the dragon-handled jugs. Schweigger evidently erroneously,[38] asserts that Murad III, "unlike his predecessors", ate only off porcelain, some of it green, not plate: "diese geschirr bringt man aus Persia".

The Ottoman porcelain table services had very limited influence on Ottoman pottery or metalwork. Relatively low-fired ceramics are capable of reproducing only a narrow range of shapes and, as far as we know, satisfactory imitations of celadons were never produced at Iznik. The Sultans' passion for porcelain in the earlier 16th century also meant that practically all of it went straight into the Treasury, so that there was very little in circulation from which to make mass-produced copies or imitations in pottery or base metalwork. Nor did the mounts made for these porcelains have much influence. As in Europe, gold or silver-gilt dragon-handles or spouts, covers with elaborate knobs or finials, and feet which have little to do with the object itself recur constantly. The closest similarities to these are the mounts of Ottoman jades and rock-crystals, but they, likewise, rarely circulated outside the Palace Treasury.

Intriguingly, the Bayazid inventory also lists various wooden vessels, *münakkaş* (probably painted); and a *kapaklı rusi ağaç çanak* (a covered Russian pot). Though there does not appear to be any evidence of Russian exports to Turkey at so early a date, Russian wooden vessels are well enough attested,[39] and the Bursa sicills contain records of Russian merchants at Bursa from the late 15th century onwards.[40] Such vessels, however, could as easily have been Turkish as Russian, for the Rudolf II inventory of 1607-11 under the heading "Türckische sachen" lists a series of wooden vessels,[41] including: "A large covered wooden dish, painted black and red, with foliate decoration and incised ornament, with a silver lock and band, containing silk-embroidered towels or napkins" and "eleven painted wooden Turkish dishes round or octagonal". What is also probable is that Bayazid's Treasury also contained mazers, either locally made or imported from Northern or Western Europe, where they were standard objects in *Kunstkammer*s from the Late Gothic onwards. In fact, the Rudolf II inventory also lists "türckische" mazers: "two vases or flasks, one of Maserholz, lidless and unpainted, the other with some painting and with a knobbed lid", and "nine drinking vessels of Maser- or Fladerinholz (cf. Ottoman *ıhlamur*/limewood) with (horn) handles, the largest in gold and silver mounts, with some enamelling" (these may well have been European), as well as "two Maserholz Turkish spoons with bone handles".

The 1505 Bayazid inventory does not ever indicate how long the objects

38. Schweigger (1608), 58-9; Gerlach (1674), 230, however, had earlier observed that Selim II ate only off porcelain, for fear of being poisoned by eating off anything else.

39. Smith and Christian (1984), 5-26.

40. Inalcık (1969), 97-140.

41. Bauer and Haupt (1976), nos.770, 788, 809-10.

listed had been in the Sultan's possession: *köhne* (old, or more probably, worn or worn out), refers to condition, not age. Almost certainly, however, some of the silver, despite the lure of the Mint and accidental destruction, was heirlooms. Among these may have been the *tikam-i Evrenusi* (a set of Evrenos vessels), a technical term of unknown force which may be a topical allusion. It recalls the spectacular gifts from Evrenos Gazi on the occasion of the marriage of the future Bayazid I to a princess of Germiyan.[42] Neşrî states that his gifts were immediately distributed among the members of a Mamlūk embassy which was conveniently present, and among the *'ulamā'*. Whether or not, a century later, some of the plate he gave was still in the Treasury, his magnificence must have become a cliché in describing splendid silver offered as an official present.

In contrast to the Bayazid inventory and foreigners' reports of the splendour of plate at the Ottoman Court in the later 16th century, Palace accounts for the year beginning 3 Muharram 981/5 May 1573[43] contain no mention of plate; instead there is a list of assorted new copper vessels (*bakır*, though some must obviously have been brass) for the Imperial apartments and for the princes, to the Spartan tune of only 7,381 akçe. This was presumably a periodic expense, principally to replace worn-out vessels, not a complete re-equipment. Vessels for the Sultan's table included covered bowls (*tas ma'a kapak*), incense-burners (*buhurdan*), rose-water sprinklers (*kumkuma*), candlesticks, jugs (*ibrik*, *maşraba*), some with lids, covered plates and dish-covers (*serpuş*) for porcelains and *çini* (China-ware, first and foremost blue and white pottery), and a *lüle-i şem'dan* (probably not the shaft of a candlestick but a torch-holder, *maş'ale*). The selection rather gives the lie to Gerlach's assertion that Selim II ate only off porcelain, but this category of metalwork is not at all well documented, for, being so cheap, it was often melted down and refashioned rather than simply melted down. Some of it obviously followed the shapes of the dishes in Lala Mustafa Paşa's feast in the *Nüsretname* (see above) and increasingly in the 17th century was gilt (*altın yaldızlı*). There are also references to gilt metalwork in registers of gifts offered to the Sultan on great feasts, but they are mostly trivial knick-knacks, not large vessels.[44]

This modest list of copper for the Imperial table is surprisingly reminiscent of the household effects of Alvise Odoni, son of the famous Venetian collector,

42. According to Neşrî's account Evrenos Beg presented a hundred Greek slave-boys and slave girls (evidently a hundred of each, in groups of ten). Each of the first ten slaves bore a gold salver with gold coins, and the next ten silver salvers with silver coins: these were to be scattered over the bride. The remaining eighteen (detachments) bore gold and silver ewers and basins, enamelled dishes and cups, jewelled beakers and glasses. Even if the account is a considerable exaggeration it shows Evrenos Gazi's legendary status in the eyes of the Ottoman chroniclers. Hammer-Purgstall, I, (1827-35), 183-4.

43. Barkan (1979), 116.

44. Meriç (1963): Topkapı Sarayı Archives D9602, D6503, D4104, all datable to the reign of Süleyman the Magnificent.

date 23 June 1555,[45] where, in contrast to the rich collections of antiquities he inherited and luxury cloths, clothing and furnishings, the only silver was cutlery, and the vessels were of wood, bronze, copper (*rami*), pewter (*lattone*), brass (*ottone*) and horn, with practically no glass either. There were also a few porcelains with gilt copper mounts, listed together with Odoni's collection of hardstones, as well as part of a service of porcelains, white wares, celadons and blue and white. Particularly suggestive is the absence of the terms for "damascening" (cf. Ottoman *şami*)[46] which are so frequent in Italian 15th-century inventories, as well as in the 1505 Bayazid inventory. Spallanzani[47] has ably argued that much of this was actually Mamlūk inlaid or gilt brass, though the Italian usage of *alla damaschina* is inconsistent and sometimes obscure.[48] But this fashion evidently waned after 1500, and mid-16th-century Ottoman inventories scarcely ever refer to the Levantine-Italian Azzimina metalwork which superseded it.

In the Palace accounts there is little variation in the types of vessels listed, the material (*bakır*/copper) of which they were made, and the strict economy practised in the kitchens, from the reign of Mehmed II right up to the end of the 16th century. Household accounts of Mehmed II for Zilhicce 873/June-July 1469 and Rabi' I 874/September-October 1469 both contain items relating to the tinning of pots and pans, 716 akçe for 117 pieces and 233 akçe for 87 pieces, respectively.[49] Tinning must have been done in rotation and with heavy use would have been an annual affair: the only item for the Sultan's table seems to have been a *sini-i Hassa* (Imperial tray, perhaps merely an extra-large one). Purchases were to replace worn-out vessels, the old pieces being sold by weight as scrap to defray part of the cost.

Miscellaneous Palace accounts for the year beginning 1 Muharram 963/1555-6[50] also list expenditure on tinning kitchen vessels, as well as purchases for high officers in the Imperial apartments (Dârüs' Seâdet). Here, both the weights and the sums allocated show certain discrepancies. Why, for example, should two *kefgir* and *kepçe* (strainers and ladles) weighing more than

45. Ludwig (1911), 55-71.

46. The general term in the Ottoman sources is *zarneşanlı*, evidently for damascening on steel. The register of Court craftsmen for the early part of the reign of Süleyman the Magnificent groups them with the staff of the Court jeweller, Çağman (1984), 51-87. More mysterious is the group of *dımışkçıyan*, who figure among the craftsmen offering knick-knacks to the Sultan for the great feasts of the Muslim year, Meriç (1963), 764-86. The descriptions of their gifts suggest that these were not damascened steel at all but decorated glass baubles, somewhat similar to Christmas tree ornaments.

47. Spallanzani (1980), 95-115.

48. For example, the inventory of the estate of Leonello Lomellino, Pandiani (1915), 247-54, dated 4 December 1458, includes utensils, a candlestick and a basin as *damasche cum argento*, others being described as *sine argento*: the force of the distinction is obscure. And some pewter (*latonum*) is even described as *damasche sine argento*.

49. Barkan (1979), 198, 216, 226.

50. Barkan (1979), 13, 25-6, 33-4.

20 okka cost 510 akçe, when 9 *kefgir* and *kepçe* weighing 16 okka only cost 227 akçe?—but there is no limit to the games one can play with accounts of this type. The list includes dish-covers (*serpuş-i sahan*) and four large tripods, evidently feet for three large *sini* (large tray-tables). Accounts for the same year for the Ibrahim Paşa Sarayı (by this time not a private residence but an official guest house) and for the Müteferrikas in the Galata Sarayı also cover the expense of retinning and purchases of assorted kitchen pots, as well as dish-covers, a jug and various trays. These are priced by weight and the most expensive, not surprisingly, are cauldrons. Nor were the table-vessels likely to have been elaborate. Officers' messes have traditionally tended to equip themselves in style: but this has generally been through their members' own contributions, not the conversion of official funds. Government issue has always been utility, not luxury.

A different aspect of the Ottoman attitude to plate is that shown in inventories of the estates of persons deceased (*tereke defter*s), drawn up by the Kadi's court for the proper distribution of the proceeds among the legal heirs. Unfortunately, many of them have been lost, destroyed or misplaced,[51] and those published for 16th-17th-century Edirne are sometimes patently incomplete. Barkan has suggested three main explanations for such inadequacies, and there may well be others: (a) because each of the spouses may have retained certain personal possessions in the connubial home, over and above the legally stipulated dowry of the wife, which on the death of one of the partners would not necessarily figure in the inventory; (b) because certain possessions, particularly valuables, could well have been distributed as gifts *inter vivos*; or (c) because certain objects, again mostly valuables, could well have been mulcted by the heirs before the inventory came to be drawn up. In addition, when people died abroad or *en poste*, the lists of their possessions in either of their domiciles would probably be complementary and would not repeat each other.

Despite these reservations, which are still far from explaining why some inventories appear to ignore pots and pans entirely, they generally reflect a balance of consumers' choices. Barkan has principally chosen the bourgeoisie of Edirne for study—junior Janissary officers; cloth merchants or manufacturers; *mütavellis* (officials administrating *vakf* property and other institutions); prosperous druggists (*'attar*); jewellers with shops in the Bedesten; and Christians, including a Slav rakı-distiller. He has also included a few more important officials—an ex-Bostancıbaşı, a provincial governor (*mir liva*), and a Janissary Ağa—all with gross estates of more than a million akçe. The period covered by his selection, mid-16th to mid-17th century, was one of chronic price inflation, which is reflected in both the gross valuations and the

51. Barkan (1966), 1-479; Faroqhi (1984), 1-19.

contents of estates. Valuations take little account of quality, age, condition or size, so that although it would be simple to present them in tabular form the results might well be misleading. However, it may be relevant to observe that *batteries de cuisine,* to judge from later Ottoman metalwork published from Hungary,[52] are highly conservative in their evolution and are only rarely influenced by contemporary pottery or porcelain shapes. This is scarcely surprising, for *batteries de cuisine* have no real substitute.

The uniformity of the mid-16th-century inventories is rather striking. Silver is rarely listed. Glass is even rarer. And though practically all estates include some luxuries—chiefly, felts, furs, textiles, clothing and slaves—*çini* (China-ware) actually occurs as rarely as porcelain (*çini-i fağfuri*). Though inflation makes the comparison rather difficult, price and size may have little to do with one another: a silver cup (*kadeh*)[53] at 200 akçe may be worth more than twice a cauldron[54] at 81 akçe; while two porcelain dishes at 60 akçe are worth almost six Iznik *çini* dishes.[55] So great is the difference in price between Iznik and porcelain that the Iznik pottery must mostly have been cracked, chipped or broken. Its relative infrequency, however, is extremely surprising, since, as its appearance in the kitchen accounts of Mehmed II[56] and quite a lot of extant pieces suggest, much of it was kitchen ware. Exceptionally, a druggist[57] had a large collection of pottery *hokka*s, presumably druggists' jars or *albarelli*. This is a very rare shape in Iznik pottery, but the inventory of a Florentine druggist published by Spallanzani[58] shows that the term *albarello* covered a large number of shapes, and *hokka* may be a general equivalent. The valuations of the pots appear to take some account of their contents. Thus a *hokka* full of terebinth and mint preserve is valued at 33 akçe, while other *hokka* were as little as two for 7.5 akçe, or as much as 80 akçe each.

The infrequency of porcelain in the earlier inventories shows that the booty captured in Iran was not shared out but went straight to the Palace Treasuries in Istanbul. It also shows that porcelain imports into Ottoman Turkey, either via Syria and Egypt or the Hijaz *or* via the Portuguese and the Mediterranean, were negligible in the 16th century. In the circumstances,

52. Fehér (1975).

53. Barkan (1966), no.3, dated mid-Receb 953/mid-September 1546, 207, 950 akçe gross.

54. Barkan (1966), no.82.

55. Barkan (1966), no.4, dated 1 Muharram 955/15 February 1548, 46, 555 akçe gross.

56. Barkan (1979), 187-208.

57. Barkan (1966), no.8, dated Receb 956/30 July 1549, 26,386 gross. Interestingly, the shop of a Venetian Muschier (perfumer) of the same period, Ludwig (1906), 317-41, who also sold druggists' materials, contains no *albarelli*, but, instead, all sorts of alabaster pots. Those were evidently for conspicuous consumers.

58. Spallanzani (1978), 155-8, no.14: *4 alberegli spianati azurri; 12 alberegli azurri cho' manico e senza manico; 5 alberegli da unguenti bianchi e gialli; alberegli bolongniese; 2 alberegli chon viso; 1 albereglo di Domascho o di Maiolicha; 4 alberegli di Domascho tondi; 43 alberegli di più ragioni.*

therefore, it is hardly explicable that the Edirne bourgeoisie was so neglectful of Iznik pottery as a substitute.

As for silver, there is some indication that soldiers were in a better position to amass it. Hızır Çelebi, for example,[59] died on campaign and the remainder of his effects were sold in the Bazar at Edirne. His silver, which was partly disposed of on campaign, included a *şiş* (probably a rapier, here 675 akçe); a *bozdoğan* (battle mace, 129.5 akçe); a chain (682.5 akçe); and various ornaments—a *başlık* (headdress, 568.5 akçe), a *burunsalık* (for an animal's muzzle, 322.5 akçe); a *sinebend* (stomacher, 532.5 akçe); and a *sorguçluk* (turban pin, 84.5 akçe). The weapons, which were obviously not wholly silver but of damascened steel, possibly in silver-plated sheaths, may well have been his own; but the ornaments, some of them female, must have been booty, or looted on his own initiative. The silver sold at Edirne, which may have been laundered loot, consisted of some expensive jewellery and a series of vessels—a *tepsi* (tray, 548 akçe); two cups (174 akçe); and a *maşraba* (jug, 506 akçe). These were sold by weight and probably therefore were bought for melting down. In contrast, his pots and pans were modest, though with some duplicates and a special set for the campaign, including dishes, a metal flask in a case (*ğilaf*), kettle, ewer and basin, and a horse-bowl (*at tası*).

Even more impressive is another soldier's estate,[60] that of Yunus Beğ, *mir liva* (military governor) of Köstendil (Velbužd) in Bulgaria. His silver included weapons and horse-furniture, doubtless all with silver plaques and evidently appropriate to his official rank or position. His silver utensils included four *tepsi* (1,575 akçe); two *maşraba*, valued by weight at 881.5 akçe; a cup and basin (1,505 akçe); a candlestick (1,783 akçe); a *dipli üsküre* (footed dish or tazza, 1,742 akçe); as well as various pieces of jewellery—a belt (1,050 akçe), a *hotoz* (aigrette, 95 akçe), three *bazubend* (brassards, or would they have been for a lady? 545 akçe), three chains (altogether 1,495 akçe), a *tablbaz* (hawker's drum, 2,001 akçe) and a dress saddle (2,000 akçe). On the other hand, although his library was important, he scarcely had any *batterie de cuisine* at all, nor any pots or porcelain.

Contemporary civilians were evidently different. The estate of a rich draper[61] who, like Yunus Beg, left more than a million akçe gross, contained no silver but three glass bowls, a good collection of *çini* (*sahan*, *tepsi*, *tabak*, *kâse*, *legen* and *ibrik*) and four porcelain dishes valued at 600 akçe. The lists suggest, in fact, that there is an inverse proportion between holdings of silver, and of glass, porcelain and *çini*. Thus, Mahmud Beşe ibn Hasan[62] left no silver, but

59. Barkan (1966), no.13, dated 16 Zilhicce 961/8 November 1554, 153, 123 akçe gross.

60. Barkan (1966), no.19, dated Zilka'da 979/March-April 1572, well over one million akçe gross.

61. Barkan (1966), no.66, dated early Rabi' II 1005/late October 1596, more than one million akçe gross.

62. Barkan (1966), no.62, dated 10 Şa'ban 1051/14 November 1641, 402, 560 akçe gross.

owned porcelains including a *tabak* valued at 1,150 akçe, cups, two *yekmerdi kâse* (meaning unknown) valued at 500 akçe, and two flasks (*sürahi*) valued at 300 akçe. Whereas the inventory of Abu Bakr Ağa[63] sets a silver mace (*debbus*) at 4,165 akçe, horse-trappings (18,000 akçe), sword-belt (16,000 akçe) and scrap silver to the tune of 78,000 akçe against a miserable 130 akçe for glass.

The comparison and contrast is not, of course, metal for metal, pot for pot, but between general preferences for one rather than the other: hence, ratios may also reflect different opportunities for acquisition. This emerges, for example, in the estate of Sünbül Hasan,[64] a jeweller with a shop and storeroom in the Edirne Bedesten, who owned two *çini* dishes (184 akçe), silver horse-trappings (4,800 akçe), and various silver vessels worth together almost 10,000 akçe, but whose principal assets were evidently jewellery in pawn (466,993 akçe), together with silver vessels, mirror-cases and chains, valued by weight and basically raw material for his craft. But a minor Court official, like Süleyman Ağa, who had been Bostancıbaşı at the Palace in Edirne,[65] was much more of a consumer. His silver included a *gaddare*, (according to Redhouse, *ḳidr*)(kettle), a censer (*micmer*), a rosewater sprinkler and a *hokka* (together 1,500 akçe). He also had Iznik dishes and bowls (200 akçe) and porcelains (together 1970 akçe), including a *tabak-i münakkaş*, a collector's item valued at 200 akçe alone and very probably one of the jewelled porcelains with gold tracery mounts executed for the Ottoman Palaces from the later 16th century onwards.[66] Among the pots and pans are a novelty, three coffee-pots (*ibrik-i kahve*, 300 akçe). Hürrem Beg,[67] a dyer, also illustrates the tendency of the 17th-century inventories to inclusiveness, for he had porcelains (2,150 akçe); Iznik and Kütahya vessels (400 akçe), and a lot of silver—three *maşraba*, four *bilezik*, an incense-burner, horse-trappings and a cup, together with 42,000 akçe worth of scrap silver, making a total of 56,714 akçe. In contrast, the estate of another Bostancıbaşı, Hasan Ağa,[68] has a *batterie de cuisine* valued practically as highly as the silver (7,500 akçe). But that, exceptionally, is because he had relatively little silver. This inventory is one of the latest published by Barkan, and it may be that because of inflation the pay or perquisites of Court officials was no longer sufficient to keep them in the manner to which they had become accustomed.

Practically all the inventories contain some imported items, mostly cloth. Silver also is very occasionally labelled as *Firengi*. Among utensils some dishes

63. Barkan (1966), no.92, dated late Zilhicce 1033/mid-August 1624, 2,136,740 akçe gross.

64. Barkan (1966), no.29, dated mid-Şa'ban 1012/January 1604, 939,000 akçe gross.

65. Barkan (1966), no.35, dated 2 Muharram 1014/20 May 1605, 1,217,816 akçe gross.

66. Ünal (1963), 676-714.

67. Barkan (1966), no.89, mid-Cumada II 1032/mid-April 1623, 751,152 akçe gross.

68. Barkan (1966), no.87, dated 21 Şevval 1069/2 July 1659, with a much lower gross valuation of 583,865 akçe.

are described as *türki*[69] which is odd because one would expect Ottoman inventories to take Turkishness for granted: it may be a trade term and the origin of the "türckische sachen" of the Rudolf II inventory. There is one mention of a *şami* bowl or basin (*tas*), at a mere 14 akçe.[70] This looks like a calque on Italian *alla damaschina*; but may we then conclude that another single mention of an *'Acemi sahan* is a calque on Azzimina work?[71] Almost the only term which plainly refers to decoration is *dendanlı*,[72] toothed. This could well refer to serrated edges, but it probably corresponds to the *taraklı* (toothed, zig-zag) ornament on wood, bone or ivory in the 1640 *narh defter*. Strangest of all, however, there is only one mention in the whole series of gilt vessels, a *yaldızlı tas*, at 60 akçe,[73] which is not markedly more valuable than any of the other pots and pans in the inventory. This cannot reflect the real distribution of *tombak* in Ottoman Turkey in the 17th century; but, equally curiously, the 1640 *narh defter* only refers to gilt metalwork once in the detailed lists it gives of copper, tin (*kalay*), brass (*pirinc*) and bronze vessels, and which also indicate size, shape and decoration.[74]

The weighing of plate against base metal in the Edirne inventories has been difficult to do in detail, because the lack of indication of what was made of what raises the question how much of the *batteries de cuisine* was crockery, either glazed or unglazed. If the reason for the omission of crockery (*kavanoz*/pots, *testi*/pitchers, *güvec*/baking dishes or stew-pots) was that secondhand it was practically valueless, this was not at all the case with vessels of terra sigillata, which were highly esteemed as a specific against internal disorders[75] and which, to judge from the 1607 inventory of Rudolf II, were far more famous in Europe than Iznik pottery.[76] The Bayazid inventory of 1505 contains references to miscellaneous *münakkaş toprak bardak* (decorated or painted drinking vessels), which are evidently unglazed. However, perplexingly, they are attributed to Konya, which is not known to have been any sort of a pottery centre in the Ottoman period. This is evidently another crux. For the remarkably comprehensive 1640 *narh defter* also ignores the pottery made by the *çömlekçiyan* on the Golden Horn, which Evliya Çelebi reports, was partly terra sigillata, and confines itself to listing Thracian pottery from Ainos

69. Barkan (1966), no.4: 2 *sahan* for 40 akçe; no.5, 18 Receb 955/27 April 1548; 1 *sahan* for 12 akçe; no.6, 6 Cumada I 955/13 June 1548, 1 large *sahan* for 40 akçe; no.13, 19 Zilhicce 961/8 November 1554, 2 *sahan* for 16 akçe.

70. Barkan (1966), no.9, dated 19 Zilka'da 956/9 December 1549.

71. Barkan (1966), dated 1005/1596, 1 *sahan* for 50 akçe.

72. Barkan (1966), no.15, Rabi' I 975/September 1567; no.18, Muharram 977/June-July 1569, dishes (*sahan*) at 41 akçe, 69 akçe or 85 akçe.

73. Barkan (1966), no.41, dated early Zilhicce 1045/mid-May 1636.

74. Kütükoğlu (1983), 195-202.

75. Hasluck (1929) and references.

76. Bauer and Haupt (1976), 56-7, nos.1061-8.

(Inoz, Enez), Selânik, Midye and Dimetoka.[77] Some of it is stated to be glazed, plain green or yellow, but it is priced at no more than an akçe or two per piece and it must have been little more than peasant-ware. Where did the fine glazed or unglazed wares disappear then?

There are doubtless many other cruces which further detailed study of the Edirne *tereke defters* would bring to light. The present survey, however, shows their general utility, and some of their limitations. On balance their contents are substantially similar to those of 16th-17th-century Italian inventories, which show comparable weighting to plate, metalwork in base alloys and *batteries de cuisine*, pottery or maiolica of various types, and possibly porcelains too. The estate of the Medici cloth-merchant, Giovanni di Francesco Maringhi, who died at Pera in 1506,[78] is not only remarkably similar to Florentine inventories of that date; it is also very similar to 16th-17th-century Ottoman inventories. The only obvious difference is that Maringhi owned more glass than his Ottoman merchant contemporaries. But, for Maringhi, as for the Ottomans, plate, pottery, porcelain and kitchen wares were essentially complementary, not substitutes for one another in any large sense.

77. Hammer, I/2, (1835-46), 31-2;
Kütükoğlu (1983), 74, 266-7.

78. Richards (1932).

Bibliography

Allan & Raby (1982) — Allan, J. and Raby, J., "Metalwork" in *Tulips, Arabesques and Turbans. Decorative Arts of the Ottoman Empire*, ed. Y. Petsopoulos, London, 1982, pp.17-48.

Anatolian Civilizations (1983) — *Anadolu Medeniyetleri/Anatolian Civilizations*, exhibition catalogue, Istanbul, 1983.

Anhegger & Inalcık (1956) — Anhegger, R. and Inalcık, H., *Ḳānūnāme-i Sulṭānī ber Mūceb-i 'Örf-i 'Osmānī. II Mehmed ve II. Bayazid Devirlerine ait Yaşaknāme ve Ḳānūnnāmeler*, Ankara, 1956.

Babinger (1956) — Babinger F., "Reliquienschacher am Osmanenhof in XV. Jahrhundert", *Bayerische Akademie der Wissenschaften, Phil.-hist. Klasse, Sitzungsberichte*, 1956, Heft, 2.

Barkan (1942) — Barkan, Ö. L., "XV. Asrın Sonunda Bazı Büyük Şehirlerde Eşya ve Yiyecek Fiatlarının Tesbit ve Teftiş Hususlarının Tanzim Eden Kanunlar. II Kanunname-i Ihtisab-i Bursa (1502)", *Tarih Vesikaları*, 2, 1942, pp.15-40.

Barkan (1966) — Barkan, Ö. L., "Edirne Askerî Kassam'îna ait Tereke Defterleri", *Belgeler*, 3, 1966, pp.1-479.

Barkan (1972-9) — Barkan, Ö. L., *Süleymaniye Camii ve Imareti Inşaatı*, I-II, Ankara, 1972-9.

Barkan (1979) — Barkan, Ö. L., "Istanbul Saraylarına ait Muhasebe Defterleri", *Belgeler*, 9, 1979, pp.1-380.

Bauer & Haupt (1976) Bauer, R., and Haupt, H., "Das Kunstkammerinventar Kaiser Rudolfs II, 1607-1611", *Jahrbuch der Kunsthistorischen Sammlungen in Wien*, 72, 1976, xi-xlv, pp.1-191.

Bonito Fanelli (1980) Bonito Fanelli, R., "I Drappi d'Oro: Economia e Moda a Firenze nel Cinquecento", *Le Arti nel Principato Mediceo*, Florence, 1980, pp.407-26.

Çağman (1984) Çağman, F., "Serzergerân Mehmet Usta ve Eserleri", *Kemal Çığ'a Armağan*, Istanbul, 1984, pp.51-87.

Dalsar (1960) Dalsar, F., *Türk Sanayi ve Ticaret Tarihinde Bursa'da Ipekçilik*, Istanbul, 1960.

Dummett (1973) Dummett, M., "Notes on a 15th-Century Pack of Cards from Italy", *Journal of the Playing Card Society*, 1, 1973, pp.1-6.

Dummett & Mann (1980) Dummett, M. and Mann, S., *The Game of Tarot, from Ferrara to Salt Lake City*, London, 1980.

Düzdağ (1972) Düzdağ, M.E., *Şeyhülislâm Ebussuûd Efendi Fetvaları Işığında 16. Asır Türk Hayatı*, Istanbul, 1972.

Faroqhi (1984) Faroqhi, S., *Towns and Townsmen of Ottoman Anatolia. Trade, Crafts and Food Production in an Ottoman Setting, 1520-1650*, Cambridge, 1984.

Fastes (1981) *Les Fastes du Gothique. Le Siècle de Charles V*, exhibition catalogue, Paris, 1981.

Fehér (1975) Fehér, G., *Craftsmanship in Turkish-ruled Hungary*, Budapest, 1975.

Gerlach (1674) *Stephan Gerlachs des Aeltern Tagbuch in der Türkey 6-Jahrigen römischkayserlichen Gesandschaft*, Frankfurt-am-Main, 1674.

Grésy (1868) Grésy, E., "Inventaire des Objets d'Art Composant la Succession de Florimond Robertet, Ministre de François Ier, Dressée par sa Veuve le 4e Jour d'Août 1532", *Mémoires de la Société des Antiquaires de France*, 30, 1868, pp.1-66.

Hammer-Purgstall (1827-35) Hammer-Purgstall, J. von, *Geschichte des Osmanischen Reiches*, Pest, 1827-35.

Hammer (1834-46) Hammer, J. von, tr. *Narrative of Travels in Europe, Asia and Africa in the Seventeenth Century by Evliyá Efendí*, London, pp.134-46.

Hasluck (1929) Hasluck, F.W., "Terra Lemnia", *Christianity and Islam under the Sultans*, I-II, Oxford, 1929; New York 1973, II, pp.671-88.

Hind (1933) Hind, A.M., "Italian Engravings of the Fifteenth Century at Constantinople", *Print Collectors' Quarterly*, 20, 1933, pp.279-96.

Inalcık (1969) Inalcık, H., "Capital Formation in the Ottoman Empire", *Journal of Economic History*, 19, New York, 1969, pp.97-140.

Ivanov, Lukonin & Smesova (1984) Ivanov, A.A., Lukonin, V.G., and Smesova, L. S., *Yuvelirniye Izdeliya Vostoka. Drevniy, Srednevkovy Period*, Leningrad, 1984.

Kreiser (1978) Kreiser, K., "'...dan die Türckhen leiden khain Menschen Pildnuss': Über die Praxis des Bilderverbots bei den Osmanen", *Fifth International Congress of Turkish Art*, ed. G. Fehér, Budapest, 1978, pp.549-56.

Kütükoğlu (1983) Kütükoğlu, M.S., *1640 Tarihli Narh Defteri ve Osmanlılarda Narh Müessesesi*, Istanbul, 1983.

Lightbown (1978) — Lightbown, R.W., *Secular Goldsmiths' Work in Medieval France*, London, 1978.

Ludwig (1906) — Ludwig, G., "Restello, Spiegel und Toilettenutensilien in Venedig zur Zeit der Renaissance", *Italienische Forschungen, Herausgegeben vom Kunsthistorischen Institute in Florenz*, 1, Berlin, 1906, pp.187-388.

Ludwig (1911) — Ludwig, G., *Archivalische Beiträge zur Geschichte der Venezianischen Kunst*, Berlin, 1911.

Malaguzzi Valeri (1917) — Malaguzzi Valeri, F., *La Corte di Lodovico il Moro III. Gli Artisti Lombardi*, Milan, 1917.

Manno (1874) — Manno, A., "Arredi ed Armi di Sinibaldo Fieschi da un Inventario del MDXXXII", *Atti della Società Ligure di Storia Patria*, 10, Genoa, 1874, pp.706-811.

Menavino (1551) — Menavino, G., *I Costumi et la Vita de Turchi*, Florence, 1551.

Meriç (1963) — Meriç, R.M., "Bayramlarda Padişahlara Hediye Edilen San'at Eserleri ve Karşılıkları, Türk San'atı Tarihi Vesikaları", *Türk San'atı Tarihi, Araştırma ve Incelemeleri*, 1, Istanbul, 1963, pp.764-86.

Miller (1977) — Miller, N., *French Renaissance Fountains*, New York, 1977.

Oreficeria (1977) — *Oreficeria nella Firenze del Quattrocentro*, exhibition catalogue, Florence, 1977.

Österreich (1983) — *Österreich und die Osmanen*, exhibition catalogue, Vienna, 1983.

Pandiani (1915) — Pandiani, E., *Vita Privata Genovese nel Rinascimento*, Genoa, 1915.

Raby (1984) — Raby, J., "Mehmed II Fatih and the Fatih Album", *Between China and Iran. Paintings from Four Istanbul Albums*, ed. E. Grube and E. Sims, London-New York, 1984, pp.42-9.

Raymond & Wiet (1979) — Raymond, A., and Wiet, G., *Les Marchés du Caire. Traduction Annotée du Texte de Maqrīzī*, IFAO, Cairo, 1979.

Refik (1935a) — Refik, A., *On Altıncı Asırda Istanbul Hayatı (1553-1591)*, 2nd ed., Istanbul, 1935.

Refik (1935b) — Refik, A., *Hicrî on Ikinci Asırda Istanbul Hayatı (1000-1200)*, Istanbul, 1935.

Richards (1932) — Richards, G.R.B., *Florentine Merchants in the Age of the Medici*, Cambridge, Mass., 1932.

Rogers (forthcoming, a) — Rogers, J.M., "An Ottoman Palace Inventory of the Reign of Bayazid II", CIEPO Cambridge 1984 Proceedings, (forthcoming).

Rogers (forthcoming, b) — Rogers, J.M., "Ottoman Luxury Trades and their Regulation", (forthcoming).

Schweigger (1608) — Schweigger, S., *Ein newe Reysbeschreibung auss Teutschland nach Konstantinopel und Jerusalem*, Nürnberg, 1608; Graz, 1964.

Smith & Christian (1984) — Smith, R.E.F., and Christian, D., *Bread and Salt. A Social and Economic History of Food and Drink in Russia*, Cambridge, 1984.

Spallanzani (1978) — Spallanzani, M., *Ceramiche Orientali a Firenze nel Rinascimento*, Florence, 1978.

Spallanzani (1980) — Spallanzani, M., "Metalli Islamici nelle Collezioni Medicee dei Secoli XV-XVI", *Le Arti del Principato Mediceo*, Florence, 1980, pp.95-115.

Steingräber (1961-3) — Steingräber, E., "Studien zur Venezianischen Goldschmiedekunst des 15. Jahrhunderts", *Mitteilungen des Kunsthistorischen Institutes in Florenz*, 10, 1961-3, pp.147-92

Ünal (1963)	Ünal, I., "Çin Porselenler Üzerindeki Türk Tarsiatı", *Türk San'atı Tarihi, Araştırma ve Incemeleri*, 1, Istanbul, 1963, pp.676-714.
Ursu (1909)	Ursu, I., ed., *Donado da Lezze, Historia Turchesca (1330-1514)*, Bucharest, 1909.
Vecellio (1590)	Vecellio, C., *Habiti Antichi et Moderni di Tutto il Mondo*, Venice, 1590.

Silver, Copper and Ceramics in Ancient Athens

MICHAEL VICKERS

O.G.S. Crawford has described the "archaeological thrill" to be experienced in finding, tracing and interpreting the remains of antiquity in the modern landscape. It is, indeed, one of the pleasures of a walk in the English countryside to be able to recognize in a row of trees or a footpath the course of a road built by the Romans two thousand years ago, or to be able to see in grass-grown mounds an Iron Age earthwork or a deserted medieval village.[1] While the past as a whole has disappeared, we can use its vestiges to reconstruct a picture of what used to exist. In similar vein, V. Gordon Childe has written of "skeuomorphism", the manufacture of vessels in one material intended to evoke the appearance of vessels regularly made in another, and has commended its study to archaeologists since "(it) often gives us a glimpse into productive activities and artistic media of which no direct evidence survives".[2] Many features of ancient Greek pottery, such as vestigial rivets, strengthening bands, or sharply angled forms, are undoubtedly skeuomorphic. Another way of looking at such features is to regard them as being in a sense like footprints in snow. Even though the wayfarer may have passed on, his former presence can be inferred. These matters will be pursued later in this paper; first it may be necessary to remind some members of the audience that silver and gold were important elements in ancient social and economic life, and that the fact that they are now for the most part missing from the archaeological record, far from being grounds for scepticism, is only to be expected.

Throughout history, whenever plate came to be considered old-fashioned by its owners, or it was badly worn, or the market price of bullion changed to such an extent that it suddenly became an attractive proposition to cash in a valuable asset, silver and gold have gone into the melting pot. Those who could afford to do so set their tables with gold or silver, but when their plate became old-fashioned or worn, they changed it for something more up-to-date.[3] If their wealth increased, they would invest in vessels of a higher gauge metal; if they became poorer, they might be forced to content

1. Crawford (1953).

2. Childe (1956), 13-14—a reference I owe to Dr Andrew Sherratt.

3. Reitlinger (1963), 14.

themselves with a finer gauge metal, or having to do without it altogether.[4]

This is to put matters at their baldest. It does not take account of the greed, avarice or sheer thuggery that the desire for possession of precious metals can generate. Ancient Sicily provides a case in point. This island has seen more than its fair share of violent crime committed in the pursuit of precious metals.[5] We need only think of the Roman procurator C. Verres, who commandeered all the silver plate he could lay his hands on, intimidating whole communities until they had produced the goods.[6] Rather earlier, in the 460s BC, we hear of the tyrant Thrasybulus confiscating the possessions of many of the more prominent citizens of Syracuse into the state treasury, and employing a large body of mercenaries with the proceeds.[7] Thucydides describes in great detail how an Athenian embassy was tricked into believing that Segesta and its allies in western Sicily were richer than they really were: the Segestans borrowed gold and silver cups from neighbouring cities and used them in every household in which their guests were entertained. Thucydides himself owned a gold-mine in Thrace, and was not so impressed. After describing the plate in a temple at Eryx, he remarked that "most of the vessels were only of silver, and therefore they made a show quite out of proportion to their value".[8]

In mainland Greece, too, there was a long tradition of gold and silver vessels both in sanctuaries and in the home. The first major objects of which we hear in historical times are the gold and silver offerings made by Gyges of Lydia in the seventh century B.C.[9] Alyattes was the second of his family to send a present to Delphi—a *kratera argureon megan*.[10] His immediate successor Croesus dedicated amongst other things a huge silver crater, which could hold six hundred amphoras of wine and weighed nine and a half talents.[11] An approximate idea of the scale of this crater may be gained from the huge silver vessel still extant today in a temple in Jaipur and which weighs 300 kilos.[12] Croesus' crater was destroyed and replaced in the third century B.C. by another silver vessel which weighed six and a half talents and which was so big that when Delphi was sacked by the Roman general Sulla in 84 B.C. "no

4. Citroen, van Erpers Royaards, and Verbeek (1984), especially nos. 111, 112. Contrast the later catalogue entries. It is to be regretted that no weights are given in an otherwise excellent catalogue. cf. the golden cups made in mid-eighteenth-century Amsterdam; de Iongh (1982).

5. Even in modern times: Professor Dieter Metzler has kindly drawn attention to a story in the *Ipswich Journal* for November 1848, according to which two Englishmen were held ransom by Sicilian banditti for 4,000 ounces of silver.

6. Cicero, *In Verrem*, 4, *passim*.

7. Diodorus Siculus, 11, 67, 5.

8. Thucydides 6, 46.

9. Herodotus 1, 14.

10. Herodotus 1, 25.

11. Herodotus 1, 51. An Attic-Euboeic talent weighed 25.86 kg., an Aeginetic 37.80 kg.

12. Seemann and Ward (1984), 72-3—a reference I owe to Dr Adrienne Lezzi-Hafter.

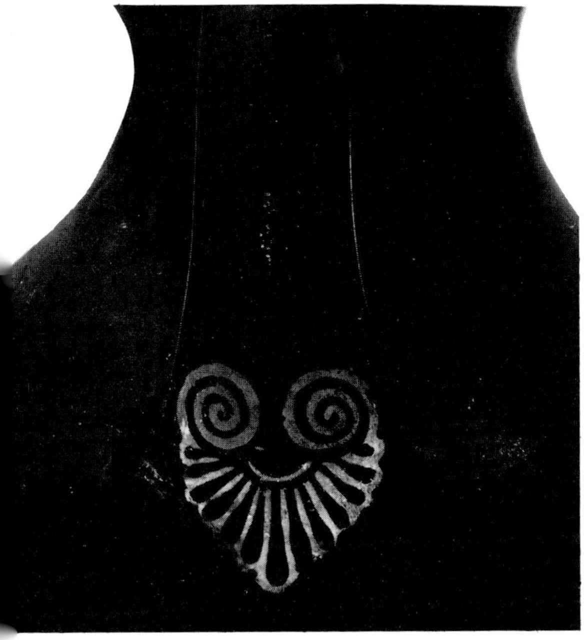

gure A. Attic black-figure *oinochoe*, detail of handle. Ash-
olean Museum, 1965.122.

Figure B. Attic black-figure *oinochoe*, detail of rim. Ashmolean Museum, 1965.122.

gure C. Attic black-figure *olpe*, detail of handle and rim.
hmolean Museum, 885.658.

Figure D. Attic black-figure amphora, detail of handle. Ashmolean Museum, 1885.668.

wagon could bear it" and the Delphian authorities "were obliged to cut it in pieces".[13]

There was plenty of silver, and gold, at Athens, at least before the city was impoverished by the expenses of the Peloponnesian War. A considerable amount of gold must have gone into the construction of the colossal chryselephantine statue of Athena in the Parthenon.[14] This kind of artistic activity can probably be interpreted as indicating the success of tribute-raising in the Athenian empire, and also perhaps the profitability of Athenian-owned gold mines in Thrace. Athenian silver, mined at Laurium in southern Attica, was still famous in Polybius' day as the purest available.[15] Queen Atossa's informant in the *Persae* of 472 was near the truth when he declared that Athens possessed "a fountain of silver buried beneath her soil".[16] Immense fortunes were made by the owners of mining contracts. Callias Laccoplutus, for instance, is said to have been worth "the enormous but nevertheless credible figure of 200 talents"—equivalent to more than five tons of silver—and we know that part of his wealth came from his mining interests.[17] It was rumoured that Alcibiades inherited a fortune worth 100 talents.[18] As a young man, Alcibiades raided the house of his would-be lover whose tables, we are told, were full of "silver and gold cups".[19] At the Olympic games of 416, not only did he purloin a fellow citizen's team of horses, value eight talents, but he used the gold and silver plate of the official Athenian delegation, as though it were his own.[20] The prizes at the Marathonian games consisted of silver plate—*argurides*.[21] Large drinking cups were proverbially known as "silver wells", and Socrates is said to have drunk from one at Plato's Symposium.[22] It is clear that the liturgy-paying class at Athens—those in the highest income tax bracket—were accustomed to using vessels in precious metal, not least from the fact that when the Athenian fleet left for Sicily in 415, libations were poured on every deck from gold and silver cups, and the "whole circumference of the Piraeus was filled with incense burners and silver craters".[23] Not long before this, the general Nicias, who also owed his wealth to the Laurium silver mines, had decked with gold a bridge linking the island of Rheneia with Delos.[24]

Athenian aristocrats clearly lived high on the hog. How far down the

13. Plutarch, *Sulla*, 12, 6.

14. Eddy (1977).

15. Polybius, 21, 32, 8 and 43, 19.

16. Aeschylus, *Persae*, 240.

17. Davies (1971), 260-1; cf. Nepos, *Cimon*, 1, 3: *magnas pecunias ex metallis fecerat.* Jones (1957), 87, 90, gives details of large fortunes made from mining in the fourth century B.C.

18. Lysias 19, 52.

19. Plutarch, *Alcibiades*, 4.

20. Andocides, *In Alcibiadem*, 29; Plutarch, *Alcibiades*, 13.

21. Pindar, *Olympians*, 9, 90.

22. Plato, *Symposium*, 223c; Athenaeus, 5, 192a.

23. Thucydides 4, 105; Diodorus 13, 3, 2.

24. Plutarch, *Nicias*, 3, 5.

igure E. Attic black-figure amphora, detail of neck. Ashnolean Museum, 1965.126.

Figure F. Attic black-figure amphora, detail of foot. Ashmolean Museum, 1965.126.

social scale did such a pattern of behaviour exist? We are given a valuable clue in Herodotus' account of the division of the spoils after the battle of Plataea, which included many golden bowls, goblets and other drinking vessels, and gold and silver water containers. The gods were given their share and the rest was divided among the soldiers, "each of whom received less or more according to his deserts".[25] A similar division will have occurred after Marathon, Salamis, Mycale and especially the Eurymedon, where, we are informed, the Athenians won "pavilions full of rich spoil".[26] We may safely conclude that the use of plate was common even among members of the hoplite class, at least during Athens' wealthiest period.

Most Athenian gold and silver will have remained above ground, to be used as a means of exchange, to be passed on from one generation to another, or to be seized as booty.[27] A few pieces have survived, in Thrace and Scythia, and these help us to understand the literary and epigraphic sources relating to Athenian metalwork, and also throw much light on the rôle of pottery.[28] That we are fortunate to have even these scanty remains of the art of the Athenian silversmith is clear when we consider the account of a magnificent procession held in the "Golden Age" of Hellenistic Alexandria which included amongst many other marvels "400 cart-loads of silver plate, and 20 of gold".[29] Not a scrap survives in its original form.

I shall not raise any chronological questions here. To do so would make a complex topic even more complicated. The phenomena I shall be discussing

25. Herodotus 9, 81; cf. Vickers (1986).

26. Plutarch, *Cimon*, 13, 2.

27. cf. The astute observation in Kurtz (1975), 70: "Large metal vases were probably prized in the rites of death as they were in the service of the living, and if few have been found in excavated Athenian graves it is probably because the living felt their need was greater".

28. For a useful list of extant pieces, see Reeder (1974), 212-14.

29. Athenaeus 5, 202f; cf. Rice (1983).

should, I trust, speak for themselves. The exhibition held in conjunction with this colloquium was designed in part to illustrate the close affinities between Attic pottery and silverware,[30] and they have been studied elsewhere in this volume.[31] The survival pattern of Athenian silver has induced some scholars to think that the silversmiths copied shapes devised by potters.[32] There are two empirical reasons why this is unlikely: the general rule in most societies for fashions to be created by and for wealthy élites, and the equally general rule that expensive products are frequently copied in cheaper materials. We have already seen something of Athens' wealthy élite, and their taste for precious metals. It is a straightforward matter to establish the price in antiquity of an object in precious metal: it is simply worth its weight in silver or gold as the case may be. It is the weight of an object which is usually recorded in temple inventories. The cost of working constitutes but a small percentage.[33] We also have the prices of enough ancient pots to be able to work out very approximately the relative values of identical vessels in ceramic, silver and gold. Employing as a basis for calculation the figures recorded by A.W. Johnston, it seems that if a pottery vessel, whether black-glaze or decorated, cost one unit, an equivalent silver vessel would cost between 750 and 1,000 units.[34] David Gill, however, has found new evidence to suggest that these figures may be too high, but believes nevertheless that "the overall impression of a large difference between the values of the two media remains unchanged".[35]

Most sensible scholars have regularly drawn attention to the obvious dependence of certain kinds of pots, and of certain features of pots, on metalwork. Thus, for example, Professors Arias and Shefton comment on the "blue metallic sheen" of a hydria in Munich, and state that the handle attachments copy metal forms; they also ask us to "note the vertical handle which even has two imitation rivets above".[36] Arthur Lane says of a fourth-century amphora: "With their shiny coat of uniform black or red colouring, such wares can only have been regarded as cheap substitutes for bronze".[37] And the metal which scholars usually choose for comparison *is* bronze, a metal which has, unlike the precious metals, survived in some quantity. The reason for its survival is simple: the value of bronze is comparatively low—around 1 per cent. of the value of silver.[38] We thus hear of body strippers after a fourth-century battle paying "little attention to

30. See Vickers, Impey and Allan (1986).

31. See Gill's contribution in this Volume.

32. e.g. by Hill (1947); Sparkes and Talcott (1970) 15; Sparkes (1977), 24; Oliver (1977), 29, 31.

33. Lewis (1968).

34. Johnston (1979), 33; Vickers (1984), 90, n.26.

35. See Gill's contribution in this Volume.

36. Arias, Hirmer and Shefton (1962), 310.

37. Lane (1963), 58.

38. Price (1968), 103 estimates that the ratio of the values of unworked silver and bronze was between 93:1 and 120:1.

'igure G. Attic black-glaze *lekythos*, detail of neck. Ashnolean Museum, 1938.126.

Figure H. Attic black-figure cup fragment. Ashmolean Museum, 1984.1082.

bronze or iron, so great was the abundance of silver and gold".[39] It is time that silver and gold were considered in relation to Athenian pottery, for these were the materials which apparently were used by those who could afford to do so at Athens. On general principles, it is likely that work in silver and gold set standards which craftsmen in other media, and especially potters and pot-painters, tried to emulate. There are several indications in extant literary sources that this was probably the case. Golden stars against a silver background are said to have been an appropriate way of bringing out the contrast between the night sky, "which is like unto silver" and the fiery nature of stars.[40] For Theocritus, the theft of the tarnish from a silver vessel represented the depths of petty thievery, and the pre-Socratic philosopher Thrasyalces actually states that "silver is black".[41] This is where the close relationship between silver and black glaze comes into play. The effect which the Greek potter was usually attempting to evoke was that of oxidised silver. This fact was noted by Sir Arthur Evans a hundred years ago when he discussed a class of South Italian black-glaze cups with tondo ornaments cast from silver decadrachms of Syracuse. The metallic black glaze extends over both the tondo and the rest of the cup and shows what a silver vessel could look like in antiquity.[42] If the ubiquitous black of Greek pottery can be thus

39. Plutarch, *Timoleon*, 29.

40. Athenaeus 11, 488b.

41. Theocritus 16, 16-17; D. Hughes and P.J. Parsons, *Papyri Oxyrhynchi*, 52, (1984), no.3659, 5-8.

42. Evans (1891), 319-20; in general, see Vickers (1985).

accounted for, what about the others: the orange, the white and the purple? The existence of silver vessels decorated in gold-figure is highly suggestive in the context of Attic red-figure.[43] Some exquisitely decorated Attic silver vessels have been found in graves in Thrace and Scythia. The technique involved in their manufacture has been known for some time: the design is engraved on the surface of the silver, and then figures cut out in gold leaf are applied and impressed into the incisions with a burnishing tool.[44] It is difficult to avoid the conclusion that the artisans employed to decorate red-figure pots conducted their craft with gold-figure vases very much in mind. The scenes on our extant pots have been described as "pictures of high society made for high society",[45] but this is only half true: the pictures painted on the pots still reflect aristocratic values, but were made for another market altogether.

It is something of a puzzle why there are not more frequent references to gilded silver vessels in Athenian temple inventories. We occasionally read the words *epichryson*, *perichryson*, *katachryson*, but not that often.[46] It could be that the amount of gold involved was not worth recording, and Thucydides' words about the silver vessels in the temple at Eryx making a show out of all proportion to their value may be relevant here.[47] Again, both the pottery and silver vessels which have survived are secular in character, whereas the objects mentioned in temple inventories are nearly always religious. Given the way in which surviving vessels, whether of pot or precious metal, all seem to have been designed for a specific purpose within the secular sphere, it would not be surprising if liturgical implements had their own peculiarities, and these may have included, in democratic Athens of the 430s, the absence of the kind of decoration which might too readily be associated with the values of a discredited aristocracy. We might note, too, that the pottery found in the Athenian Agora inscribed *DE*—that is *demosion*, "state property"—is undecorated.[48] At all events, we are extremely fortunate in having several actual pieces of fifth-century Attic silver to help us envisage the furnishings of private, if not necessarily public, tables.

I have argued elsewhere for white on pots having been intended to evoke ivory, a luxury material often spoken of in the same breath as gold, though by no means as expensive.[49] Another frequent colour is purple (frequently, though misleadingly, referred to as "added red"), and again I have alluded

43. Reeder (1974), 212-14; Vickers (1985), n.20; Vickers, Impey and Allan (1980), pls. 4 nd 7.

44. Blümner (1887), 311.

45. Webster (1972), 298.

46. e.g. *IG* 1^3, 331; *IG* $2^2/2$, 1425, 70.

47. Thucydides 6, 46.

48. e.g. Lang (1960), fig.5; Thompson and Wycherley (1972), 89.

49. Vickers (1983), 33; (1984); (1985), 111-12.

gure I. Attic black-glaze standlet. Ht. 7.6cm. Ashmolean Museum, 1928.320.

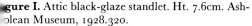

Figure J. Attic black-glaze cup. Ht. 6.3cm. Ashmolean Museum, 1915.264.

elsewhere to the likelihood that it was intended to evoke copper.[50] Copper, as everyone knows, "is a brilliant metal of a peculiar red colour which...(is) purplish when the metal contains cuprous oxide...It takes a brilliant polish, is in a high degree malleable and ductile, and in tenacity it only falls short of iron, exceeding in that quality both silver and gold".[51] Purple is added to painted pots at the points where one might well expect to find copper on silver vessels. It is ubiquitous on black-figure pots, but its use become progressively less frequent in red-figure. For the rest of this paper I propose to examine in greater detail than before the likely significance of purple in Athenian ceramics.

The purity of Attic silver was famous, as we have seen: 98 per cent. was the norm.[52] Sterling silver, by contrast, only contains 92.5 per cent. of the precious metal. The remainder is copper, added to make the metal harder and to withstand the wear and tear of everyday use. There was a brief period at the end of the seventeenth century when the fineness of British silver was raised to 95.9 per cent., but this "Britannia standard metal" was soon abandoned since objects made from it had a very short active life.[53] At 98 per cent., Attic silver will have been very soft indeed, and it seems that the silver vessels of which black-figure pots are the ceramic analogues were strengthened at the points at which they might have been expected to have worn most quickly, or at which extra strength was required, with copper. This can be

50. Vickers (1983), 32-3; (1985), 111. The term "added red" ultimately depends on the Comte de Caylus (1756), 90, where a figure on a black-figure cup is described as follows: "le soldat est peint avec une couleur rouge, assez haute pour se detacher, et faire effet sur la couleur de la terre qui occupe le champe".

51. *Encyclopaedia Britannica*, 11th edition, 7, (1910), 102, s.v. "Copper".

52. Gale, Gentner and Wagner (1980), 14-15, record Athenian silver coins of an average purity of 98.25 per cent.

53. cf. Craddock (1983), 132.

observed on the handle palmette on a jug in Oxford (**Fig. A**).[54] The purple heart, a feature which is quite common on black-figure palmettes, is probably intended to evoke a copper rivet of a kind employed to fasten the end of the handle to the body on a silver jug. Copper rivets are famous for their strength even today, whether it be on blue jeans or on battleships.[55] It so happens that a rivet on an archaic bronze vessel in the Ashmolean when analyzed recently proved to be 98 per cent. copper.[56] The rim of the Oxford jug (**Fig. B**) illustrates yet another use of copper: this time to strengthen the mouth of an analogous silver vessel. The rims of silver jugs would have received a good deal of wear; a copper sheathing would have provided some protection. Many black-figure amphora lids bear added purple around their edges and also on the very tip of the knob.[57] In metal, a relatively soft silver lid would have been strengthened against knocks and had its knob attached by means of a copper rivet.

The upper parts of handles on ceramic vessels often bear purple spots at the points at which one could plausibly postulate the use of copper rivets in metalwork. **Figure C** illustrates one example in Oxford, chosen from among several. Note too that the rim is edged with purple as well. Another frequent use to which purple is put on clay vases is on the edges of the handles of quite large amphoras (**Fig. D**). On silver vessels, these are points which would receive the most wear; a good reason for strengthening them with a harder and more durable substance.

Another point at which purple regularly occurs on pots is at the junctions of neck and body (**Fig. E**) or of body and foot (**Fig. F**). While the individual parts of pots will usually have been thrown separately,[58] there is no compelling reason for the points of junction on ceramic vessels to have been consistently painted purple. In the case of metal vessels, however, if a strong joint were called for, copper might well have been used. The presence of purple on pots was doubtless intended to evoke the appearance of copper on a metal vase. The same feeling probably underlies the presence of purple both at the rim and on the rather prominent handle junction on a black-figure oil-jar (**Fig. G**).

54. The detail (though not its purpose) was first noted by Clark (1981) 45.

55. cf. the *Hull Advertiser*, 9 July 1796, where one may read: "She is copper-fastened and copper-bottomed, and a remarkable fine ship".

56. Craddock (1977), 118. It is interesting, too, to note that the metal used in antiquity to repair Greek pots was frequently an alloy with a very high copper content: e.g. Ashmolean G.244: Cu 90 per cent., Zn 5 per cent., Pb/Sn 5 per cent.; 1913.2 Rivet: Cu 98.58 per cent., Pb 0.66 per cent., Ag 0.32 per cent., Sb 0.44 per cent., Upper surface: Cu 91.11 per cent., Pb 1.49 per cent., Ag 0.09 per cent., Sn 7.19 per cent., Sb 0.12 per cent.. Many thanks are due to Miss Fiona Macalister for conducting X-ray fluorescent analyses.

57. There are drawers full of such lids in the Campana Reserves in the Louvre. I am most grateful to M. Alain Pasquier for granting me access.

58. Noble (1965), 9-30.

gure K. Attic black-figure amphora. Ht. .5cm. Ashmolean Museum, 1965.126.

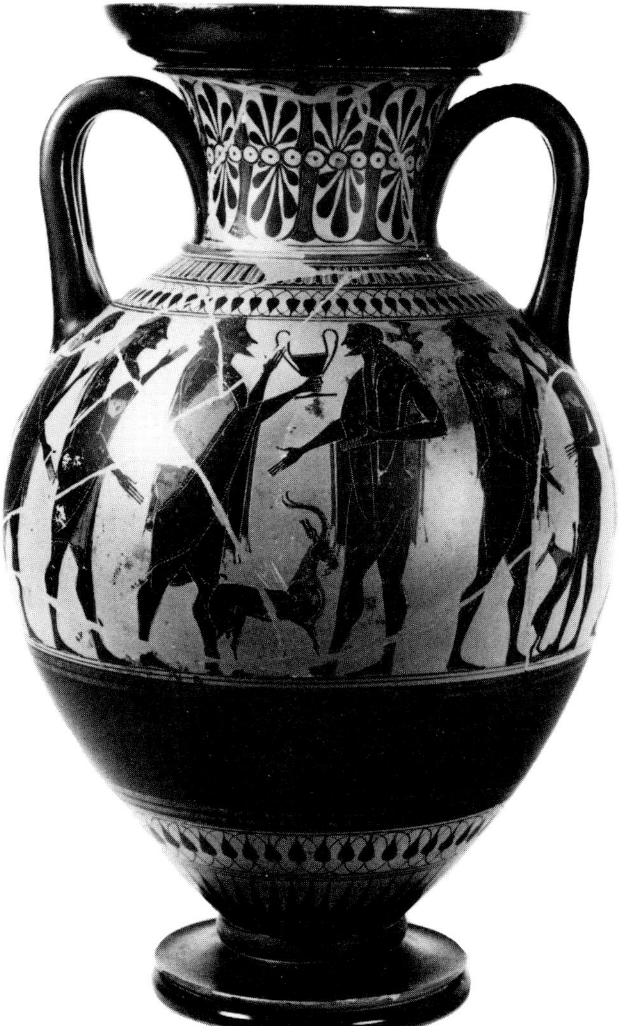

ure L. Attic silver cup from Semibratny. 6cm. Hermitage Museum, Leningrad.

The phenomenon is, however, pretty well universal on black-figure pots: purple frequently appears at the points where we might expect a need to have been felt for strengthening on an analogous metal vessel. On cups and stands of the relevant period, we regularly find purple bands at the point where the foot is joined to the body (**Figs. I and J**). A metalworking explanation probably underlies the presence of the purple band on a fragmentary foot, if that is the word, of a cup recently presented to the Ashmolean (**Fig. H**).[59]

A related feature calls for comment, namely the universal presence of encircling purple bands on black-figure pots, often at the points where there is a major change in the overall colour scheme. In metalwork, these would correspond to the points where one part of a vessel was joined to another; in some cases different metals (**Fig. K**), in others the same (**Fig. F**). It would seem that the points of junction on metal vessels were somehow strengthened with copper; indeed, it may well be that the tensile strength of copper wire was employed to hold the different pieces together at the start of the relevant stage of the manufacturing process. When the vessel was heated in the flame, the higher melting point of copper (1083 degrees C) would mean that the copper would retain its form when it embedded itself in the softer silver, the melting point of which is 960 degrees C.[60] This is probably the kind of feature to which the encircling purple bands on pots allude.

Although the practice of using purple in what we might describe as structural contexts was carried over into red-figure, it did not survive long there. It occurs on some of the earliest red-figure, but its use on vessels made in this technique tends to be confined to lettering and subsidiary features such as streaks of blood, black eyes or cocks' combs. Red-figure, as we have already seen, was probably made under the influence of silver vessels decorated with gold figures. Junctions on gold-figure vessels are strengthened with silver, as on the cup from Semibratny in the Hermitage (**Fig. L**). We might suppose that even the restrained use of copper on vessels which were supposedly made of precious metal was tantamount to advertising the fact that their value was not equal to their weight, and we must not overlook the fact that the ancients, like their modern counterparts in the Worshipful Company of Goldsmiths, set great store by such considerations.

Finally, a glance at the decorative, rather than structural, use of purple. Two examples will suffice to illuminate the lost world of decorative metalwork

59. Accession number 1984.1082; presented by Dr Herbert Hoffmann in memory of the late Sir John Beazley.

60. For the high tensile strength of copper, see Untracht (1968), 464; for melting points Untracht (1968), 463. Professor George Sines, of the Department of Materials Science and Engineering, UCLA, has suggested to me that the purple effect at points of junction may be attributable to the presence of copper oxides in the silver solder used to join different parts of silver vessels. It is an effect which modern silversmiths counter by polishing or by the use of an acid.

Figure M. Attic plastic head-vase. Ht. 14.5cm. Ashmolean Museum, 1920.106.

Figure N. Attic black-figure *oinochoe*, detail of figure decoration. Ashmolean Museum, 1965.122.

to which our black-figure pots are witnesses. A moulded jug in the Ashmolean in the form of a woman's head recalls a vessel of silver with gold and ivory decoration for the face, volutes, eyes and hair. The lips are rendered in purple (**Fig. M**), a practice which recalls the use of copper for lips and nipples on such works of sculpture as the Riace bronzes.[61] This in turn recalls the widespread practice of rendering nipples on black-figure pots in purple (**Fig. N**). Moreover, figures in black-figure frequently have purple bands around their heads (**Fig.N**). This feature can also be matched in sculpture, this time in the copper band in a roughly contemporary head of a youth from the Athenian Acropolis.[62] If there is a connection, then there is a clear implication that the figure decoration on black-figure pots also depends on metal prototypes.[63]

61. cf. Houser (1982), 8: "...lips and nipples are made of copper to give red colour to those areas..."; Bol (1985), 148-54.

62. Bol (1985), 152, fig.110.

63. For surviving examples of archaic Greek silver figures on bronze, see the cheek-pieces of the helmets from Olympia, Kunze (1958), fig.107, pls.57-2; and Trebenischte, Kunze (1958), fig.108.

Bibliography

Arias, Hirmer & Shefton (1962)	Arias, P., Hirmer, M. and Shefton, B.B., *A History of Greek Vase Painting*, London, 1962.
Blümner (1887)	Blümner, H., *Technologie und Terminologie der Gewerbe und Künste bei Griechen und Römern*, 4, Leipzig, 1887.
Bol (1985)	Bol, P.C., *Antike Bronzetechnik, Kunst und Handwerk Antiker Erzbilder*, Munich, 1985.
Caylus (1766)	Comte de Caylus, *Recueil d'Antiquités Egyptiennes, Etrusques, Grecques, Romaines et Gauloises*, 2, Paris, 1756.
Childe (1956)	Childe, V.G., *Piecing Together the Past; the Interpretation of Archaeological Data*, London, 1956.
Citroen, van Erpers Royaards, & Verbeek (1984)	Citroen, K.A., van Erpers Royaards, F., and Verbeek, J., *Meesterwerken in Zilver: Amsterdams Zilver 1520-1820*, Museum Willet-Holthuysen, Amsterdam, 1984.
Clark (1980)	Clark, A.J., "The Earliest Known Chous by the Amasis Painter", *Metropolitan Museum Journal*, 15, 1980, pp.35-52.
Davies (1971)	Davies, J.K., *Athenian Propertied Families 600-300 B.C.*, Oxford, 1971.
Craddock (1977)	Craddock, P.T., "The Composition of the Copper Alloys Used by the Greek, Etruscan and Roman Civilizations 2. The Archaic, Classical and Hellenistic Greeks", *Journal of Archaeological Science*, 4, 1977, pp.103-24.
Craddock (1983)	Craddock, P.T., "A Roman Silver Mirror 'Discovered' in the British Museum: a Note on its Composition", *Antiquaries Journal*, 63, 1983, pp.131-2 and p.134.
Crawford (1953)	Crawford, O.G.S., *Archaeology in the Field*, London, 1953.
Eddy (1977)	Eddy, S., "The Gold in the Athena Parthenos", *American Journal of Archaeology*, 81, 1977, pp.107-11.
Gale, Gentner & Wagner (1980)	Gale, N.H., Gentner, W. and Wagner, G.A., "Mineralogical and Geographical Silver Sources of Archaic Greek Coinage", *Metallurgy in Numismatics*, 1, 1980, pp.3-49.
Hill (1947)	Hill, D.K., "The Technique of Greek Metal Vases and its Bearing on Vase Forms in Metal and Pottery", *American Journal of Archaeology*, 51, 1947, pp.248-56.
Houser (1982)	Houser, C., "The Riace Marina Bronze Statues, Classical or Classicizing", *Source, Notes in the History of Art*, 1/3, 1982, pp.5-11.
de Iongh (1982)	de Iongh, M.L., "Twee Gouden Bokalen Door Louis en Philippe Metayer", *Bulletin van het Rijksmuseum*, 30/3, 1982, pp.115-31.
Johnston (1979)	Johnston, A.W., *Trademarks on Greek Vases*, Warminster, 1979.
Jones (1957)	Jones, A.H.M., *Athenian Democracy*, Oxford, 1957.
Kirchner (1931)	Kirchner, J., ed., *Inscriptiones Graecae*, 2, 2nd edn., part 1, Berlin, 1931.
Kunze (1958)	Kunze, E., *6. Bericht über die Ausgrabungen in Olympius*, Berlin, 1958.
Lane (1963)	Lane, A., *Greek Pottery*, London, 1963.
Lang (1960)	Lang, M., *The Athenian Citizen*, Princeton, 1960.

Lewis (1968)	Lewis, D.M., "New Evidence for the Gold-Silver Ratio", in C.M. Kraay and G.K. Jenkins eds., *Essays in Greek Coinage presented to Stanley Robinson*, Oxford, 1968, pp.105-10.
Lewis (1981)	Lewis, D.M., ed., *Inscriptiones Graecae* 1, 3rd edn., Berlin, 1981.
Noble (1965)	Noble, J.V., *The Technique of Attic Painted Pottery*, New York, 1965.
Oliver (1977)	Oliver, A. Jr., *Silver for the Gods: 800 Years of Greek and Roman Silver*, Toledo, Ohio, 1977.
Price (1968)	Price, M.J., "Early Greek Bronze Coinage", in C.M. Kraay and G.K. Jenkins eds. *Essays in Greek Coinage presented to Stanley Robinson*, Oxford, 1968, pp.90-104.
Reeder (1974)	Reeder, E.D., *Clay Impressions from Attic Metalwork*, Diss. Princeton, 1974.
Reitlinger (1963)	Reitlinger, G., *The Economics of Taste*, 2, London, 1963.
Rice (1983)	Rice, E.E., *The Grand Procession of Ptolemy Philadelpheus*, Oxford, 1983.
Seemann & Ward (1984)	Seemann, H. and Ward, F., "Silber, Metall für alle Tage", *Zeit Magazin*, 2 November 1984, pp.72-5.
Sparkes & Talcott (1970)	Sparkes, B.A. and Talcott, L., *Agora*, 12, *Black and Plain Pottery of the 6th, 5th and 4th Centuries B.C.*, Princeton, 1970.
Sparkes (1977)	Sparkes, B.A., "Quintain and the Talcott class", *Antike Kunst*, 20, 1977, pp.8-25.
Thompson & Wycherley (1972)	Thompson, H.A. and Wycherley, R.E., *Agora*, 14, *The Agora of Athens, the History, Shape and Use of an Ancient City Center*, Princeton, 1972.
Untracht (1968)	Untracht, O., *Metal Techniques for Craftsmen*, New York, 1968.
Vickers (1983)	Vickers, M., "Les Vases Peints: Image ou Mirage?" in F. Lissarague and F. Thelamon, *Image et Céramique Grecque. Actes du Colloque de Rouen 25-26 novembre 1982*, Rouen, 1983, pp.29-44.
Vickers (1984)	Vickers, M., "The Influence of Exotic Materials on Attic White-Ground Pottery", *Ancient Greek and Related Pottery: Proceedings of the International Vase Symposium Amsterdam 1984*, (Allard Pierson Series, 5), pp.88-97.
Vickers (1985)	Vickers, M., "Artful Crafts: the Influence of Metalwork on Athenian Painted Pottery", *Journal of Hellenic Studies*, 105, 1985, pp.108-28.
Vickers (1986)	Vickers, M., "Athenian Symposia after the Persian Wars", in O. Murray ed., *Sympotica*, Oxford, 1986.
Vickers, Impey & Allan (1986)	Vickers, M., Impey, O., and Allan, J., *From Silver to Ceramic*, Oxford, 1986.
Webster (1972)	Webster, T.B.L., *Potter and Patron in Classical Athens*, London, 1972.

Pottery and Precious Metals in the Roman World

MICHAEL FULFORD

This paper seeks to discover how highly the best pottery of the Roman world was regarded by Roman society, particularly in comparison with tableware in other materials. We can look for insights to the raw materials out of which the vessels were fashioned, to commentary on literary sources, to the artefacts themselves and the contexts in which they were found. For the most part vessels for use at table were made of metal (gold, silver. bronze, pewter), glass, pottery or wood. The intrinsic value of these materials varied enormously, with items of precious metal retaining a basic bullion value. Whereas even a damaged bronze or pewter vessel had scrap value, sherds of broken pottery and glass were of minimal use or value. Partly for this reason, perhaps, some people took great pains to repair broken vessels; pottery sherds with traces of lead rivets or with holes drilled to receive them are often found. The value attached to the craftsmanship displayed in pottery or glass could, of course, surpass the intrinsic scrap value of a bronze or pewter vessel.

If the material was one fundamental factor governing value, three others should not be overlooked. The Roman Empire at its most extensive contained many different societies, not all of whom shared the same taste in tableware; and it existed over many hundreds of years during which fashions and values might change. What was cherished and sought after by one social class may have been despised by another. The poor who were in the majority in the Roman world, could not aspire to the more expensive forms of tableware. Pottery vessels were the best that most people could hope for.

Precious metal, particularly silver, was abundant in Rome from the beginning of the second century B.C., because of the defeat of the Carthaginians in the second Punic war, and Roman expansion into Spain.[1] As Donald Strong wrote:

" The importance of silver plate in the domestic, political and economic life of the Roman Empire cannot be overestimated. The evidence of literary and legal texts gives proof of the vast quantity of silver in private hands, the changes in fashion, the enthusiasm of collectors, the ostentation of owners. A middle-class family of the Empire would probably have a complete set of table silver for dining, besides a quantity of show-plate acquired as heirlooms,

1. Strong (1966), 123-4 with references.

wedding presents, and so on. There was hardly any family that did not possess some item of table silver and to have been brought up in a family that had none was a sign of the most abject poverty.[2] " Although, simply because of its scrap value, relatively little Roman silver survives today, (except for hoards deposited in antiquity), the number of finds of silver from Pompeii, a modest Campanian town, preserved by the eruption of A.D. 79, suggests that, for the upper and upper-middle classes at least, Strong is right.[3] Two hoards of silver were also buried by the eruption: a collection of 109 pieces was recovered from the villa at Boscoreale and one of 118 from the Casa del Menandro in Pompeii.[4] The villa and the town house can scarcely be regarded as luxury residences. Pompeii has also yielded many bronze vessels.[5] Yet it would be unwise to suppose that the situation in first-century Italy was the same as that in, say, Gallia Belgica or Africa Proconsularis. Unfortunately, because of the bias of both our material and literary sources (as we shall see) towards first-century Italy, it is impossible to evaluate contemporary provincial values. Yet, patchy as our sources are, the evidence of fourth-century hoards from the British Isles, Kaiseraugst and elsewhere implies strongly that the land-owning aristocracy and the Church at the periphery of the Empire possessed a wealth of silver.[6] Table silver, it seems was widely available throughout the Empire, for those who could afford it, by the fourth century, if not considerably earlier.

What of pottery tableware? Unlike silver and bronze, pottery was not hoarded; where large collections have been found in excavations it has been deduced from their general context that they were the stock of shops or stalls.[7] Invariably they are associated with the destruction that overtook them; separate concealment, such as we find for hoards of precious metal, is not recorded. Although Pliny devotes one whole book of his *Natural History* to gold and silver[8] and another to metals such as copper, bronze, lead,[9] pottery (excluding bricks) is discussed in one short passage in the following chapter.[10] After remarking that many choose to be buried in pottery containers, Pliny observes that "maior pars hominum terrenis utitur vasis". Of tableware, samian pottery is praised, and Pliny mentions the pottery of Arretium as an example. The term *samian* occurs earlier, in the writings of Plautus, apparently because it was believed that good quality pottery originated in the island of Samos.[11] Exactly what kind of pottery—and of what data—is meant is unclear, but the term is best understood from Plautus onwards as the equivalent of our word "china". In one passage of the *Stichus*, written about

2. Strong (1966), 124.
3. Strong (1966), 125; Appendix 2.
4. Villefosse (1899); Maiuri (1933).
5. Carandini (1977), 157-68.
6. Kent and Painter (1977).
7. e.g. at Colchester, Hull (1958); at Pompeii, Atkinson (1914); at Aquinum, Juhász (1936).
8. *Natural History*, xxxiii.
9. *Natural History*, xxxiv.
10. *Natural History*, xxxv, 46.
11. *Menaechmi*, 178.

200 B.C., Plautus would have the rich drink "scaphio et cantharis batiocis", and slaves from "nostro samiolo poterio", "our little samian jug".[12] Since samian in Pliny's time was equated with Arretine, the implication of Plautus' remark is that fine pottery (which in his time would have been black-glazed ware) was not for the rich. Although Pliny mentions a number of places in Italy, as well as in Spain and Asia, which produced fine pottery cups, it is really only the pottery of Arretium and Pergamon that we can securely identify today in the archaeological record.[13] Arretine ware is characterized by its fine red fabric and red glossy slip and a repertoire of forms which includes both plain and decorated shapes. The latter were produced from pottery moulds which had been decorated with the impressions of individual punches to make a coherent narrative; when the vessel was turned out of its mould, the decoration stood out in relief. Decorative themes included scenes of dancing, feasting, love-making, vine-harvesting, in narrative sequences. Pergamene vessels were generally plain. Arretine appeared about 30 B.C. and was at its best in the Augustan and Augustan-Tiberian period; by the middle of the first century the technical quality had seriously declined and, although still produced when Pliny was writing, in the third quarter of the first century A.D., it was clearly inferior to *sigillata*,[14] made in and around la Graufesenque in the south of Gaul from the reign of Tiberius.[15] As the crate of brand new vessels found at Pompeii so vividly demonstrates, south Gaulish ware was making serious inroads into the Italian market in the second half of the first century.[16] There is no hint of this in Pliny. Obviously anachronistic references to Arretine can be found in Martial, writing towards the end of the first and at the beginning of the second centuries A.D. By this time the undistinguished work of both Italian and Gaulish producers of red-slipped ware was giving way to *sigillata* from North Africa.[17] Given that Arretium was only one of several sources of *sigillata* in Italy in the first century A.D., it is possible that by Martial's time red wares, *sigillata*, generally had become synonymous with Arretine. In one poem he refers to Arretine degrading glass, "sic Arretinae violant crystallina testae",[18] and a second reference implies that this pottery was not thought of very highly: "Arretina nimis ne spernas vasa monemus: lautus erat Tuscis Porsena fictilibus".[19] After the passage on

12. *Stichus*, 692-5.

13. Brief introductions to these wares with useful bibliographies may be found in Johns (1971) and King (1983), 183-87.

14. A general term used for plain and decorated red-slipped wares derived from Arretine.

15. Johns (1971), 21-4.

16. Atkinson (1914).

17. Hayes (1972 and 1980).

18. *Epigrams*, i, 53, 6. It is also worth noting that the importance attached to the "Arretine" name encouraged some Italian potters making *sigillata* in the first century to incorporate the name in the stamp which marked their vessels and even, in a few cases, to employ the stamp ARRET(inum) VER(um) - true Arretine! (Oxé and Comfort (1968), no.132).

19. *Epigrams*, xiv, 98.

tableware, Pliny's section on pottery focuses on the exceptional. Mention is made of a special dish for the Emperor Vitellius costing one million sesterces and for which a special furnace had to be made, about which Pliny remarks: "quoniam eo pervenit luxuria, ut etiam fictilia pluris constent quam murrina".[20] One might reasonably deduce from this that pottery was usually comparatively cheap.

Limited though the literary sources are, they suggest that while Arretine pottery did make a considerable impact, it could not be a serious rival to glass or metal tableware. Its impact on pottery-making was considerable, for the tradition of red-slipped tableware spread throughout the Empire, surviving the collapse of the western Roman Empire, to disappear eventually in the seventh century.[21] Although we must be careful about how much Isidore of Seville (writing in the early seventh century) borrowed from Pliny, he does say that "postea inventum et rubricam addere et ex rubra creta fingere" and, later, "Arretina vasa ex Arretio municipio Italiae dicuntur, ubi fiunt; sunt enim rubra".[22] Clearly the colour of the pottery was important, as its long history suggests, but Isidore, like Pliny, was not aware of the contemporary sources of this pottery, which included North Africa (Tunisian), Phocaean (Asia Minor), Cypriot and Egyptian production centres.[23] The impact of Arretine on the manufacture of pottery tableware may be connected with the failure of other kinds of decorative techniques to gain popularity; glazed wares, for example, though produced in many workshops in east and west, never gained more than a small section of the market.[24]

It is clear that the Arretine shapes and decorative themes were derived from Hellenistic and late Republican silver vessels, including those richly ornamented with *repoussé* reliefs.[25] Convincing proof of the direction in which ideas travelled is difficult to obtain because such metalwork is rarely found in an independently dated archaeological context. The fact that the decoration of an Arretine vessel matches closely but not precisely that of a silver cup from Hoby in Denmark illustrates this difficulty.[26] In more general terms, though, the shapes and decorative themes of Arretine can be paralleled, closely but not exactly, on both Hellenistic and the little Republican silver that survives.[27] In a wider sense Arretine fully belongs to the tradition of late Republican art and craftsmanship. Its achievement was the widespread diffusion of relief decoration on pottery, along with the shapes that were associated with

20. *Natural History*, xxxv, 46, 163.

21. Hayes (1972).

22. *Etymologiae*, xx, 4.3-6.

23. Hayes (1972).

24. King (1983).

25. Strong (1966), 123-59; Henig (1983a), 140-43.

26. Strong (1966), 139; for later Roman pottery, Hayes (1972), 283-87.

27. As Roth-Rubi (1984) has shown in her comparison of the forms of silver vessels represented in the Hildesheim hoard with those of early Roman *sigillata*.

metalwork, in a red fabric and finish.[28] It is noticeable that by the later first century A.D. virtually all the more difficult and angular shapes had given way to those more suited to the ceramic medium.[29]

Since the literary sources provide only limited help, we can turn to archaeological evidence for another perspective. In the case of Arretine, which probably represents the high point of the Roman tableware tradition, we find many examples from archaeological excavations in Italy and the Mediterranean littoral. The number of recorded examples of potters' stamps, mostly from plain vessels, runs into thousands.[30] Decorated wares, particularly early examples, however, are comparatively rare, presumably because not so many were made.[31] This might mean that it was more expensive than the plain wares, and thus sought after by the well-off as a minor luxury. Pliny may have noticed Arretine for this reason. Although never as numerous as the plain ware, decorated Arretine does have a wide provincial distribution.[32] Yet wide distribution and mass production should not be seized on as clear evidence of the importance attached to Arretine. Recent careful excavation of Roman wrecks has shown that pottery for domestic consumption never formed a major element of ships' cargoes. These were largely given over to the transport of perishable substances, often carried in the ubiquitous amphora, and raw materials such as metal ingots.[33] The widespread distribution of Arretine and other types of pottery can be seem in relation to the general volume of traffic moving around and beyond the Mediterranean. The value of such pottery fits in with its regular shipment as a part of other cargoes, but not as a cargo in its own right. In fact the widespread distribution of some tablewares can be correlated with that of contemporary amphoras originating from the same province or district. Thus, for example, Italian black-glazed tableware (Campana A) is found alongside Italian amphoras of Dressel 1 type; Arretine alongside wine amphoras of Dressel 2-4 types; and the North African red-slipped wares alongside the olive-oil amphoras of Tunisia.[34] In contrast, a province such as Greece, only a modest producer of foodstuffs and other commodities in the Roman period, does not seem to have generated sufficient volume of exports to carry such distinctive manufactured goods as pottery. That we should not attach too much importance to the widespread distribution of tableware is the lesson of the wide distribution of certain cooking wares. African (Tunisian) casseroles and lids, and Pantellerian

28. Arretine itself can be seen as a development of the Hellenistic tradition of relief-decorated "Megarian" bowls, King (1983), 182-83.

29. Oswald and Pryce (1920).

30. Oxé and Comfort (1968).

31. Compare, for example, collections from Luni in Italy, Frova (1977); Corinth in Greece, Hayes (1973); Berenice in Libya, Kenrick (1985); Conimbriga in Portugal, Alarcão and Etienne (1975).

32. As, for example, from Rhineland military sites, Oxé (1933).

33. Pucci (1983).

34. Blake (1978), 438-39.

hand-made cooking wares, for example, are found widely in the western Mediterranean.[35] Now that we understand better how pottery travelled in the Roman world, we can use distributional studies of different kinds of pottery as a way of gaining insight into the changing directions and volumes of trade as a whole; in this context pottery represents more precious goods.

If wealth was more concentrated among the land-owning classes of Italy and the Mediterranean regions than, say, in the frontier provinces, it would be reasonable to expect a higher value to be attached to pottery tableware imported from the centre of the Empire. As an example we may consider pre-Roman Britain. We may note the occurrence of Republican wine amphoras of Dressel 1 type from settlements and rich burials in southern England, yet there are no published examples of the contemporary black-glazed pottery.[36] The earliest imported Mediterranean tableware is Arretine from the closing decade of the first century B.C., and it is found predominantly in rubbish deposits of the major settlements or oppida of southern England.[37] Interestingly, although other types of pottery, both imported and local, are found in the rich burials of the Welwyn type, Arretine is conspicuous by its absence.[38] Bronze and silver vessels were available, and (along with the wine amphoras) they take pride of place in these burials. As Wheeler observed in his general survey of Roman trade beyond the frontiers, the same is true in Free Germany, where there is an extreme scarcity of Arretine and Italian *sigillata* in comparison with bronze vessels, which are found frequently as grave goods in the early Empire.[39] In southern India, notably at Arikamedu where Arretine was imported, Wheeler noted that, as in Britain, amphorae preceded the arrival of the tableware.[40] Numerically more important than either amphorae or Arretine are the finds of first century A.D. gold and silver coin.[41] Thus, even in regions where one might have imagined its very scarcity would have given it greater value, tableware pottery does not appear to have been highly regarded.

Although our sources are biased in favour of the higher classes of Roman, provincial and barbarian society, the evidence consistently indicates that even the best pottery ranked well below tableware of precious metal, bronze and glass. The memory of the finely produced early Arretine of Augustus and Tiberius lingered in places until the end of the first century A.D. Nevertheless, for the silent majority—the poor—the acquisition of fine pottery may have been the height of ambition. Although there may have been some sharing of a common pool of ideas, it is generally agreed that metalwork and glass inspired

35. Hayes (1972), 206-9 and 455; Fulford and Peacock (1984), 8-10.

36. Peacock (1971).

37. As at Camulodunum, Hawkes and Hull (1947); Skeleton Green, Partridge (1981).

38. Stead (1967); Whimster (1981).

39. Wheeler (1954), 63-94.

40. Wheeler (1954), 148.

41. Wheeler (1954), 134-45.

the form and decoration of tableware pottery. This one would expect if the most sought-after items were in precious metal and glass and can scarcely be regarded as the "luxusgeschirr" of the Roman world.[42] Perhaps the conservatism of Roman pottery, reflected in the domination of the red-slipped ware tradition over seven centuries is, largely due to dependence on fashions set by metal and glass-ware.

42. Garbush (1982).

Bibliography

Alarcão & Etienne (1975)	Alarcão, J. and Etienne, R., eds. *Fouilles de Conimbriga IV, Les Sigillées*, Paris, 1975.
Atkinson (1914)	Atkinson, D., "A Hoard of Samian Ware from Pompeii", *Journal of Roman Studies*, 4, 1914, pp.27-64.
Blake (1978)	Blake, H., "Medieval Pottery: Technical Innovation or Economic Change?" in H. McK. Blake, T.W. Potter and D.B. Whitehouse, eds., *Papers in Italian Archaeology I: The Lancaster Seminar*, British Archaeological Reports, Supplementary Series, 41, Oxford, 1978, pp.435-72.
Carandini (1977),	Carandini, A., ed., *L'Instrumentum Domesticum di Ercolano e Pompei*, Rome, 1977.
Frova (1977)	Frova, A., *Scavi di Luni: Relazione Preliminare delle Campagne di Scavo 1972-1973-1974*, Rome, 1977.
Fulford & Peacock (1984)	Fulford, M.G., and Peacock, D.P.S., *Excavations at Carthage: The British Mission*, 1, (2), Sheffield, 1984.
Garbush (1982)	Garbush, J., *Terra sigillata: ein Weltreich im Spiegel seiner Luxusgeschirrs*, Munich, 1982.
Hawkes & Hull (1947)	Hawkes, C.F.C., and Hull, M.R., *Camulodunum*, Report of Research Committee of the Society of Antiquities, London, 1947.
Hayes (1972)	Hayes, J.W., *Late Roman Pottery*, London, 1972.
Hayes (1973)	Hayes, J.W., "Roman Pottery from the South Stoa at Corinth", *Hesperia*, 42, 1973, pp.416-70.
Hayes (1980)	Hayes, J.W., *Supplement to Late Roman Pottery*, London 1980.
Henig (1983a)	Henig, M., "The Luxury Arts: Decorative Metalwork, Engraved Gems and Jewellery" in Henig, 1983b, pp.139-65.
Henig (1983b)	Henig, M., ed., *A Handbook of Roman Art*, Oxford, 1983.
Hull (1958)	Hull, M.R., *Roman Colchester*, Report of Research Committee of the Society of Antiquities, London, 1958.
Johns (1971)	Johns, C., *Arretine and Samian Pottery*, London, 1971.
Juhász (1936)	Juhász, G., "A Lezouxi Terrasigillata Gyárak Aquincumi, Levakata", *Archaeologiai Értesitö*, 49, 1936, pp.33-48.
Kenrick (1985)	Kenrick, P.M., *Excavations at Sidi Khrebish, Benghazi (Berenice), 3, (1), The Fine Pottery*, Tripoli, 1985.

Kent & Painter (1977)	Kent, J.P.C., and Painter, K.S., eds., *Wealth of the Roman World*, London 1977.
King (1983)	King A., "Pottery" in Henig (1983b), pp.179-90.
Maiuri (1933)	Maiuri, A., *La Casa del Menandro e il suo Tesoro di Argenteria*, Rome, 1933.
Oswald & Pryce (1920)	Oswald, F., and Pryce, T.D., *An Introduction to the Study of Terra Sigillata*, London, 1920.
Oxé (1933)	Oxé, A., *Arretinischer Reliefgefässe vom Rhein*, Frankfurt, 1933.
Oxé and Comfort (1968)	Oxé, A., comp. and Comfort, H., ed., *Corpus Vasorum Arretinorum*, Bonn, 1968.
Partridge (1981)	Partridge C., *Skeleton Green*, London 1981.
Peacock (1971)	Peacock, D.P.S., "Roman Amphorae in Pre-Roman Britain" in D. Hill and M. Jesson, eds., *The Iron Age and Its Hill-Forts*, Southampton, 1971, pp.161-88.
Pucci (1983)	Pucci, G., "Pottery and trade in the Roman World", in P. Garnsey, K. Hopkins and C.R. Whittaker, eds., *Trade in the Ancient Economy*, London, 1983, pp.105-17.
Roth-Rubi (1984)	Roth-Rubi, K., "Der Hildesheimer Silberschatz und Terra Sigillata—eine Gegenüberstellung", *Archäologisches Korrespondenzblatt*, 14, 1984, pp.175-93.
Stead (1967)	Stead, I., "A La Tène III Burial at Welwyn Garden City", *Archaeologia*, 101, 1967, pp.1-62.
Strong (1966)	Strong, D.E., *Greek and Roman Gold and Silver Plate*, London, 1966.
Villefosse (1899)	Villefosse, H. de, "Le Trésor de Boscoreale", *Monuments Piot*, v, 1899-1902, pp.79-83.
Wheeler (1954)	Wheeler, M., *Rome Beyond the Imperial Frontiers*, London, 1954.
Whimster (1981)	Whimster, R., *Burial Practices in Iron Age Britain*, B.A.R., Oxford, 1981.

Precious Metal—Its Influence on Tang Earthenware

W. WATSON

While lead-glazed earthenware made in metropolitan China can be related at almost every point to the imitation of metal forms, it is only in rare cases that gold or silver can be verified as the immediate prototypes. On the whole the manufacture of lead-glazed ware aimed at a luxury market, exploiting the potters' skills in structural rather than wheel-thrown or other ceramic forms. Characteristic features are on the one hand the exclusion of lead-glazed pottery from the range of bowls and other utilitarian pieces (from the 8th century A.D. it ceases to be used for the tea-ware which was rapidly expanding and largely determining the course of ceramic development, and on the other the correspondence of its periods of high production with phases of patrician patronage. Rare though finds of Tang and earlier gold and silver have been in China, these metals assume in Chinese decorative arts forms which are not found in other branches of craft. Gold seems not to have been plentiful in north China before the Han unification, and in coinage appears only in the Chu state, whose proximity to the Yunnan sources of the metal, aided by a political threat if not an occupation, presumably ensured a supply that was denied to other states.[1]

The employment of massive gold and silver is confined to buckles, bosses and rings.[2] While both metals appear in the decoration inlaid in bronze vessels and accoutrement during the period of the Warring States (mainly in the 4th Century B.C.), the gold in nearly every case proves to be no more than the thinnest layer covering a thin sheeting of bronze or copper. Similar designs were painted on lacquer and carved in jade, but it is arguable that the use of metal foil had its peculiar influence on the ductus of pattern with the metallic inlay setting the fashion.[3] The spirals of thin strips (not wire), the angular breaks in curving figures and the geometric precision over all are eloquent of the metal worker, and they mark a break with the more plastic figures of the earlier iconic tradition. Meanwhile, if gold was scarce, silver was no doubt in such demand as specie, as it was at all later times, that its chance of survival in

1. *Historic Relics* (1972), 70.

2. Jenyns & Watson (1963-65), pls.7, 8; Eskenazi (1985), 28, no.7.

3. Watson (1973), nos.127, 129-131.

art was minimal.[4] Before the opening of the Han period gold-dipping of bronze or copper gave way to fire-gilding through amalgam; and in the later Han specific gold-working techniques make their appearance: the parcel-gilding of bronze vessels (a gold wash coinciding approximately with an engraved design, or a design made in reserve by cutting away parts of a gold "slip",[5] and granulation, the adoption of which in China seems to mark a remote contact with the gold industry of the Bosporan kingdom on the Black Sea.[6]

What connection can be found between these crafts and the decoration of pottery? The imitation in unfired pigments of the designs inlaid on bronze enjoyed a brief fashion in Hunan in the early 4th century B.C., but had no notable sequel.[7] Just before the opening of the Han period there is evidence of designs chased on vessels cast wholly of silver, the motifs corresponding closely to what is see on the contemporary lacquerwork;[8] and when in the western Han period (2nd and 1st centuries B.C.) in south China close-knit geometric pattern appears on bronze vessels (where it resembles engraved line) there is a presumption that this ornament derives originally from silver-working, for it seems to be more appropriate to the chasing and beating of that metal. Pottery then imitated this style of ornament, roughly on low-fired ware and with greater exactitude on a class of high-fired, brown-glazed vessels peculiar to Hunan and Guangdong in the early and middle Han period.[9] It thus appears that the effect claimed for the precious metals on the potter's art was mediated by bronze. After the Han period we observe a decline in bronze vessels finely cast and decorated, and the argument for this mediated influence can no longer be sustained. Three centuries later a more direct ceramic imitation of gold and silver in north China, now linked to an extraordinary resumption of lead-glazing.[10]

A rather unaccountable aspect of the employment of lead flux in China is its recurrent connection, guessed at or demonstrable, with the ceramic practice of central and western Asia. It is still uncertain exactly when this technique was adopted in China, though it may go back to the century or two before Han, when some rare vessels made to imitate ritual bronzes were covered with what appears to be the soft glaze.[11] An old theory that the use of lead flux was introduced to the Far East from Parthian Persia in the course of

4. It is possible that silver was exported in quantity in payment for goods imported from the west from Han times onwards. The return in silk and iron alone may not have balanced the trade.

5. Watson (1973), nos.150, 151, 167, 169; Watson (1979), fig.616.

6. Gyllensvärd (1953), nos.15, 16; *I.A.P.* (1981), pl.114, no.9.

7. *Kaogu*, 1, (1959), 46.

8. Loehr (1965), 73.

9. For the comparison of pottery and bronze: Tokyo (1973), 91-92; *I.A.P.*, 1, (1962), 131, 229, 437; *Kaogu*, 2, (1958), 39.

10. Watson (1984), 26-28, 50-56 and *passim*.

11. *S.T.Z. 10*, pl.56.

igure 1. White stoneware bowl decorated with iitations of precious stones and metal florets. Excavated at Hansenjai, Shaanxi, from a tomb dated to D.667. Collections of the People's Republic of hina.

Figure 2. Vase with relief medallions, covered with green lead-glaze. Late 6th century. Ht. 59.8cm. Freer Gallery of Art, Smithsonian Institution, Washington, D.C., (Acc. no.30.32.) (Photo courtesy of the Freer Gallery of Art.)

Han diplomatic and military contacts in the 2nd or 1st century B.C. is unproven and seems unlikely, although it is plausible that knowledge of lead-glazing should have spread through Central Asia during Han times and perhaps a little earlier.[12] In China lead-glazing next appears on pottery towards the end of the 6th century, under the Sui dynasty, applied to the imitation of more or less exotic shapes and ornament, all of strongly westernizing types. It is convenient to distinguish three phases, in each of which models wrought in silver or gold determined the main trends, and caused pottery to reflect styles of ornament which had reached China from the Sasanian territory (probably from the north-eastern province of Sogdiana) and from the Iranized city-states of Central Asia.

12. For Iran-China relations, Watson (1983).

The First Westernizing Style: Late 6th and 7th Century

It becomes clear that the Chinese of the Sui and Tang capitals were acquainted, among a great variety of exotic goods, with ewers, bowls and cups which were traded eastwards along the northern route through Xinjiang (Central Asia), the Silk Route as it has been called in recent western writing. A striking illustration of the foreign style is to be seen in a spherical footed bowl of white stoneware found near Xian in Shaanxi and dated from a funerary tablets to A.D. 637 (**Fig.1**).[13] On this bowl two horizontal bands are decorated at intervals with alternating ovals/roundels and squares, imitating respectively precious stones set in cabochon, and a squared eight-petalled floret, all set within narrow granulated lines. Both ornaments are commonplace in the Iranian tradition, reaching back into Achaemenid times. There can be little doubt that the setting imitated is gold granulation, and that the florets imitate an original repoussé of silver or gold. Almost a century before this bowl was buried similar decorative elements were introduced on jars and ewers covered with the low-fired lead-glaze. It has been suspected, judging in part from the Sogdian murals, that Sasanian goblets and other feasting vessels were in some instances made of wood covered with cloth (or painted) and encrusted with jewelled ornaments of the kind just described from the Xian pottery bowls. In one instance a silversmith's method was to cover a bowl with plain textile over which he laid openwork ornament of lotus cut from thin silver sheet. Pottery of the 6th-8th centuries from the site of ancient Khotan shows a common practice of ornamenting even utilitarian pots with small relief motifs, either animal masks or shapes resembling mounted stones.[14] Pottery prolonging this tradition into China belongs at the earliest to the last quarter of the 6th century, and is found in both the lead-glazed and high-fired varieties. That repoussé silver or gold underlay the ceramic ornament is hardly to be doubted: the swelling lobed petals of the flowers, symmetrical and emblematic, the leaves of the palmettes, the masks of lions and horned monsters, bear the unmistakable character of this method, at whatever remove, though cast-silver or bronze and carved materials, from the fountain-head of the style.[15] The motifs in question, particularly the geometricized florets, were not confined to metalwork. They supplied a chief ornament to textile embroidery, and eventually made a large contribution to the minor ornament of the Tang International style, as it was disseminated through the Buddhist east. In view of what was to develop in lead-glazed

13. Watson (1984), fig.3; *S.T.Z. 11*, pl.13.

14. Watson (1970), 214f; Azarpay (1981), figs.36, 40, 48, pl.13; Trever (1947); for the Khotan pottery cf. D'yakonova & Sorokin (1960), pl.1/3, 8, 19; also Trever (1947).

15. *S.T.Z. 10*, pl.2; Gray (1953), pl.15; Watson (1979), pl.153.

Figure 3. Silver-gilt cup, eight-sided, with standing figures in relief. First half of 8th century. Ht. 6.5cm. Excavated in 1970 at Hejiacun, Xian, Shaanxi. Collections of the People's Republic of China.

Figure 4. Base of gold bowl, lobed in repoussé and chased with floral ornament. First half of the 8th century. Diam. 13.5cm. Excavated at Hejiacun Xian, Shaanxi, Collections of the People's Republic of China.

Figure 5. *Wannian* jar of earthenware with relief medallions. Blue, green, red and yellow, on white ground, in lead-glaze. First half of the 8th century. Ht. 24.5cm. Seikadō Bunko, Tokyo.

pottery in north China, it is interesting that pottery from before 700 with encrusted ornament seems not to have been intended so exclusively for funereal ostentation as the early 8th-century ware. The stoneware green-glazed vases and ewers, which are sometimes grotesquely overloaded with the ornament, rather suggest luxury for the living.

The Classical Phase of Lead-Glazing: c.700-750

Thus far the revived lead-glazing of the Sui and Tang periods has been monochrome, usually a muddy-green which no doubt owes its lack-lustre appearance to failure to produce a glaze of the necessary viscocity (**Fig.2**). Towards 700 the lead-fluxed greens and browns grow clearer; then in the last decade of the century and possibly not until a year or two before 700, the polychrome lead-glazes make their appearance. In itself of course the introduction of bright colours—brown, red, green, blue—did not necessarily bring the pottery closer to models made of silver or gold, though the new work belongs to a much more varied and intense commercial and intellectual exchange between China and the Iranian west. The influx of Buddhist religion, iconography and crafts through the Xingjiang was at its height, and

Figure 6. Phoenix-head ewer with petals, soaring phoenixes and floral medallions in relief. Trailed yellow, green and brown lead-glaze over buff earthenware. First half of the 8th century. Ht. 33.5cm. Hakutsuru Art Museum, Kobe.

Chinese awareness and emulation of western fine art in gold and silver reached a degree that was never surpassed. The Tang International style diffused elements of the Buddhists' art, particularly the linear brush-style of Chinese painting, through a vast territory stretching from Pandjikent in Sogdiana to Nara in Japan. But the disruption caused by rebellion and a realignment of ruling forces within metropolitan China after the first half of the 8th century almost put an end to the entry of exotic goods and influence. Sasanian silver coins have been found in comparative plenty, but Sasanian gold and silver vessels seem not to have survived, although we can see their influence on Chinese work.[16]

Among the *sancai*, "three-colour", i.e. polychrome lead-glazed, vessels found in such quantity in the noble tombs at a short distance from the Tang capital Changan, small cups are fewer than larger bowls and ewers; but since they copy the shape of wine-cups they are more readily matched with their equivalents in gold and silver (**Figs.3, 4**).[17] Pedestal cups in gold and silver have been found in tombs outside the city walls in a tomb of Sui date. They were closely copied in earthenware about a century later, though more commonly it is the type with low ring-foot, sometimes ring-handled, which

16. For a summary of the Sasanian material found in China see Xia Nai in *Kaogu*, 2, (1978), 11.

17. Watson (1984), figs.125-128; Tokyo (1973), fig.148; Rawson (1982).

appears in the lead-glazed ware. Of this last shape an example exists in gold decorated on the sides with large rosettes of cloisons and surrounding granulation.[18] This design resembles ornament common on dishes, but impossible to produce in lead-glaze on the vertical sides of small vessels, though on larger pieces, as mentioned below, the rosettes were moulded in low relief. Naturally the punched, engraved and chased ornament of the silver and gold bowls and cups was beyond the capacity of the potters. Instead they resorted to the splashed polychrome which constitutes the predominant decoration of *sancai*. The profiles of cups and small drinking-bowls form the segment of a circle, bulge slightly, or show an offset typical of work in the precious metals.[19] Small boxes with vertical lobed sides and vegetal scrollery in relief on the lid were readily imitated from gold or silver.[20] It is notable that one of these minor items were imitated, either in earthenware or in high-fired ware, as the 8th century went on, whereas tea-drinking, and with it the demand for tea-cups, increased in popularity. Neither vessels executed in the precious metals not their close copies can have been in popular demand, except to some degree the white porcelain dishes with foliated rims (the form named "five-petal marshmallow") which spread from north-east China in the 10th century.[21]

In lead-glazed ware the great demand around the Tang capital at Changan was for impressive funerary urns, ewers and jars (in addition to the figurines of servitors and apotropaic genii (**Figs.5, 6**); and when relief motifs appearing on these vessels are imitated from Iranian types (which permits us to infer that the originals were gold or silver) these are often splashed with colours without regard to the detail of the design.[22] The majority of pieces are content with a gay and imprecise pattern of lines, rosettes and random splash, suggesting the effect of dyed stuffs imported from Xinjiang. The relief motifs were borrowed and transferred to different shapes, as when figures of lions and birds set in a beaded circle and placed centrally inside a dish (a superb example of this still exists, in gold) are taken to decorate the sides of a vase or ewer.[23] One class of ornament used on the sides of such vessels includes phoenixes, lions, dancing figures, fruit and flowers arranged in close profusion. These motifs are strongly suggestive of work in gold or silver, of a Hellenizing type, and can be paralleled in repoussé and cast-silver belonging to the Iranian sphere. A silver bowl reputed to have been long preserved in Lhasa is a perfect exemplar of the kind of lingering Hellenistic style which found its way into Tang ceramics, occasionally on lead-glazed pottery, and more

18. Tokyo (1979), 46.

19. Watson (1984), figs.8, 168-170.

20. Watson (1984), figs.128, 186, 187; for silver cf. *I.A.P.* (1962), pl.105, no.1.

21. Watson (1984), figs.115, 116.

22. Watson (1984), esp. figs.1, 5, 7, 12, 30, 122; and *S.T.Z. 11*, *passim*, figs.47, 48.

23. *S.T.Z. 11*, pls.33, 34; for silver and gold cf. Tokyo (1973), 141.

Figure 7. Detail of a flat tripod dish showing lead-glaze of different colours separated by grooved lines. Ashmolean Museum.

frequently on such pieces as the stoneware "pilgrim flasks".[24] In silver and on the pottery the stance of the human figures and the casual treatment of trees and fronds are characteristic. The Chinese artist's handling of the post-Hellenistic and the Iranian themes are quite eclectic, and his unfamiliarity with the rhythms and proportions of the exotic ornament is betrayed by an improper relation of the parts. The colour trailed or splashed over relief ornament on the earthenware vessels is in a way the equivalent of the parcel-gilding used on silver dishes which were contemporary with them. On flat dishes deeply grooved lines defining the ornament helped to confine the colours to the appropriate areas (**Fig.7**). The various roundels of lotus and magical fungus *ling-zhi* were probably frequent also on dishes made of the precious metals, for one design popular on the earthenware dishes—the ring of elaborate cordiform petals formed of divided palmettes—is attested for silver by a box excavated on the site of the palace at Changan.[25] In the effort to reproduce in earthenware some elaborate censers, the potter advanced his already age-old skill in structural ceramics. The relief ornament of the metal prototypes could be imitated in *sancai* pottery, but not the openwork figures on the sides and lid of the censer.[26] The potter was content with a crown-like lid formed of arching ribs.[27]

After the rebellion of 756 and the devastation of the capital, Tang decorative art betrays clearly the withdrawal of the metropolitan patronage, with its unprecedented exotic and liberal taste, which had dominated for half a century. In the lead-glazed earthenware this change of direction is specially noticeable; its history through the remainder of the Tang period is obscure, and most obviously its dependence on the craft of silversmith and goldsmith

24. Denwood (1973); Watson (1984), figs.4, 7, 30, 76, 304.

25. Tokyo (1973), 142.

26. Tokyo (1979), 49.

27. Watson (1984), fig.24.

Figure 8. Vessel in the shape of a duck, with three-colour lead-glaze. 8th century. Ht. 24.8cm. Seikadō Bunko, Tokyo.

Figure 9. Square dish with impressed ornament under green lead-glaze. 9th or early 10th century. Diam. 14.2cm. Private collection, Japan.

has altered and declined. Some small zoomorphic vessels (usually geese or rhytons), and small lobed bowls and dishes, certainly recall work in silver or gold, their surface being covered with the raised lines and seeded ground imitative of chasing and punching (**Fig.8**).[28] Glaze of a single colour, green, brown or rarely blue, became the rule, and on some pieces the glaze is washed over a floral or abstract design incised or scratched on the surface of the clay. The origin of this technique calls for explanation, since it hardly belongs to ceramic tradition. In the Han period designs of phoenix, clouds and vegetation were engraved in thin line under the hard glaze of the so-called "proto-porcelain" bottles and jars,[29] and these arguably are descended from the kind of linear ornament which may, as was suggested above, derive from tracing and chasing on gold and silver. On middle and late Tang pieces thread-like *raised* lines define ornament under uniform lead-glaze, and this technique may also have been adopted in imitation of silverwork, foreign as it is to normal Chinese methods (**Fig.9**). It is worth remarking that the three-colour lead-glazed dishes unearthed at Samarra on the Tigris include pieces with linear figures *incised* under the glaze. It is uncertain how far this latter method was followed, if at all, in China, and it cannot have been frequent before the appearance of a coarser equivalent in the Liao period. While an origin in Tang China for the Samarran pottery can no longer be

28. Watson (1984), figs.2, 134, 195, 263.

29. Watson (1984), fig.641.

accepted, the approximate coincidence of technique with that of the later Tang does suggest a remote connection.[30] Ornament in engraved line is, however, occasionally seen on Chinese stoneware, as early as Sui on a green-glazed flat tripod dish, and on a rare cream-glazed dish of the 9th or early 10th century.[31] In the latter piece the peony scrolling resembles the linear flowers found on silverwork credibly attributed to the late 8th or 9th century.[32]

The Revival of Lead-Glazing under the Liao Dynasty

Pottery found in Inner Mongolia and dating from the reign of the house of Liao includes much that was imported from China, but the types peculiar to the Liao kilns prolong styles and techniques of Tang tradition rather than emulating the contemporary products of Song. In particular the lead-glazed ware is distinct and forms a recognizable pendant to Tang work.[33] It is difficult, however, to trace a historical continuity, the most important part of the Liao lead-glazed earthenware being separated by a century and a half from the latest Tang and giving the impression of a deliberate revival sponsored by the Liao court. On phoenix-head bottles, bird-mouth ewers and various floreate-lipped vases, all covered with green or brown glaze, the underglaze engraved designs of peony scrolls show the technique known at Samarra but not found in Tang, with the same suggestion of derivation from work on silver and gold vessels. On the typical pilgrim bottles made in imitation of sewn leather, some abstract scrolling and developed leaves and blooms appear to come from the silversmith's pattern book (**Fig.11**). These pieces date from the 10th and the earlier 11th century. To the period between about 1050 and 1100 are attributed the small lead-glazed dishes which stand for something quite different artistically and technically (**Fig.10**).[34]

Probably made at the Nanshan kiln at Shangjing in the Liao territory, these pieces record the potter's effort to imitate the silver equivalent as closely as his medium allowed, in a spirit unlike the eclectic and carefree invention of his Tang predecessor. The silver dishes, like the pottery ones, have a broken oval outline or the "marshmallow" outline popularized by the superior white-ware of Hebei which reached the Liao cities. A group of silver pieces, consisting of an ewer, deep and shallow bowls and a foliate dish, was placed in a tomb of about 1100 near Bairin Youqi in Inner Mongolia, and these shapes with their ornament of floral scrolling and roundels demonstrate the fidelity of

30. Watson (1984), figs.187, 275.

31. Watson (1984), fig.118; *S.T.Z. II*, colour pl.4.

32. Gyllensvärd (1953), no.116.

33. Watson (1984), 220.

34. Watson (1984), 234-5, figs.279, 280.

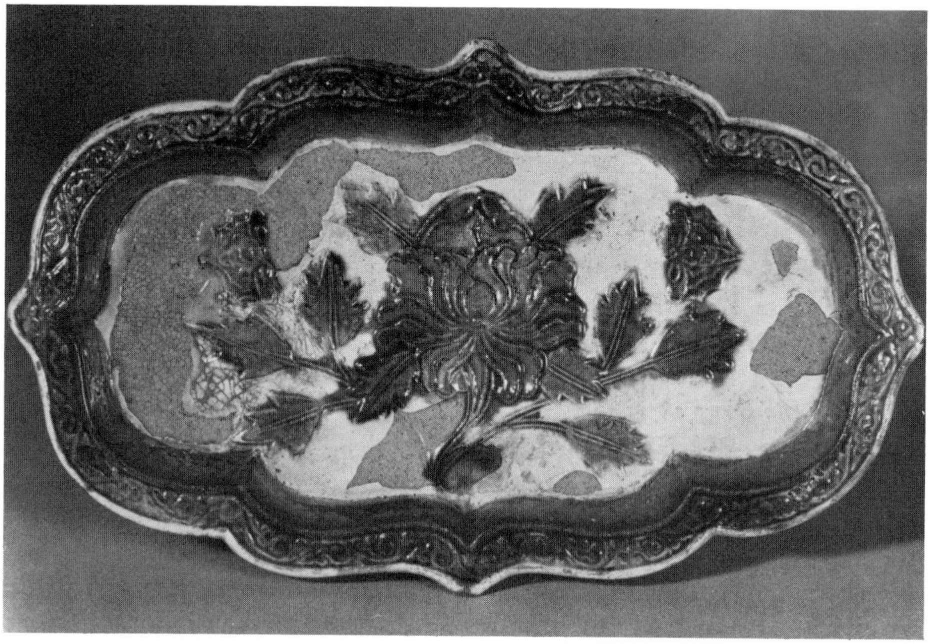

Figure 10. Earthenware dish with impressed floral ornament picked out in white, brown and green lead-glaze. Mid-11th century. Length 26.5cm. Tokyo National Museum.

the earthenware imitations.[35] The latter succeeded in confining their green, brown and cream-coloured glazes appropriately to borders, petals and leaves.

Conclusion

A generalized conclusion about Chinese work in the precious metals is made hazardous by the paucity of surviving ancient examples. Our idea of the use made of silver is perhaps less accurate than our picture of the use of gold, since silver, in standard ingots, was less normal specie, which gold was to a limited extent, and only for a short time in the pre-Han period. But some features of this long history can be discerned. Whenever particularly fine gold and silver vessels were made and then copied in pottery, an exotic influence was at work. In isolated examples, the Chinese craftsman tried to imitate closely a model of western origin, either a creation of the metropolitan Iranian industry or a modified version of that tradition transplanted to Iranized cities in Central Asia. The reflection in ceramics of this process of part-imitation and part-reinvention also suggests an exotic fashion of comparatively short duration, and limited to a narrow sphere surrounding a capital city. Changan

35. Watson (1984), line fig.11 on 228.

Figure 11. Earthenware pilgrim flask decorated with peony flower and leaves in grooved line under cream-coloured lead-glaze. 10th-early 11th century. Ht. 25.5cm. British Museum.

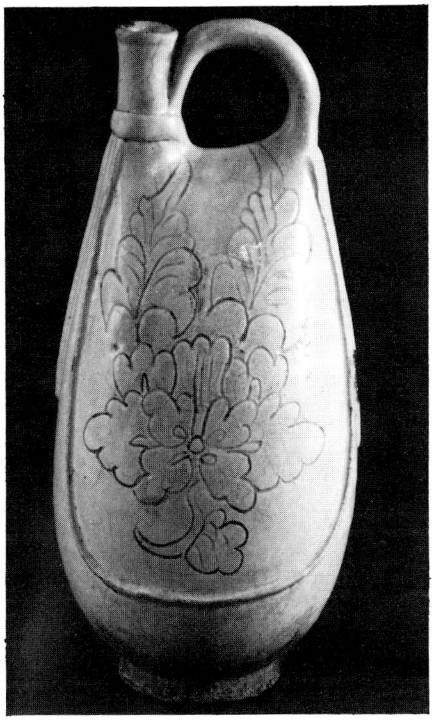

Loyang and (Liao) Shangjing received this influence directly, while other centres took it in at second hand or even less directly. We have seen how much lead-glazed earthenware was used in those pottery imitations and developments which derived from a gold or silver vessel.

From the beginning the habit of *constructing* pottery forms, rather than *turning* them brought a large proportion of Chinese pottery close to shapes associated with other materials, bronze, precious metal, basketwork, gourds or even leather. Once a shape or a trick of detail originating in non-ceramic material was conventionalized and established, it joined a long-lived repertoire of purely ceramic resource, all consciousness of indebtedness to the original having disappeared. The transient influence of the precious metals on Chinese pottery becomes indistinguishably integrated into the tradition which the ceramic historian analyses. In the Chinese treatment of gold and silver, as such, there is no intelligible continuous evolution to be perceived. Inlay, foil-work, casting and repoussé, granulation and filigree tend to appear unheralded and depart unlamented, leaving slight traces in pottery. As for the sensuous luxury of possession, gold and silver could not in China compete among connoisseurs with jade or calligraphy.

Bibliography

Azarpay (1981)	Azarpay, G., *Sogdian Painting*, London, 1981.
Denwood (1973)	Denwood, P., "A Greek Bowl from Tibet", *Iran*, 11, 1973, pp.212-27.
D'yakonova & Sorokin (1960)	D'yakonova, N.V., and Sorokin, S.S., *Khotanskie Drevnosti*, Leningrad, 1960.
Eskenazi (1985)	Messrs Eskenazi, *Eskenazi Twenty-Five Years*, London, 1985.
Gray (1953)	*Early Chinese Pottery and Porcelain*, London, 1953.
Gyllensvärd (1953)	Gyllensvärd, B., *Chinese Gold and Silver in the Carl Kempe Collection*, Stockholm, 1953.
Historic Relics (1972)	*Xin Zhongguo Chutu Wenwu, (Historic Relics Unearthed in China)*, Peking, 1972.
I.A.P. (1962)	Institute of Archaeology, *Xin Zhongguo di Kaogu Shouhuo*, Peking, 1962.
I.A.P. (1981)	Institute of Archaeology, *Guangzhou Han-Mu*, Peking, 1981.
Jenyns & Watson (1963-65)	Jenyns, R.S. and Watson, W., *Chinese Art: The Minor Arts*, New York, 1963-65.
Kaogu	*Kaogu*, Peking.
Loehr (1965)	Loehr, M., *Relics of Ancient China from the Collection of Dr Paul Singer*, New York, 1965.
Rawson (1982)	Rawson, J., "The Ornament on Chinese Silver of the Tang Period", *British Museum Occasional Paper No.40*, London, 1982.
S.T.Z. 10 (1962)	Okazaki Takashi, *Sekai Tozi Zenshū 10 Chūgoku Kodai*, Shōgakkan Tokyo, 1962.
S.T.Z. 11 (1976)	Satō Masahiko and Hasebe Gakuji, *Sekai Tozi Zenshū 11 Zi Tu*, Shōgakkan Tokyo, 1976.
Tokyo (1973)	*Chūgoku Jinmin Kyōwakoku Shutsudo Bunbutsuten*, Tokyo National Museum, Tokyo, 1973.
Tokyo (1979)	*Chūgoku Jinmin Kyōwakoku. Shiruju Rōdo Bunbutsuten*, Tokyo National Museum, Tokyo, 1979.
Trever (1947)	Trever, K.V., "Sasanidskiy Serebryannyy Kubok iz Urdonskogo Ushchel'ya v Severnoy Osetii", *Trudy Otdela Istorii Kul'tury i Iskusstva Vostoka*, 4, Leningrad, 1947.
Watson (1970)	Watson, W., "Overlay and *p'ing-t'o* in T'ang silverwork", *Journal of the Royal Asiatic Society*, 1970, pp.210-15.
Watson (1973)	Watson, W., *The Genius of China. An Exhibition of Archaeological Finds of the People's Republic of China*, Royal Academy, London, 1973.
Watson (1979)	Watson, W., *Art of Dynastic China*, New York, 1979.
Watson (1983	Watson, W., "Iran and China", *Cambridge History of Iran*, ed. E. Yarshater, vol.3, (1), Cambridge, 1983, pp.537-58.
Watson (1984)	Watson, W., *Tang and Liao Ceramics*, London, 1984.

Tenth Century Yue Ware and Silver and Gold

MARY TREGEAR

Influences exchanged between metal and ceramic in the 10th century in China differ in degree and nature from those of previous times. By the 10th century, the ceramic tradition of north Zhejiang, the site of the Yue kilns, had long been established.[1] Behind it lay some eight centuries of technical and stylistic development. Several times there had been periods of influence, particularly of influence on style, which appear to have been derived from metalwares. These metalwares were not always of local or even of Chinese manufacture, for Chinese potters have always been ready to take in exotic stylistic ideas from any source. The metal would most often have been bronze, as can be seen in much of the 2nd-century north Zhejiang green glazed stoneware. By the 4th century near-eastern shapes had arrived, possibly in precious metals, with ewers and tall-necked vase shapes and elaborate decoration. Alongside such stylistic borrowing runs a tradition of technical skills peculiar to the Chinese potter, his handling of stoneware clays and glazes and the management of kilns. By the 10th century most technical discoveries necessary for the successful production of high-fired ware had been made, notably the balancing of clay and glaze to produce a fine quality stoneware with an elegant hard glaze. The kiln for firing this was now reliable and, as far as one can judge, very similar to the kiln used in later centuries. The type most popular in Yue seems to have been the climbing "dragon", which was developed and used in this part of China.

So behind the 10th-century Yue ware there is a firmly founded tradition of Chinese technology and potters' skills, used in a tradition of styles based partly on much older borrowing from metalwares and partly on what was by the 10th century a ceramic tradition of shapes and decoration. In some cases stylistic borrowing had brought problems of construction for the potter. In the construction of spouts and handles in Zhejiang greenware, there is a reminder of the close relationship, for the Chinese potters seem never to have made thrown spouts or pulled handles, which would be natural to the European potter. These parts of the ewer were made around a mould, in the same way that a metal worker made them. This technique had been absorbed at an early period by the Chinese potters, and become a part of the Chinese

1. Tregear (1976) and Watson (1984).

tradition which has persisted. By the 10th century pottery was a craft with styles of its own which were beginning to be shared by several kilns in widely separated parts of the country. Where borrowing from metal, made in earlier centuries, had become detached from the metal tradition and accepted as part of ceramic technique and design, they were by this time being adapted and developed as part of the pottery traditions which led to the classic Song stoneware.

Yet during the 10th century there does appear to have been a change in style in the wares of the Yue kilns of north Zhejiang. Yue ware was made in at least three styles, two of which seem close to the silver and gilt pieces now associated with the later Tang period. In a general way, the influence appears in the introduction of very thin-walled potting. In bowls the tiny thickened rim, often nicked rather than indented to form a foliation, and the slight mark of indentation on the wall are also reminiscent of the metal bowls of Tang, and even the thin neat foot may be associated with silver wares. The very fine line incised decoration, which apparently soon fell out of favour, resembles a technique used on metal. Many of these characteristics were thoroughly assimilated, though not always all together, and passed into the vocabulary of potters in other centres. It is interesting that the potters were turning to a silver ware which, as far as we can tell, was not "the latest thing" but a style of some age and standing. This could be a comment on the position of the Yue area and the metropolis. North Zhejiang was well beyond the metropolitan centre of the Tang state, but in the Five Dynasties Period of the 10th century the court of the Wu Yue state was situated near to present-day Nanking and very close to the kiln area. From being a provincial centre of Tang, Yue had become a centre of some importance, with a notable court at Nanking . Perhaps this court was a refuge for wealthy families escaping from the troubles accompanying the breakdown of the Tang, who brought metropolitan styles with them. This might account for the somewhat old-fashioned echo of Tang silver in the now sought-after Yue ware. Besides these possible associations with metropolitan Tang, one may look to the Korean courts of the unified Silla at Kyongju of the 11th century for a further extension of the style, and indeed, of the technique of 10th-century Yue.[2] At this time the two states, Wu Yue and Silla, were closely allied politically, and ideas of craftsmanship seem to have been exchanged. The grey-green stoneware tradition of Yue and Korea might almost be regarded as one at this time. The Korean ware, a little lighter grey in body and a little bluer in glaze, is really the apotheosis of this ware.

While one can see a relationship with silver and precious metal in the thin walls and delicately tooled decoration of the ceramic ware, one is always conscious of the presence of the two major crafts of China: jade and lacquer.

2. Goepper & Whitfield 1984.

Figure 1. Covered jar. Yue Ware, 10th century. The shape is derived from a much earlier bronze, the decoration and the finish of the cover may well come from more closely contemporary silver inspiration. Ht. 41.90cm. Ashmolean Museum, 1956.1221.

Because of their status, perhaps, they display the period style most distinctly, and there is a stress on thin walls and fine decoration in these wares too. A contemporary value judgement is illuminating: "Yue ware is like jade, Xing ware is nothing like it".[3] The Chinese connoisseur has accepted the thin wall in jade and silver and ceramic, and is looking at the glaze, yet he apparently does not see (or appreciate) that Ding (or Xing) ware is like silver. The small incense boxes of neat profile and "secret" decoration recall painted lacquer boxes made on a fine-turned wood matrix and painted in a spidery vegetable scroll motif. So that although this fine and influential group of green-glazed stonewares can be looked at with an art historian's eye, finding and recording borrowing from metalwares, it seems to me too much of a simplification to see the mature Yue ware as a mere replica of silver or gold. It may be taking in some of the borrowed characteristics at second hand through another craft. More importantly, the 10th century sees the rise of the potter's trade, especially that of the Zhejiang and Ding kilns, to the rank of a major craft, valued highly, and standing only a little below jade and lacquer production in the social scale. The position of a craft, not necessarily its monetary valuation, is of interest, especially when it moves from an inferior position to become serious and valued in its own right. During the period of serious valuation, influences are likely to be fewer and more subtle. The position of ceramics has altered frequently in China. During the 10th century the foundation was laid for the classic period of the 11th-14th centuries, when monochrome stoneware held a position of importance never to be repeated, yet continuing to influence world ceramics to this day. So 10th-century Yue ware is a complex of old and long-digested influences, and some "new" ideas from many sources, all joining to produce a style or styles which should not be regarded as originating in any one other craft.

3. Lu Yu, *Chajing*.

Bibliography

Goepper & Whitfield (1984)	Goepper, R., and Whitfield, R., *The Treasures of Korea*, 1984.
Lu Yu	Lu Yu, *Chajing*.
Tregear (1976)	Tregear, M., *Catalogue of Chinese Greenwares in the Ashmolean Museum*, 1976.
Watson (1984)	Watson, W., *Tang and Liao Ceramics*, 1984.

Looking for Silver in Clay: A New Perspective on Sāmānid Ceramics

JULIAN RABY

The influence of Chinese ceramics has long been regarded as formative in at least three of the major periods of Islamic pottery production, the 9th and 10th centuries A.D. in 'Abbāsid Iraq, the late 12th and early 13th centuries in Seljuq Iran, and the late 15th and early 16th centuries in Ottoman Turkey. Insistence on a ceramic influence from abroad has, however, distracted attention from the rôle of local, Muslim metalwork in the development of pottery forms and decoration.

The blue-and-white palette and soft-paste porcelain body, as well as the fineness of execution and the scale of the first Iznik frit-wares, the so-called *Abraham of Kütahya* wares, were certainly a response to Yuan and Ming Chinese porcelains. On the other hand, the shapes and decorative motifs were largely Ottoman. The same motifs occur on the few surviving Ottoman silver objects of the period, while the shapes of the earliest examples betray a metallic prototype in their use of sharply articulated profiles, offset lips and torus mouldings. This is not surprising, since *Abraham of Kütahya* wares mark an abrupt break with earlier pottery traditions in Turkey, and the potters must have looked beyond the ceramic sphere for inspiration.[1] Precious metal vessels were the obvious source, especially as they were prevalent at court, to judge from a Treasury register of 910/1505 in which they outnumbered Turkish ceramics by some 5 to 1.[2] It was only in a later phase, following Selim's conquests of Tabriz in 1514 and of Damascus and Cairo in 1517, when he seized quantities of Chinese porcelain, that Chinese blue-and-white began to have an appreciable effect on Iznik pottery.[3]

Iznik pottery, therefore, drew initially on indigenous metalwork and only later on Chinese porcelain. The inverse is true of Seljuq frit-wares. The white-wares Lane attributes to the earliest phase are those most indebted to Chinese models, imitating the forms and restrained aesthetic of Qingbai ware.[4] The elaborate decorative techniques and compositions of the subsequent *mīnā'ī* and lustre types owe nothing, on the other hand, to China, and it is noticeable how Islamic metalwork shapes become current in these pottery types, as Oliver Watson has shown elsewhere in this volume. It is worth adding, though, an area in which metalwork decoration also influenced

1. Raby and Yücel (1983); Raby (1982).

2. For a discussion of this register, see Michael Rogers' contribution in this volume; cf. Raby & Yücel (1986), 79-81.

3. Raby & Yücel (1983).

4. Lane (1946-7); Lane (1947), 29-36.

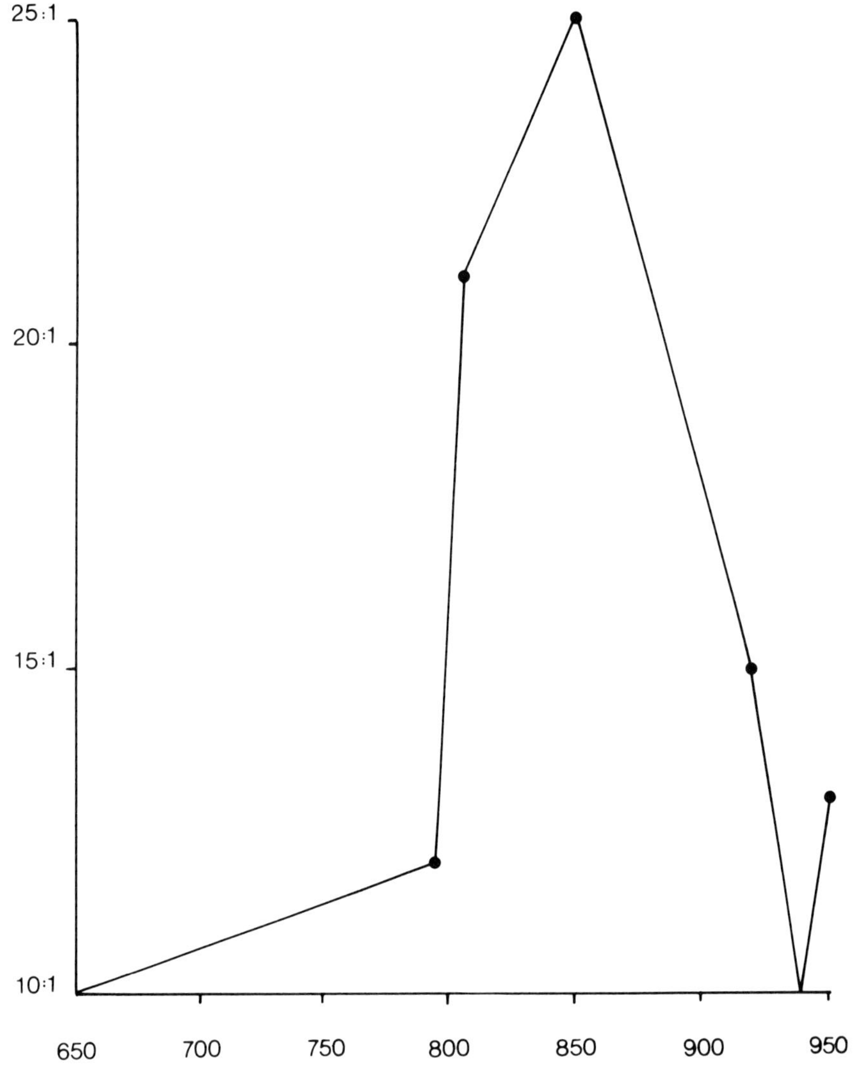

Table 1. The Dīnar-Dirham Ratio in Irac A.D.650-950, from figures given by Ashtor (1961).

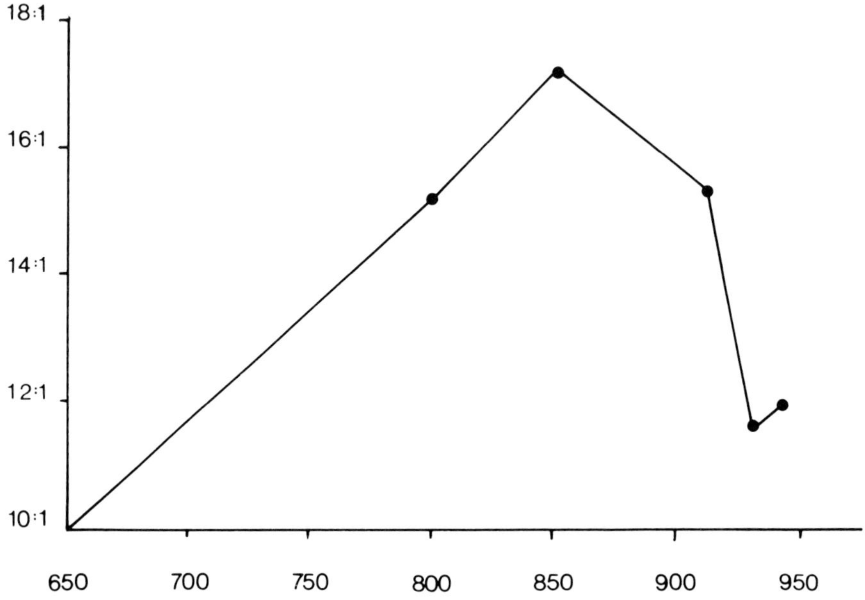

Table 2. The Value Gold to Silver in the Central Islamic Lan A.D.650-950. (After Bolin.)

Table 3. The chronological distribution of Muslim coins found in hoards in Gotland. 560 determinable Kufic coins, with the most recent coins being of the period A.D.978-1016. (After Sawyer.)

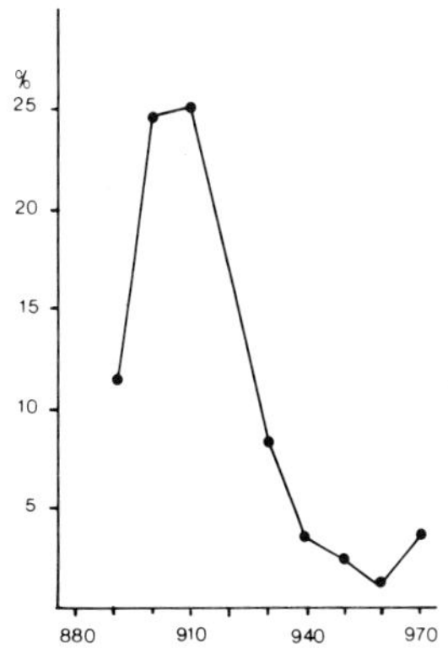

the Seljuq potter. A curious sub-group of *mīnā'ī* ware has raised bosses, usually pierced and gilded, which give the vessels a tectonic rather than organic appearance, one more common in metal than ceramic (**Fig.1**).[5] The same effect can be seen in a repoussé silver jug made for a certain Ḥusayn ibn 'Alī, according to Marshak in 10th-century Khurāsān or Transoxiana (**Fig.2**).[6]

The focus of this paper is, however, on the 9th and 10th centuries A.D., on 'Abbāsid Iraq and, in particular, north-east Iran and Transoxiana. In this period 'Abbāsid Iraq produced three main types of glazed pottery. Of these the so-called *relief-wares* owe nothing to China in terms of either shapes or decoration. The inspiration instead is from local metalwork, in the use of sharply everted rims, vestigial handles and, on occasion, feet, as well as in the geometric designs and what Sarre describes as the "sharpness and angling" of the relief.[7] On the other hand, both the *white-wares*, most often with cobalt decoration, and the *lustre-painted-wares* look, as we shall see later, to Chinese models for their typical bowl shape. Their decorative techniques, however, are Middle Eastern developments, while their decorative styles and motifs are heterogeneous, and in some cases show influence from metalwork.[8]

A characteristic of early Islamic metalwork was the beaded or hatched border, which was usually in relief and could take the form of continuous strapwork, roundels or arcades. The best known type of Iraqi *relief-ware* is afigural and decorated with interlaced strapwork with relief beading. Although a silver prototype seems highly probable, the only known silver

5. Grube (1976), 206-7, who compares the decoration to "gilded and painted stucco relief"; cf. *Survey*, (1938-39) pls.677-85.

6. Smirnov (1909), pl.lxxii, no.128; Marshak (1976), 155.

7. Lane (1939); Sarre (1925), 32, pl.x; Rosen-Ayalon (1974), 212, fig.501. It is generally overlooked that most of the relief-ware found at Samarra by the German excavators came from one of the latest palaces, the Qaṣr al-'Āshiq: Sarre (1925), 33.

8. Lane (1947), 13-16; Grube (1976), 35-80.

Figure 1. Mīnā'ī ceramic jar, painted with overglaze enamels and gold. Iran, 12th century. Ht. 14.5cm. Ashmolean Museum, Barlow Gift, 1956.152.

Figure 2. Silver repoussé jug, made for Ḥusayn ibn 'Alī. Khurāsān or Transoxiana, 10th century. Leningrad, Hermitage. (After Smirnov.)

comparandum is an octagonal tray in Berlin which has animals enclosed within a hatched interlacing frame (**Figs.3 & 4**).[9] Beaded roundels occur on a green-glazed bowl in the Keir Collection; here, again, a precise silver parallel does not survive, but the main design element recurs on a great bronze charger of the same period (**Figs.5 & 6**).[10] On the base of the Keir pottery bowl is an eight-lobed rosette, for which silver parallels do survive, several in conjunction with a beaded border (**Figs.7a-c**).[11] When a painted design of beaded roundels occurs, therefore, on an 'Abbāsid *white-ware* bowl, an influence from metalwork seems likely, particularly since the design allows the painter little freehand expression (**Fig.8**).[12] Finally, the arcading and the beaded frame found on several early Islamic bronze chargers finds an echo in the lustre decoration of a fragmentary dish in the Ashmolean (**Fig.9 & 10**).[13]

Indeed, it has often been suggested that the lustre technique itself, in particular monochrome lustre, was an attempt to emulate the effect of gold

9. Smirnov (1909), pl.lxx, no.126; *Survey* (1938-9), pl.238; Hayward (1976), cat. no.157. Parallel hatching also occurs on the 'Abbāsid relief-ware ceramics, e.g. Rosen-Ayalon (1974), pl.xli, f.

10. Grube (1976), 29-35; *Survey* (1938-9), pl.195A and vol.ii, 675.

11. Darkevich (1976), pls.12 and 13; Smirnov (1909), pl.lxi, no.97, pl.lxii, no.103, pl.lxviii, no.122, pl.lxxx, no.134, pl.lxxii, nos.312, 314; cf. pl.lxxviii, no.138. cf. *Survey*, i, (1938-9), 676-7 and 765 esp.

12. Grube (1966), 21, fig.7.

13. Pézard (1920), pl.cxv.

ure 3. 'Abbāsid relief-ware ceramic bowl, with yellow-wn glaze and green splashes. Iraq, 9th century. Diam. ?cm., ht. 4.9cm. Oxford, Ashmolean Museum, Reitlinger lection, 1978.2143.

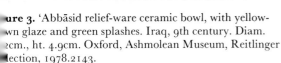

Figure 4. 'Abbāsid silver dish, beaten and chased. 9th-10th century. Diam. 35.8cm., ht. 3.0cm. Berlin-Dahlem Museum für Islamische Kunst, no.I.4926.

and parcel-gilt, the use of which was open to the censure of theologians.[14] Be that as it may, a point of interest in this context is the stippled background (**Fig.9**). It seems such a laborious, even laboured, technique for a painter that it seems unlikely to have been developed in a pottery context. It makes sense, however, as a transfer from precious metalwork, where ring or dot-matting is common as a means of providing a textural contrast in an essentially monochrome medium (**Figs.27a,c**). The most frequent type of stippling in 'Abbāsid monochrome lustre pottery consists, however, of "arrow-head" motifs, rather than of round dots which one would expect in a derivative from precious metal. Yet this is not a surprising modification, because a painter in order to produce a series of consistently round dots has to raise his brush and his hand from the surface for each dot, whereas he can produce "arrow-heads" with quick horizontal strokes and with his hand resting on the surface of the pot.

The Iraqi wares were widely distributed, and sherds have been found from Pakistan to Spain, and from north-east Iran to Sri Lanka.[15] The contemporary "Sāmānid" potteries from Khurāsān and Transoxiana were, by

14. Sarre (1925), 32, writes unreservedly of relief-ware with monochrome lustre: "Es ist kein Zweifel, dass es sich hier um eine direkte Nachahmung von Goldgefässen handelt; man wollte, um das religiöse Gebot zu umgehen, dem Tongefäss den Anschein des Goldgefässes geben".

15. Grube (1976), 35-37.

contrast, of limited distribution.[16] As Iraqi wares have been found in the north-east, notably at Nīshāpūr, but no Sāmānid ceramics have been found in Iraq, it might be assumed that Sāmānid epigraphic-wares were influenced from Iraq. Sāmānid ceramics with inscriptions divide, however, into two sharply contrasting groups. One is tin-glazed and so evidently derivative from imported Mesopotamian models that it need not delay us; in what follows I shall reserve the term *Sāmānid epigraphic-ware* to the second type, the lead-glazed, slip-painted calligraphic vessels which are among the most majestic achievements of the Islamic potter (**Fig.11**).[17]

Leaving aside the obvious distinction in technique between the tin-glazed 'Abbāsid white-wares and the lead-glazed Sāmānid epigraphic-wares, the differences in the *contents*, *location* and *morphology* of their respective inscriptions are striking.

The 'Abbāsid inscribed-wares consist mostly of artists' signatures and simple blessings, whereas the Sāmānid carry no signatures and frequently bear lengthy, somewhat trite, aphorisms such as: "He who professes the faith will excel; and to whatever you accustom yourself you will grow accustomed to. Blessing to the owner"; another reads: "To keep your temper at first is bitter to the taste, but in the end it is sweeter than honey. Peace."[18] On twenty-six 'Abbāsid examples studied by Vera Tamari, the inscriptions are located in a variety of positions, but the majority are central. None are fully concentric, although one has an inscription around part of the bowl's circumference.[19] No such figures are yet available for Sāmānid pottery, but the overwhelming majority have concentric inscriptions around the outer edge of the object. What is more, the 'Abbāsid and Sāmānid calligraphic styles differ markedly, as we shall see shortly. In other words, there is nothing apart from the basic concept of an inscription on a white ground, to link 'Abbāsid and Sāmānid epigraphic pottery.

An explanation as to why the Mesopotamian and north-east Iranian inscribed-wares are so different can be found in their shapes. The inscribed 'Abbāsid white-wares consist mostly of small bowls with an undulating profile derived from Yue and Yue-type green-wares and Tang white-wares.[20] There is nothing Chinese, however, about the shapes of Sāmānid epigraphic pottery. The double curve of the small 'Abbāsid bowl (**Fig.8**) contrasts with the carinated shape of the large Sāmānid platter, whose sharp angles and thin,

16. Williamson (forthcoming) on distribution; cf. Rosen-Ayalon, (1974), 211, note 3, 240-41.

17. Wilkinson (n.d.), 90-127, 179-204.

18. Herzfeld in Sarre (1925), 83-86; Atil (1973), cat. no.8; Volov (1966); Grube (1976), 38-40, 59; *Survey*, ii, (1938-9), 1752; Ventrone (1974), 224, who also discusses a possible "signature" on a Sāmānid bowl.

19. Tamari (1984), 43.

20. Medley (1976), 100; Tregear (1976), esp.46ff; Lane (1947), 15.

igure 5. 'Abbāsid green-glazed relief-ware ceramic owl. Iran or Iraq, 8th-9th century. Diam. 18.6cm., t. 7.0cm. Richmond, Keir Collection. (After harleston.)

Figure 6. Bronze repoussé salver. Probably Iran, 8th century. Diam. 73.5cm. Leningrad, Hermitage Museum. (After *Survey*.)

igure 7a. Roundel from the centre a silver bowl, found in Wiatka, ossibly 8th century. Leningrad, ermitage Museum. (After mirnov.)

Figure 7b. Silver bowl, found at Klimowa, Perm. Leningrad, Hermitage Museum. (After Smirnov).

Figure 7c. Detail of repoussé roundel on base of silver bucket. Sogdian, 8th-9th century. cf. Fig.27a & 27c. (After Smirnov.)

igure 8. Opacified white-ware bowl with cobalt ainting. Iraq or Iran, 9th-10th century. Diam. .3cm. New York, Private Collection. (After rube.)

straight walls seem more appropriate to precious metal (**Figs.11, 13, 14**)).[21] No silver platters of this shape survive, but two other shapes common in Sāmānid epigraphic pottery do have extant silver parallels.

The flat-based dish with shallow rising sides can be compared to a silver salver which was found at Izgirli in Bulgaria, but which is held to be Islamic (**Figs.16 & 21**).[22] If it comes from early 11th-century Khurāsān as Melikian-Chirvani and Allan have argued, it would provide a silver prototype for the ceramic shape which was close both geographically and chronologically.[23] The second shape is the deep bowl with straight-flaring sides and, on occasion, a sharply inset foot (**Figs.15 & 19**).[24] The straightness of the thinly pared sides immediately suggests a metal prototype, and this is confirmed by the three silver bowls from the Ḥamadān hoard (**Fig.20**). A third parallel is provided by a small jug found in Samarqand which compares in shape and decorative layout with the jug from the Ḥamadān hoard (**Figs.17 & 18**).[25]

If the shapes of the Sāmānid epigraphic-wares point to an inspiration from metalwork, so too does the calligraphy. Whereas the letter forms on the 'Abbāsid pots are rounded and their outlines blurred, those on the Sāmānid are crisply delineated against the white ground. The result is reminiscent of plain, polished silver with sparse niello engraving, an aesthetic which is found on Late Roman and Byzantine silver and which, more importantly,

21. Wilkinson (n.d.), eg. 97, cat. no.17, 104, cat. no.53, 131, cat. no.1; Atil (1973), cat. nos.7 & 8.

22. Migeon (1922), who describes the salver as footless, 31 cm. in diameter and parcel-gilt. Degrand (1903), also notes that it is 4 cm. deep and weighs 1 kg. 250 gr.

23. Melikian-Chirvani (1973), 13; cf. *Arts of Islam* (1976), 162, cat. no.160. Degrand (1903), attempted to connect the burial of the Izgirli hoard, which included numerous coins of the Comnene Emperors, Alexis I, John II and Manuel I, with the defeat of the Byzantines under Basil I by the Bulgars in 1189. Marshak (1982), 170-3, has argued for a more western, probably Edessan, provenance. His argument rests, however, on two points. First he compares the Izgirli interlace with that on the interior of a silver standing cup now in the abbey of St. Maurice d'Agaune. The comparison is striking, and the d'Agaune cup proves that the design was known in the west. (Oman attributes it to Norman Sicily, but the case is far from proved.) Secondly, he compares the zig-zag feathering on the border to that on western chalices such as one found in Kiev, attributed on bare circumstantial evidence to 12th-century Norman-Sicily, Oman (1959), and one attributed to 13th-century England and now in the British Museum, Read & Tonnochy (1928), 5, cat. no.12, pl.viii. This comparison, however, is weak. The western chalices have very narrow zig-zag bands, formed by walking a scorper, whereas the Izgirli salver has long tufts which fall into clumps. A closer parallel for this would be the decoration on some Sogdian silver: e.g. Smirnov (1909), pl.134. Marshak also overlooks the animal frieze, which surely helps relate the Izgirli salver to bronze salvers probably from 13th-century Khurāsān: Melikian-Chirvani (1974).

24. Wilkinson (n.d.) *passim*; Atil (1973), cat. nos.9 & 12.

25. *Survey* (1938-39), pl.1346B; *Arts of Islam* (1976), 161-2, cat. nos.158-59; Wiet (1933), 18, 20, pls.ii & iii; Pugachenkova & Rempel' (1965).

ure 9. ʻAbbāsid lustre painted dish. Iraq, 10th tury. Diam. 37cm. Oxford, Ashmolean Museum, tlinger Collection, 1978.2146.

Figure 10. Detail of repoussé bronze tray. Sasanian or early Islamic. Diam. 56cm. Leningrad, Hermitage. (After *Survey*.)

characterizes much of the extant early Islamic silver with inscriptions.[26] The concentrically disposed calligraphy of the Ḥamadān hoard provides the closest parallel, even if the scale and ductus of the lettering differ, their forms pointing to a western Iranian provenance (**Figs.11 & 12**).[27]

It is uncertain whether the relief calligraphy on the pottery was merely the result of the slip technique, or whether it reflected a relief niello tradition, for which there is some evidence.[28] The pottery technique, though, facilitated greater fluency of writing than engraving or tracing on metal. To judge from the obliquely cut terminals and tapering serifs of the Sāmānid pottery inscriptions the slip was applied with a reed pen. The result was obviously closer to calligraphy on paper than most metalworkers could achieve, but this does not preclude the ceramic's "primary descent" from metalwork, because deference to calligraphy on paper is understandable in an area which was the first to manufacture paper in the Muslim world and which prided itself on its high standards of penmanship.[29]

26. On the ʻAbbāsid calligraphy, Herzfeld in Sarre (1925), 83-86. For the Roman and Byzantine silver with niello, Strong (1966), esp. 194-6. For the early Islamic, Smirnov (1909); Darkevich (1976).

27. *Arts of Islam*, (1976), 161-2. The calligraphic treatment of the Ḥamadān hoard silver differs from that of the grandest Sāmānid epigraphic wares. The artist has paid less attention to the balance between void and decoration within the epigraphic frieze, and instead of playing with local rhythmic contrasts between the letters, has concentrated on the overall movement of the band itself. This is a result partly of reducing the relative size of the band, and partly of enclosing it, top and bottom, with a frame. The same small scale of frieze, sometimes with a double frame, can be seen on late 10th and 11th-century descendants of Sāmānid epigraphic wares: Wilkinson (n.d.), 110, fig.3, 111, figs.5 and 7, 115, fig.15.

28. Stockholm (1985), 189-90, cat.32 of *Vikingar i Sverige* section, is a hack-silver fragment of a silver dish with a *relief*-niello inscription on the rim. The silver sprinkler in the Freer Gallery of Art has a *relief*-inscription decorated with niello on the shoulder: Atil (1985), cat. no.10.

29. cf. Flury in *Survey*, (1938-9), ii, 1752-3, who notes that the occasional occurrence of red slip-painted letters alongside the black "reminds us of manuscript calligraphy".

Figure 11. Sāmānid epigraphic black-on-white ware plate with wide everted rim. Iran, 10th century. Diam. 46.8cm., ht. 6.0cm. Washington D.C., Freer Gallery of Art, 52.11. (Photo Courtesy of the Freer Gallery of Art.)

Figure 12. Silver salver with niello inscriptions in the name of Amīr Abū'l 'Abbās Valgīr ibn Hārūn. Found at Ḥamadān. Diam. 37cm. Probably Western Iran, 11th century. (After *Survey*.)

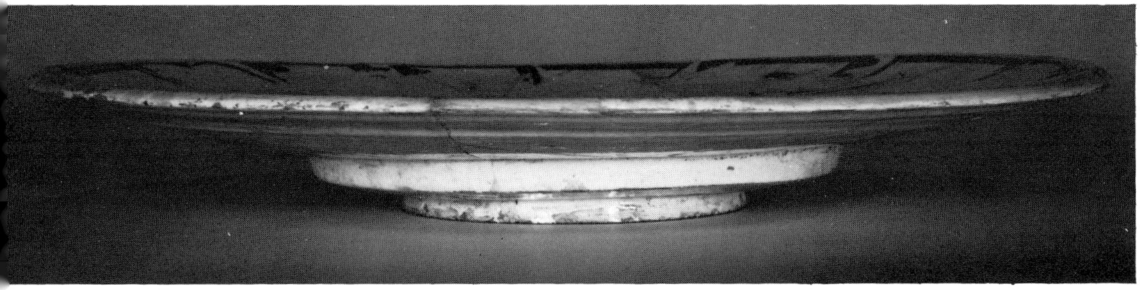

ɜure 13. Profile view of Figure 11.

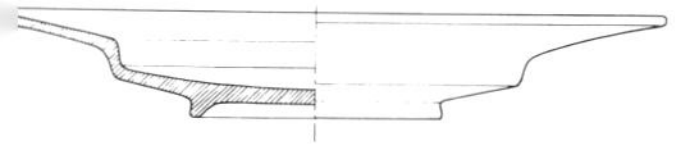

ɜure 14. Profile of Sāmānid ɡraphic black-on-white ware tter. Excavated at Nīshāpūr, h century. Diam. 42cm., ht. n. New York, Metropolitan ıseum of Art, 40.170.20. (After lkinson.)

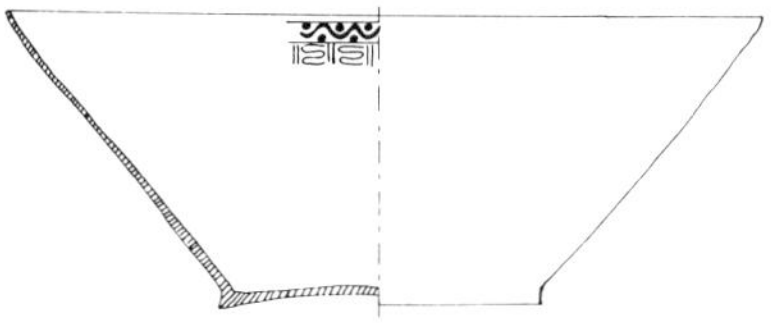

Figure 15. Sāmānid black-on-white white-ware bowl. Excavated at Nīshāpūr, 10th century. Diam. 32cm., ht. 11cm. Tehran, Muze-i Iran Bastan. (After Wilkinson.)

Figure 16. Profile of fragmentary Sāmānid black-on-white ware bowl without a footring. Excavated at Nīshāpūr, 10th century. Diam. 46cm., ht. 8cm. New York, Metropolitan Museum of Art, 38.40.246. (After Wilkinson.)

An apparent difference between the pottery and silver lies in the legends. The inscriptions of many of the niello-inscribed silver objects are dedicatory, with the patron's name and titles and standard blessings. None of the pottery, on the other hand, is personalized, and the legends often consist, as we have seen, of aphorisms. This need not be taken, though, as evidence that the pottery tradition was independent of the silver. In the first place, silver vessels were more likely to be special commissions and bear unique inscriptions, whereas mass-produced pottery required inscriptions of general appeal.[30] Secondly, at least two of the handful of extant silver vessels have aphoristic inscriptions, although, admittedly, neither is similar in shape to known Sāmānid pottery. One is a flask in the name of a high official, as yet unidentified, who styles himself "Client of the Prince of Believers" (*mawlā amīr al-mu'minīn*) and reads "Faithfulness is found with him who is not privy to

30. That silver plate was not always personalized is proved by the hoard formerly in the Harari collection and now in the L.A. Mayer Memorial Museum, Jerusalem: *Survey*, (1938-9), pls.1350-52. Ventrone (1974), 223, note 11, raises the question whether the benedictory phrases on Sāmānid ceramics reflect their use on metalwork.

cowardice".[31] The other is a flask, which was found at Malaya Anikova in 1959, and which bears the terse directive, adapted from Qur'ān IV, 4,: "Eat and drink in health and wholesomeness". Similar inscriptions occur on 10th-century pottery from Samarqand and on silver and niello spoons of the 10th-11th century.[32]

In terms, therefore, of the location and proportion of its inscriptions, occasionally in terms of their contents, and most importantly in terms of its shapes and overall aesthetic, Sāmānid epigraphic pottery, which bears little relation to previous ceramic traditions, can be related to early Islamic silverwork. No one extant silver object offers parallels for all of the characteristics of the pottery, but one may suggest that Sāmānid silver, were it to survive, would present a greater concentration of parallels. It may seem presumptuous to posit a major group of Sāmānid silver when none is in fact known, but there are several arguments in favour.

First, the Sāmānids controlled the most productive silver mines in the Muslim world in the 10th century, notably in the Zarafshān valley of Sogdia, and at Panjhīr, north of Kābul. Descriptions of the mines at Panjhīr, which were discovered in the second half of the 9th century, conjure up images of a Klondyke.[33] Secondly, silver objects are attributable to Khurāsān and Transoxiana just *after* Sāmānid rule. These are a tray inscribed in the name of a Khwarazmshāh, probably Abū Ibrāhīm who reigned between 1034 and 1041, and a flask in the name of an early 11th-century vizier of Balkh.[34] Marshak has argued that they were manufactured in Balkh, which not only was the administrative centre for Panjhīr and neighbouring mines, but also had an important silversmiths' quarter with its own mosque.[35] Although these particular objects differ in shape and calligraphic style from the 10th-century Sāmānid potteries, they share the same aesthetic principle.

Thirdly, there was a sizable production of silver vessels *before* the Sāmānids. The Sogdian merchant princes, whose territory lay at the western end of the Central Asian desert routes with capitals at Samarqand, Varakhshah and Panjikent, had a silver industry which lasted into the 8th century A.D., when they were defeated by the Muslim armies.[36] The Muslim conquerors seized quantities of silver and gold as booty, and in all probability

31. Smirnov (1909), no.142; Marshak (1976), 162. The patron's name preceded by another title, al-Amīr al-Jalīl, is Ibn 'Alī al-Ḥasan ibn Ya'qūb al-[Satawi?], van Berchem (1909).

32. Marshak (1976), and n.b. fn.39, for references to pottery; Tashkhodhzaev (1967) 41; Ventrone (1974), 226. For the spoon, *Survey* (1938-9), pl.1351C. For the use of maxims on bronze vessels from Khurāsān, Baer (1983), 213.

33. Dunlop (1957), 40-41; Allan (1979), 13-15.

34. Smirnov (1909), no.150 and 147 esp.; van Berchem (1909); the identification of the patrons is due to Marshak (1976), 163-6.

35. Marshak (1976), 164.

36. Marshak (1971).

goldsmithing continued.[37] In 125/742 the Umayyad Caliph Walīd II ordered his governor, Naṣr ibn Sayyār, to have gold and silver jugs manufactured for him in Khurāsān.[38] Some fifty years later, the governor of Khurāsān, 'Alī ibn 'Isā ibn Mahan sent the Caliph Harūn al-Rashīd a thousand Turkish slave-girls each carrying either a gold or silver goblet.[39] During the Sāmānid period, when the amīr Rashīd's palace in Bukhara was looted and burned in 350/961, al-Narshakhī writes that "everything burned including every beautiful object of gold and silver". Yet within a year the palace had been burned down again, though on this occasion "it was found that nothing had been lost save one gold cup".[40]

Sogdian silver survives in some quantity, and there is also evidence from Sogdian sites near Samarqand, in particular Kafir Kala, that silver was copied in ceramic in the seventh and eighth centuries A.D.[41] It would therefore not be surprising to find that Sogdian silver fashions continued into the Muslim period and in turn influenced pottery. The practice of copying metal forms in ceramic can be shown to have continued at Baikand, where a local green-glazed ceramic was excavated together with a kiln datable to the 10th century by associated Sāmānid coins.[42] A Sāmānid 10th-century ring-handled cup, found at Samarqand, is a further case in point: it is not only a pottery modification of a standard east Sogdian silver shape, but it has parallels in an inscribed silver cup of the 11th-century (**Figs.22 & 23**).[43]

Given, therefore, that the Sāmānids controlled the most productive silver

37. When Qutaiba ibn Muslim seized Baikand in about 705 A.D., it is related that "he found an idol of silver in a temple with a weight of 4,000 *dirhams*. He also found silver goblets. When he gathered everything it amounted to 150,000 *mithqāls*": Frye (1954), 45. In about 750 A.D. Abū Muslim's general Abū Dāwūd Khālid ibn Ibrāhīm killed the local Sogdian Ikhshīd of Kīsh and looted his treasures said to include "Chinese" engraved and gilded vessels: Ṭabarī (1879-1901), iii, 79. Kahle (1934), 5-7, strangely, takes these to be porcelain. For the attribution of several figural silver dishes to post-Sogdian workshops, Marshak (1971).

38. *Abārīq al-dhahab wa'l fiḍḍa*: Ṭabarī (1879-1901), ii, 1765. The order also included statuary: cf. Hamilton, (1972), 155.

39. Baihaqi (1345/1966), 538.

40. Frye (1954), 26-7.

41. Marshak (1961). Even an unassuming type of bronze ewer was copied in ceramic. For the ceramic analogue, *Survey* (1938-39), i, 678, fig.233, where it is dated to the 7th-9th century. For the metal, Allan (1982), 41-2; Darkevich (1976), pl.45.7. Another example was found with a hoard of Muslim coins in Birka in Sweden: Stockholm (1985), 188 cat. no.21, and colour plate, and 115, cat. no.23 for an example from the al-Sabbah collection.

42. Kondratieva (1961).

43. Tashkhodzhaev (1967), fig.8; Darkevich (1976), pl.33. For another example, but illustrated without showing its ring-handle and thumb-piece, Hayward (1976), cat. no.286. The Sogdian ring-handled cups often had a double-curve profile; this may have continued into 10th-century products, as a pottery example found in Gotland, and believed to have been buried c.900 A.D., seems to follow the older type: Arne (1914), 196-8. For the high-tin bronze example discovered by Martin at Surgut in Siberia: Arne *loc.cit*; Stockhold (1985), 183; cf. in general Baer (1983), 191.

Figure 17. Sāmānid epigraphic ware jug from Samarqand, 10th century. Ht. not recorded. Leningrad, Hermitage Museum. (After Pugachenkova & Rempel'.)

Figure 18. Silver jug from the Ḥamadān hoard with niello inscriptions in the name of Valgīr ibn Hārūn. Probably West Iran, 11th century. Ht. 12cm. Tehran, Gulistan Museum. (After *Survey*.)

Figure 19. Sāmānid epigraphic black-on-white ware bowl. Lead-glazed, slip-painted ceramic. 10th century. Diam. 21.0cm., ht. 7.4cm. Richmond, Keir Collection. (After Charleston.)

Figure 20. Silver bowl from the Ḥamadān hoard. Dia 19cm. (After *Survey*.)

Figure 21. Silver salver, engraved with areas of gilding, found at Izgirli in Bulgaria. Probably Khurāsān, 11th century. Diam. 31.5cm., ht. 4.7cm. Paris, Bibliothèque Nationale, Cabinet des Médailles. (After Migeon.)

mines in the Muslim world, and that their territories are known to have produced silver vessels both *before* and *after* the Sāmānid period, it is difficult to imagine that the Sāmānids themselves produced no silver vessels. Sāmānid industry needs, however, to be seen in a broader economic context. This requires a brief excursus on the numismatic evidence.

The distribution of Sāmānid coins points to substantial flows westwards. Massive quantities of Muslim coins have been found in Russia, Poland and Scandinavia.[44] In European Russia, for example, more than 120,000 Islamic coins have been unearthed. In Scandinavia the total is some 105,000, almost all from Sweden; the original figure must have been considerably higher, though, because analysis of Viking armlets from Birka has revealed a gold and bismuth content similar to that of Sāmānid coinage, which suggests that many were made from imported Muslim coin.[45] Indeed, before about 970 A.D., Muslim coins represent 60 per cent. of the weight of all these coin hoards.[46]

As regards chronology and provenance, two main phases of imports can be identified. The first is from the late 8th-century to about 820; the second, with a larger number of coins involved, ranges from about 850 to about 925 A.D., imports becoming rare after the 960s. There is thus a gap of about 30 years between 820 and 850, which has recently been connected with the massive architectural development at Samarra in Iraq.[47] The first phase

44. The bibliography on this subject is vast. To cite only a few recent studies: Lieber (1981); Noonan (1981); Cahen (1979); Herrmann (1982), 87-112.

45. Arrhenius (1972-3).

46. Lieber (1981), 22.

47. Hodges & Whitehouse (1983), 123-57.

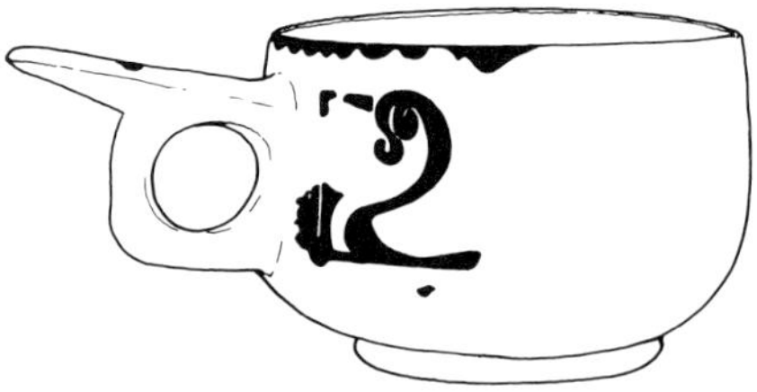

Figure 22. Sāmānid pottery ring-handled cup. 10th century. (After Tashkhodhzaev.)

Figure 23. Silver ring-handled cup. Iran, 11th century. (After Darkevich.)

consists overwhelmingly of "'Abbāsid" coins, either from Iraq or from the western provinces of the Muslim world; many of these coins were issued some considerable time before they were buried. The second phase, after about 850 A.D., sees a shift eastwards, with the majority of coins being Ṭāhirid and Sāmānid, issued for the most part shortly before they were buried.[48] This corresponds to a shift in the trade routes from the Caucasus to further east, encouraged by the development of the Panjhīr mines in the second half of the 9th century. The routes took advantage of the Russian river system, and three main centres of trade were Khwarazm, the Khazar capital of Itil, at the junction of the Lower Volga and the Caspian Sea, and the Bulgar capital, further up the Volga, the Sāmānids purchasing Russian furs and slaves in particular.[49] The decline in trade in the second half of the 10th century was due in part to external factors, such as the destruction of the Khazar emporium, and the collapse of the Bulgar state, which was attacked by the rising Varangian power of Kiev under Sviatoslav in 965 A.D. It was due also to the decline of Sāmānid power and their loss of the Panjhīr silver mines in about 975 A.D. Moreover, Dekówna's analysis of Russian explorations in silver mining regions in Central Asia has shown that the second most productive silver mines in the Muslim world after Panjhīr, those at Ilāq, declined due to the exhaustion of the beds, although other beds failed to be exploited fully, and were not reopened until later in the 11th and 12th centuries. Dependent smelting communities also declined towards the end of

48. Noonan (1981); Sawyer (1962), 83-116, 214-19, on the basis of Sture Bolin's unpublished researches. For the declining revenues of the 'Abbāsid caliphate and economic decline in 10th-century Iraq, Waines (1977).

49. For maps of Viking trade in the East and a description of the Russian river system used in east-west trade, Jones (1968), 160-61, 252-4; Foote and Wilson (1970), 224-9; Arne (1914), 14-17. For commodities traded, Jacob (1891); Dennett (1968), 137. For Khazar trade, Golden (1980), i, 107-111.

ure 24. Geometrical strapwork
oration on a Sāmānid pottery
. 10th century. (After
hkhodhzaev.)

Figure 25. Detail of the Izgirli salver. cf. Figure 21.

Figure 26. Stucco decoration from a palace of the Sāmānid period, excavated at Afrāsiyāb/Samarqand. (After Achrarov & Rempel'.)

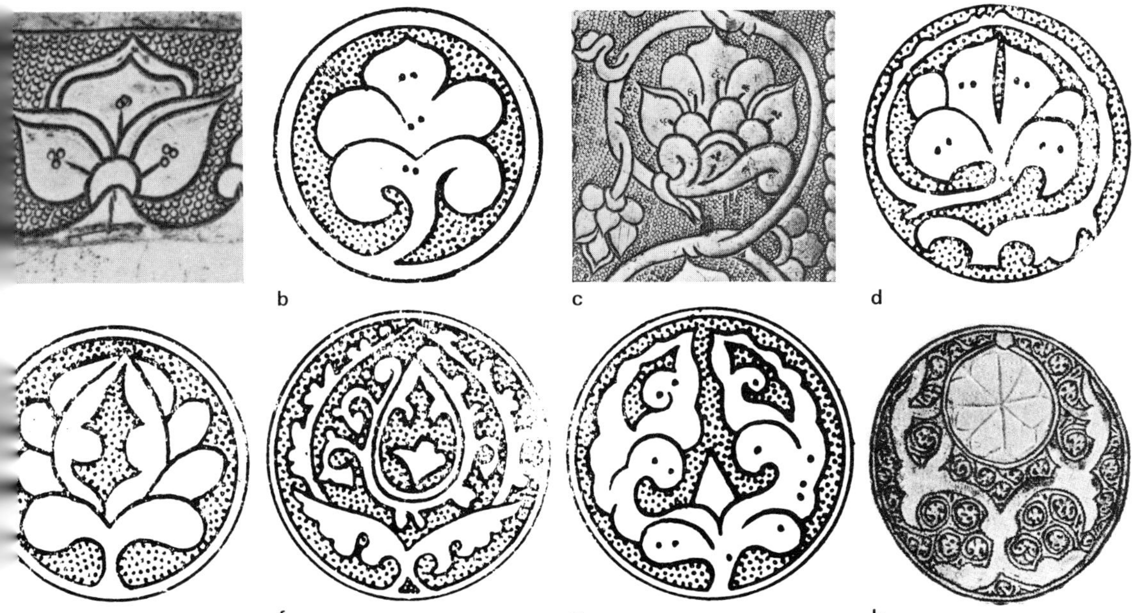

ure 27a-h. a & c. Details from a silver bucket. Sog-
, 8th-9th century. Leningrad, Hermitage. (After
rnov.) **b, d-g**. Roundels from Sāmānid pottery from
arqand. (After Tashkhodhzaev.) **h**. Roundel from a silver and niello bottle in the name of Abū Ibrāhīm. Khurāsān or Transoxiana, 11th century. Leningrad, Hermitage. (After Smirnov.)

the 10th century. Less important mining regions in the River Talus valley in Kirghizistan and in the Pamir mountains in Tajikistan were at their most productive between the 9th and 11th centuries, and especially in the 11th when the Ilāq mines were at low production.[50]

Be that as it may, the exodus of Sāmānid silver suggests that silver was much less expensive than it was in the west. This would have encouraged the operation of Gresham's law, whereby foreign merchants removed and hoarded silver coinage, and left a debased coinage in local circulation. This seems to be confirmed by the minting of alloyed coins in Bukhara, known according to al-Narshakhī as the *ghiṭrīfī*;[51] and Khwarazmian merchants imported silver from the Sāmānids which they hoarded.[52]

It might be assumed that the fluctuating value of silver in the central Islamic lands from the early 7th century to the mid-10th century was directly reflected in the changing dirham-dinar rates. A graph of these rates, **Table 1**, provides a dramatic picture, but a word of caution is essential, on three counts. First, the rates, which are cited here from Ashtor, are based on documentary evidence of dubious interpretation, because it is often unclear whether the references are to actual coins or moneys-of-account.[53] Secondly, the ratios are drawn from Iraq, but Iraqi conditions cannot be taken to have applied universally. The currency fluctuations in Khurāsān and Transoxiana, where the most productive silver mines were situated, undoubtedly differed; but comparable references for these areas have yet to be collected. Thirdly, nominal dirham-dinar rates are of little value unless one knows the variations in the fineness and weight standard of both currencies.[54]

A preliminary attempt was therefore made by Sture Bolin to establish the ratios between the real values of gold and of silver, **Table 2**. Bolin's pioneering work, based on research carried out almost fifty years ago, took account of some of the weight changes, but seems to have made no allowance for the variable of fineness.[55] It therefore requires re-examination in the light of detailed numismatic research. Meanwhile, his graph, even if inaccurate as regards *specific* ratios, provides a suggestive picture of the *general* movement of the ratios between gold and silver values. Two conclusions emerge which are of significance to the art historian.

The graph shows a rise between 650 and 850 and a marked fall between 850 and about 930. The rise indicates an increase in the value of gold and

50. Dekówna (1971); *pace* Lieber (1981), 24.

51. Frye (1949); Blake (1937), 300-305.

52. Linder Welin (1961). On the possible development of an outsize dirham coinage to replace that exported to the West, Mitchiner (1973); cf. Lowick (1977).

53. Ashtor (1961), 25; cf. Watson (1967), 22-28, 51.

54. cf. Bates (1979), esp. 10-11.

55. Bolin (1968), 237-9.

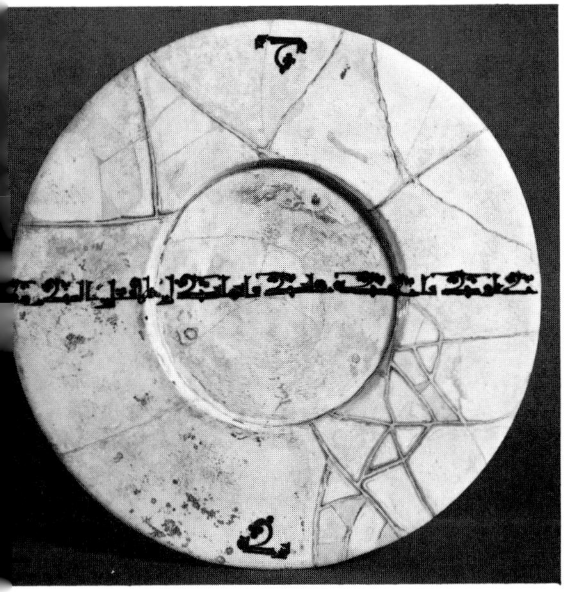

ure 28. Sāmānid epigraphic black-on-white ware tter. 10th century. Diam. 42.7cm., ht. 5.0cm. ashington D.C., Freer Gallery of Art, 54.16. (Photo urtesy of the Freer Gallery of Art.)

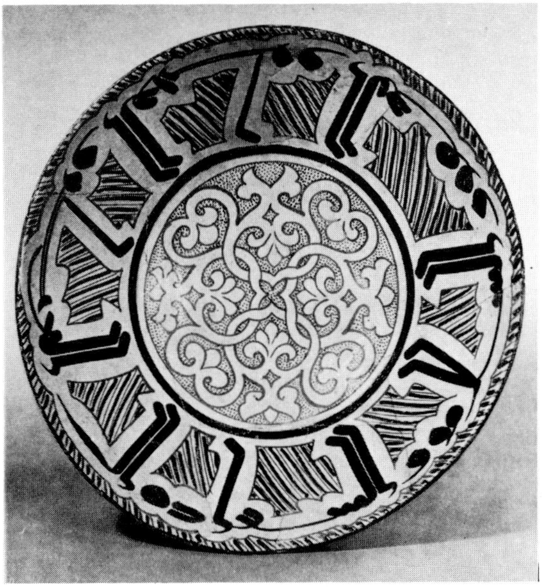

Figure 29. Sāmānid epigraphic ware bowl. Lead-glazed, slip-painted ceramic. Found at Nīshāpūr, but probably Transoxanian. Diam. 35.8cm., ht. 10.8cm. New York, Metropolitan Museum of Art, 40.170.15. (After Wilkinson.)

inversely a decline in the value of silver to gold.[56] One might suspect, first, that as silver became cheaper between 650 and 850, so it became more available for use as tableware. It is impossible, however, on the basis of surviving objects to establish any trends in silversmithing output; nevertheless, the increasing theological censure against gold and silver utensils, which Dr Juynboll has shown in this volume became codified in *ḥadīth* in the first decades of the eighth century, points to their more widespread use, for increasing licence is often echoed in increased opprobrium.[57]

The second conclusion relates to the fall in the value of gold after 850 and the corresponding rise in the value of silver. The reason may be a rapid influx of gold from Nubia and the trans-Sahara,[58] but it may also be connected with the exodus of silver already noted in precisely this period. The graph can be compared to a graph of the chronological distribution of Muslim silver coins

56. Bolin (1968), 237-9; cf. Lieber (1981), 23-24, who criticizes Bolin's theory on the grounds that an increased influx of African gold would have caused the value of gold to fall in relation to silver, at a time when Bolin argues for a fall in silver's value. In a bimetallic monetary system, however, the gold and silver ratio can be modified by adjustments to either currency or both, and it may be relevant that the Būyid Rukn al-Dawlah debased the gold coinage in the 10th century: Mez (1937), 475.

57. On some silver bowls attributable to 8th-century Mazandaran, Ghirshman (1957), Henning (1959).

58. Lombard (1977).

found in Gotland, **Table 3**.[59] This shows a rise in the level of exports after 850, that is, at a time when silver was at a low value, and a marked decline in the number of coins after 910, when silver's value had strengthened. There is also the possibility that silver flowed from the Sāmānid realm to Tang China, where, as Professor Dudbridge underlined in his contribution to the *Pots & Pans* colloquium, the ratio of gold to silver c.850 was 1:10. Silver in Tang China was, therefore, considerably more expensive than it was in the eastern Muslim world, where Bolin estimates a ratio of 1:17.[60] Some Islamic silver coins were imported into Byzantium and either restruck or melted down, particularly in the late 8th and early 9th centuries and for a few years in the late 10th century.[61]

Whatever the factors, the rise in the price of silver in the Sāmānid realm would have discouraged the production of silver vessels, and encouraged the production of substitutes. It is surely no coincidence that the 10th century, when so much silver disappeared to the west and the price of silver rose against gold, saw an upsurge in pottery production under both the 'Abbāsids and the Sāmānids. Although there is still considerable uncertainty about the details and implications of these economic developments, the evidence seems to suggest a silver production in times of plenty and a pottery production as silver prices rose. It would have been understandable for the pottery replacements to follow the aesthetic of the silver vessels.

This hypothesis can be tested by returning to the objects and considering some of the non-epigraphic decoration on the regional ceramics and silver, namely *geometrical strapwork*, *medallion motifs*, and *background devices*.

Geometrical strapwork is frequently used to define the compositional structure of Afrāsiyāb/Samarqand pottery (**Fig.24**), but rarely occurs on extant silver with the exception of the Berlin platter (**Fig.4**). There is, however, one striking parallel—the Izgirli dish (**Fig.25**) (cf. **Fig.26**).[62] Moreover, the *palmette medallion motifs* common on Afrāsiyāb/Samarqand pottery, with their often fleshy rounded leaves, and sparse dotting, are close cousins of the motifs on Sogdian silver (**Fig.27a-h**). It is common for these palmettes on the pottery to be

59. Sawyer (1962), 214-19.

60. Thirty-four finds of Sasanian coins numbering a total of 1,178 have been recorded in China; of these a quarter are Arab-Sasanian, but I am not aware whether Ṭāhirid or Sāmānid coins have also been discovered: Nai (1974); Nai (1980); but cf. Frye (1965), 72.

61. Gordus and Metcalf (1970-2).

62. For the Izgirli salver and its design, see above, notes 22 and 23. A caveat is required, however, because a comparable, though not identical, design of two interlocking triangles and circular strapwork occurs on a stucco panel from Afrāsiyāb/Samarqand (**Fig.26**). The fact that this composition was common to a variety of media weakens, but does not preclude, the argument that the pottery was indebted to the metalwork: Akhrarov & Rempel' (1971), fig.13. I am grateful to Dr Melikian-Chirvani for kindly lending me a copy of this book.

set against a stippled ground, a practice which at once recalls the dot-matting used by goldsmiths, including the Sogdian.[63]

Indeed, Sogdian silverwork has been divided into stylistic zones; the more westerly, from north-east Iran, is characterized by figures set against a plain ground, while the more easterly group makes greater use of stippled backgrounds, being more closely related to Tang silver. There are divisions according to shape as well, but these need not concern us here. The salient point is that Sogdian silver attributed to Samarqand and further east uses textured, ring or dot-matted, grounds.[64]

Whether these regional stylistic tendencies survived into 10th-century metalwork cannot be answered directly. The hypothesis that Sāmānid epigraphic-wares depended on silver prototypes allows us, however, to speculate that the use of stippling on pottery would coincide with its use on silver; in other words, that Transoxanian ceramics would use stippling more than the Khurāsāni. This is, in fact, the case. Sāmānid epigraphic-wares from Nīshāpūr have inscriptions set against undecorated grounds (**Figs.11, 19, 28**), whereas their counterparts from Afrāsiyāb/Samarqand often have the calligraphy surrounded by contour panels filled with stippling (**Fig.29**).

Sāmānid epigraphic pottery appears, therefore, to owe its distinctive shapes and decorative repertoire to local silversmithing traditions. More arguably, increased pottery production may have been a response to a decline in silversmithing which was due to a rise in the value of silver. Neither 'Abbāsid Iraqi nor Chinese ceramics exerted an influence on this one group of Sāmānid pottery, whatever their effect on other Sāmānid wares.[65]

Chinese ceramics had their rôle to play in the burgeoning of the ceramic industry in the Near East in the 9th and 10th centuries. But the *lux ex oriente* should not blind us to the brilliance of the silver close at home.[66]

63. Tashkhodzhaev (1967), pls.15-16. cf. Arne (1914), 117-19, and 130f.

64. Marshak (1971); but for relations with Tang China cf. Rawson (1982), esp. note 36

65. cf Lane (1939), 62, on the limited influence of Chinese wares in north-west Iran.

66. Since the above was written Miss Zelfa Hourani kindly drew my attention to G.B. Shiskina, *Glazurovannaya Keramika Sogda*, Tashkent, 1979. The author has also drawn parallels between Sāmānid ceramics and silver, but almost exclusively in the figural types.

Bibliography

Akhrarov & Rempel' (1971)	Akhrarov, I., and Rempel', L.I., *Reznoi Stuk Afrasyaba*, Tashkent, 1971.
Allan (1979)	Allan, J., *Persian Metal Technology 700-1300 A.D.*, Oxford, 1979.

Allan (1982)	Allan, J., *Nishapur: Metalwork of the Early Islamic Period*, Metropolitan Museum of Art, New York, 1982.
Arne (1914)	Arne, T.J., "La Suède et l'Orient. Etudes Archéologiques sur les Relations de la Suède et de l'Orient pendant l'Âge des Vikings", *Archives d'Etudes Orientales*, vol.8, Uppsala, 1914.
Arrhenius (1972-3)	Arrhenius, B., *et al.*, "Arabiskt Silver och Nordiska Vikingasmycken", *Tor*, 15, 1972-3, pp.151-60.
Arts of Islam (1976)	*Arts of Islam*, London, 1976.
Ashtor (1961)	Ashtor, E., "Essai sur les Prix et les Salaires dans l'Empire Califien", *Rivista degli Studi Orientali*, 36, 1961, pp.19-69.
Atil (1973)	Atil, E., *Ceramics from the World of Islam. Freer Gallery of Art*, Washington, 1973.
Atil (1985)	Atil, E., *et al.*, *Islamic Metalwork in the Freer Gallery of Art*, Washington D.C., 1985.
Baihaqī (1345/1966)	Baihaqī, Abū' al-Ḥasan 'Alī ibn Zaid, *Tārīkh-i Baihaq*, 2nd edn., Tehran, 1345/1966.
Bates (1979)	Bates, M., "Islamic Numismatics", *Middle East Studies Association Bulletin*, 13.1, July, 1979, pp.3-21.
Blackburn & Metcalf (1981)	Blackburn, M.A.S., and Metcalf, D.M., eds., *Viking-Age Coinage in the Northern Lands. The Sixth Oxford Symposium on Coinage and Monetary History*, Part 1, BAR International Series 122 (i), Oxford, 1981.
Blake (1937)	Blake, R., "The Circulation of Silver in the Moslem East down to the Mongol Epoch", *Harvard Journal of Asiatic Studies*, 2, 1937, pp.291-328.
Bolin (1968)	Bolin, S., "Mohammed, Charlemagne and Ruric", *Scandinavian Economic History Review*, 1, 1953, pp.5-39, reprinted in Hübinger (1968), pp.223-65.
Cahen (1979)	Cahen, C., "Contribution à l'Étude de la Circulation Monétaire en Orient au Milieu du Moyen Âge", *Annales Islamologiques*, 15, 1979, pp.37-46.
Charleston (1979)	Charleston, R., ed., *Masterpieces of Western Ceramic Art. IV, Islamic Pottery*, Tokyo, 1979.
Darkevich (1976)	Darkevich, B.P., *Khudozhestvennii Metal Vostoka VIII-XIII vv*, Moscow, 1976.
Degrand (1903)	Degrand, M., "Le Trésor d'Izgherli", *Comptes-rendus de l'Académie des Inscriptions et Belles-Lettres*, 31, 1903, pp.390-96.
Dekówna (1971)	Dekówna, M., "Stan Badan nad Górnictwen Srebra i tzw. Kryzysem Srebra w Azji Środkowej", (with a summary in French), *Archeologia Polski*, 16, 1971, pp.483-502.
Dennett (1968)	Dennett, D.C., *Pirenne and Muhammad*, *Speculum*, 23, 1948, pp.165-90, reprinted Hübinger, 1968, pp.120-59.
Dunlop (1957)	Dunlop, D.M., "Sources of Gold and Silver in Islam according to al-Hamdānī (10th century A.D.)", *Studia Islamica*, 8, 1957, pp.28-49.
Foote & Wilson (1970)	Foote, P. and Wilson, D.M., *The Viking Achievement*, London, 1970.
Frye (1949)	Frye, R., "Notes on the Early Coinage of Transoxiana", *Numismatic Notes and Monographs*, 113, New York, 1949.

Frye (1954)	Frye, R., *The History of Bukhara. Translated from a Persian Abridgement of the Arabic Original by Narshakhī*, Cambridge, Mass., 1954.
Frye (1965)	Frye, R., *Bukhara: The Medieval Achievement*, Norman, Oklahoma, 1965.
Ghirshman (1957)	Ghirshman, R., "Argenterie d'un Seigneur Sassanide", *Ars Orientalis*, 2, 1957, pp.76-82.
Golden (1980)	Golden, P.B., *Khazar Studies*, Budapest, 1980, 2 vols.
Gordus & Metcalf (1970-2)	Gordus, A.A., and Metcalf, D.M., "The Alloy of the Byzantine Miliaresion and the Question of the Reminting of Islamic Silver", *Hamburger Beiträge zur Numismatik*, 24/26, 1970-2, pp.9-36.
Grube (1966)	Grube, E., *The World of Islam*, London, 1966.
Grube (1976)	Grube, E., *Islamic Pottery of the Eighth to the Fifteenth Century in the Keir Collection*, London, 1976.
Hamilton (1972)	Hamilton, R., "Pastimes of a Caliph: Another Glimpse", *Levant*, 4, 1972, pp.155-56
Henning (1959)	Henning, W., "New Pahlevi Inscriptions on Silver Vessels", *Bulletin of the School of Oriental and African Studies*, 22, 1959, pp.132-34
Herrmann *et al.* (1982)	Herrmann, J., *Wikinger und Slawen. Zur Frühgeschichte der Ostseevölker*, Neumünster, 1982.
Hodges & Whitehouse (1983)	Hodges, R., and Whitehouse, D., *Mohammed, Charlemagne and the Origins of Europe*, London, 1983.
Hübinger (1968)	Hübinger, P.E., ed., *Bedeutung und Rolle des Islam beim Übergang von Altertum zum Mittelalter*, Darmstadt, 1968.
Jacob (1891)	Jacob, G., *Welche Handelsartikel bezogen die Araber des Mittelalters aus den nordisch-baltischen Ländern*, Berlin, 1891.
Jones (1968)	Jones, G., *A History of the Vikings*, Oxford 1968.
Kahle (1934)	Kahle, P., "Islamische Quellen zum Chinesischen Porzellan", *Zeitschrift der Deutschen Morgenländischen Gesellschaft*, 88, 1934, pp.1-45.
Kondratieva (1961)	Kondratieva, F.A., "Keramika s Zelenoi Polivoi iz Paikenda", *Trudi Gosudarstvennogo Ermitazha*, 6, 1961, pp.216-27.
Lane (1939)	Lane, A., "Glazed Relief-ware of the Ninth-Century", *Ars Islamica*, 6, 1939, pp.56-65.
Lane (1946-7)	Lane, A., "Sung wares and the Seljuq Pottery of Persia", *Transactions of the Oriental Ceramic Society*, 22, 1946-7, pp.19-30.
Lane (1947)	Lane, A., *Early Islamic Pottery*, London, 1947.
Lieber (1981)	Lieber, A.E., "International Trade and Coinage in the Northernlands during the Early Middle Ages: an Introduction", in Blackburn and Metcalf, (1981), pp.1-34.
Linder Welin (1961)	Linder Welin, U.S., "Coins from Khwārazm and the Swedish Viking Hoards", *Meddelanden fran Lunds Universitets Historiska Museum*, 1961, pp.155-79.
Lombard (1947)	Lombard, M., "L'Or Musulman du VIIe au XIe siècle", *Annales. Economies, Sociétés, Civilisations*, 2, 1947, pp.143-60.
Lowick (1977)	Lowick, N., "On the Dating of Samanid Outsize Dirhams", *Numismatic Circular*, 85, 1977, pp.204-6.

Marshak (1961)	Marshak, B.I., "Blyyanye Toreutike na Sogdyiskuyou Keramiky VII-VIII BB." *Trudi Gosudarstvennogo Ermitazha*, 5, 1961, pp.176-201.
Marshak (1971)	Marshak, B.I., *Sogdiiskoe Serebro*, Moscow, 1971.
Marshak (1976)	Marshak, B.I., "Serebrannye sosudy X-XI vv, ich znachenie dlja periodizacii iskusstva Irana i Srednej Azii" *Iskusstvo i archeologija Irana. II. Vsesojuznaja konferencija*, Doklady, Moscow, 1976.
Marshak (1982)	Marshak, B.I., "Zur Toreutik der Kreuzfahrer", *Metallkunst von der Spätantike bis zum ausgehenden Mittelalter*, ed. A. Effenberger, Berlin, D.D.R., 1982, pp.166-84.
Medley (1976)	Medley, M., *The Chinese Potter*, Oxford, 1976.
Melikian-Chirvani (1973)	Melikian-Chirvani, A.S., *Le Bronze Iranien, Musée des Arts Décoratifs*, Paris, 1973.
Melikian-Chirvani (1974)	Melikian-Chirvani, A.S., "Les Bronzes du Khorasan I", *Studia Iranica*, 3, 1974, pp.29-50.
Mez (1937)	Mez, A., *The Renaissance of Islam*, trans. Salahuddin Khuda Baksh and D.S., Margoliouth, Patna, 1937.
Migeon (1922)	Migeon, G., "Orfèvrerie d'argent de style orientale trouvée en Bulgarie", *Syria*, vol.3, 1922, pp.141-44.
Mitchiner (1973)	Mitchiner, M., *The Multiple Dirhams of Mediaeval Afghanistan*, Sanderstead, 1973.
Nai (1974)	Nai, Xia, "A Survey of Sassanian Silver Coins found in China", *Kaogu Xuebao*, 1, 1974, pp.93-109, in Chinese, with an English résumé.
Nai (1980)	Nai, Xia, "Sassanian Objects Recently Found in China", *Social Sciences in China*, 1, no.2, 1980, pp.153-61.
Noonan (1981)	Noonan, T., "Ninth-Century Dirham Hoards from European Russia: a Preliminary Analysis" in Blackburn & Metcalf (1981), pp.47-118.
Oman (1959)	Oman, C., "Two Siculo-Norman Silver Cups", *Burlington Magazine*, 101, 1959, pp.350-53.
Pézard (1920)	Pézard, M., *La Céramique Archaïque de l'Islam et ses Origines*, Paris, 1920.
Pugachenkova & Rempel' (1965)	Pugachenkova, G.A. and Rempel', L.J., *Istoriya isskusstv Uzbekistana s Drevneyshikh Vremen do Serediny Dnadnatzatogo Veka*, Moscow, 1965.
Raby (1982)	Raby, J., "Silver and Gold" in *Tulips, Arabesques and Turbans. Decorative Arts from the Ottoman Empire*, ed. Y. Petsopoulos, London, 1982.
Raby & Yücel (1983)	Raby, J. and Yücel, Ü., "Blue-and-White, Celadon and Whitewares: Iznik's Debt to China", *Oriental Art*, 29, 1983, pp.38-48.
Raby & Yücel (1986)	Raby, J., and Yücel, Ü., "The Earliest Treasury Registers", in ed. J. Ayers, *Chinese Ceramics in the Topkapı Saray Museum, Istanbul. A Complete Catalogue*, London, 1986, vol.I, pp.77-81.
Rawson (1982)	Rawson, J., "The Ornament on Chinese Silver of the Tang Dynasty (A.D. 618-906)", *British Museum Occasional Paper*, No.40, London, 1982.
Read & Tonnochy (1928)	Read, C.H., and Tonnochy, A.B., *Catalogue of the Silver Plate, Medieval and Later, bequeathed to the British Museum by Sir Augustus Wollaston Franks, K.C.B.*, London, 1928.

Rosen-Ayalon (1974)	Rosen-Ayalon, M., *La Poterie Islamique. Ville Royale de Suse, IV, Mémoires de la Délégation Archéologique en Iran*, Tome L, Paris, 1974.
Sarre (1925)	Sarre, F., *Die Keramik von Samarra*, Berlin, 1925.
Sawyer (1962)	Sawyer, P., *The Age of the Vikings*, London, 1962.
Smirnov (1909)	Smirnov, V.I., *Atlas d'Argenterie Orientale*, St. Petersburg, 1909.
Stockholm (1985)	*Islam. Konst och Kultur*, Exhibition Catalogue, Statens Historiska Museum, Stockholm, 1985.
Strong (1966)	Strong, D.E., *Greek and Roman Gold and Silver Plate*, London, 1966.
Survey (1938-9)	*A Survey of Persian Art from Prehistoric Times to the Present*, ed. A.U. Pope and P. Ackerman, Oxford, 1938-39.
Ṭabarī (1879-1901)	Ṭabarī, Muḥammad ibn Jarīr, *Annales quos scripsit Abu Djafar Mohammed ibn Djarir at-Tabari*, ed. M.J. de Goeje, 15 vols, Leyden, 1879-1901.
Tamari (1984)	Tamari, V., *Ninth-Century White Mesopotamian Ceramic Ware with Blue Decoration*, M.Phil. thesis, University of Oxford, 1984, unpublished.
Tashkhodzhaev (1967)	Tashkhodzhaev, Sh. S., *Khudozhestvennaya polivnaya keramika Samarkanda ix-nachala xiiivv*, Tashkent, 1967.
Tregear (1976)	Tregear, M., *Catalogue of Chinese Greenware. Ashmolean Museum, Oxford*, Oxford, 1976.
van Berchem (1909)	van Berchem, M., "Inscriptions Mobilières Arabes en Russie", *Journal Asiatique*, 10e série, 14, 1909, pp.401-13
Ventrone (1974)	Ventrone G., "Iscrizioni inedite su ceramica samanide in collezione italiane", *Gururājamañjarikā. Studi in Onore Giuseppe Tucci*, Istituto Universitario Orientale, vol.1, Naples, 1974, pp.221-32.
Volov (1966)	Volov, L., "Plaited Kufic on Samanid Epigraphic Pottery", *Ars Orientalis*, 6, 1966, pp.107-34.
Waines (1977)	Waines, D., "The Third Century Internal Crisis of the Abbasids", *Journal of the Economic and Social History of the Orient*, 20, 1977, pp.282-306.
Watson (1967)	Watson, A.M., "Back to Gold and Silver", *Economic History Review*, 20.1, 1967, pp.1-34.
Wiet (1933)	Wiet, G., *L'Exposition Persane*, Cairo, 1933.
Wilkinson (n.d.)	Wilkinson, C., *Nishapur: Pottery of the Early Islamic Period*, New York, n.d.
Williamson (forthcoming)	Williamson, A., "Regional Distribution of Mediaeval Persian Pottery in the Light of Recent Investigations", in ed. J.W. Allan, *Medieval Islamic Pottery: Sirjān and Tell Minis, Oxford Studies in Islamic Art*, forthcoming.

Pottery and Metal Shapes in Persia in the 12th and 13th Centuries

OLIVER WATSON

The development in Persia of a ceramic industry based upon the artificial "frit" body took place with astonishing rapidity during the second half of the twelfth century. An extraordinary fecundity of invention is shown by the potters who, by the time of the Mongol invasions in 1220, had transformed their techniques, their styles, and the very status of their product. In the process, to name but one example, they had perfected a decorative technique that was to revolutionize not only Islamic, but Chinese and eventually world ceramic decoration—the technique of underglaze-painting.

During this development, the potters examined with a critical eye the shape of their vessels. New forms were needed—both to match the characteristics of the new ceramic medium, and to provide a suitably refined range for the luxury products that were then being made. Nowhere else in the history of Islamic ceramics can we see this process so clearly —the creation of a new type of pottery, more expensive than any yet made in the Islamic world.

Of interest to us here is the identification of the source, or sources, for the new shapes which the potters used. In the range of shapes developed, we see many forms drawn from models obvious to the potters. Naturally, earlier ceramics provide the greater part of the inspiration. Shapes previously found in the crude earthenwares of "Garrus", "Amol" and "Aghkand" and other types with simple cut and incised decoration are refined and tautened to suit the new, finer material. Chinese porcelains, imported into the Middle East in considerable quantities from the 9th century onwards, provide another obvious source for shapes. We know, from textual references, that porcelain was a highly regarded and expensive commodity, and indeed the desire of local potters to cash in on such a market had given inspiration to Islamic potters from the earliest times. The 12th century in Persia was no exception —it is probable that the fritware itself was initially taken up in order to imitate imported porcelains—and Chinese shapes are commonly found among the earlier fritwares.

Other sources are perhaps less obvious. Glass, though little identified from this period in Persia, seems to be a prototype for many of the bottle shapes.

Figure 1. Ewer, inlaid bronze. c.A.D.1200. Ht. 44.5cm. Nuhad Es-Said Collection. Photograph courtesy of Sotheby's. Published: Allan (1982), no.5.

Figure 1a. Ewer, lustre painted fritware. Early 13th century. Ht. 34.5cm. Ades Family Collection. Published: Watson (1985), pl.82.

This is seen in the proportions, in features such as the sharp change of angle from body to neck, and in details such as the tooling of many of the cup mouths.[1]

Metalwork is, however, the predominant non-ceramic source that can be identified. This again is not surprising, for metalwork must have always been a more expensive commodity than ceramics, and if the new "fritware" ceramics were trying to break into a luxury market, this was an obvious field in which to poach. In view of James Allan's argument that inlaid bronzes were replacing scarce silver work in this period, one might also see the new ceramics, and in particular the lustre wares, as attempting to fill this gap in

1. Watson (1985), pl.30, also pls.33, 46, 47, 83 and 84. A wide range of shapes is illustrated in this work, many of which resemble forms in other materials—one can seldom, however, find exact correspondences; Raby and Yücel (1983).

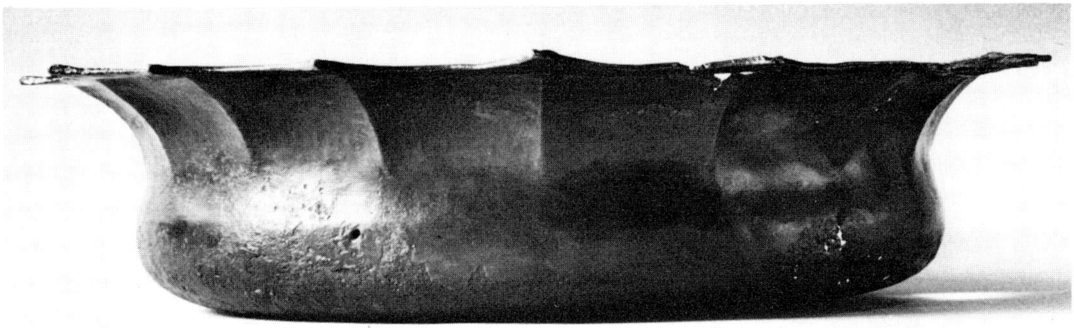

Figure 2. Basin, inlaid copper. Mid-13th century. Diam. 33.8cm. Victoria and Albert Museum, M120-1966. Published: Melikian-Chirvani (1982), no.86.

Figure 2a. Basin, lustre painted fritware. Early 13th century. Diam. c.30cm. Photograph courtesy of Sotheby's.

Figure 3a. Dish, fritware with lustre painting. Second half of the 13th century. Diam. 15cm. Ex-Kelekian Collection; al-Sabah Collection, Kuwait. Published: Kelekian (1910), no.40.

the market. Could not the demand for wares to replace the silver have stimulated the ceramic trade as much as it did the trade in inlaid metalware?

Evidence in support of this argument is provided by the fact that some metal shapes are copied so exactly that they must have been recognized by both maker and customer as imitations, even substitutes, not merely pieces inspired by the prototypes. One finds a more faithful degree of imitation of metal than of glass prototypes, for example. A similar close copying of metal in ceramics can be seen in other periods.[2]

Shown here are a number of photographs of metal objects and copies after them in fritware. The metal pieces are, with one exception, of brass, bronze or other alloy inlaid with silver. Following the arguments of James Allan, we can assume a silver model behind the bronze forms. A comprehensive or exhaustive selection is not presented here, but one which will show the possibilities of work in this field. The study of Islamic ceramics has

2. For example, Ṣafavid and Ottoman ceramics which copy metal prototypes, Lane (1957), pls.23a, 24a, 75 and 95.

Figure 3. Dish, silver with niello and gilt decoration. 12th century. Diam. 15.3cm. Ex-Kelekian Collection, present whereabouts unknown. Published: Pope (1939), pl.1354.

Figure 4. Tray, brass with engraved decoration. 12th century. Diam. 47.5cm. Victoria and Albert Museum, 558-1905. Published: Melikian-Chirvani (1982), no.20.

Figure 4a. Dish, lustre painted fritware. Dated A.D.1207. Diam. 35cm. Victoria and Albert Museum, C51-1952. Published: Watson (1985), Col.pl.E.

concentrated almost exclusively on decoration, and has virtually ignored the shapes. Such studies would be of great interest, however, not least in that, by revealing who copies what, they would help to establish the relative status of the various materials.

Figure 1 and 1a. The form and layout of the decorative scheme have been closely copied from the metal piece by the potter, though the motifs he has used, such as the leaf form on the neck, are those developed in lustre painting. Metal pieces with vertical inscriptions on the fluting of the body are known; see Pope (1939), pl.1326. Other forms of metal ewer are copied in ceramics, in particular that with a round body, often fluted, and a pronounced lip on the short neck.[3]

Figure 2 and 2a. The shape is known in metal from the 12th century; in ceramics it is apparently restricted to lustre ware.[4] A metal piece dating from the second half of the 12th century, is decorated with a geometrical design of stars filled with animals, similar to the square grid of the ceramic piece illustrated here.[5]

Figure 3 and 3a. The silver dish, at one time on loan to the Victoria and

3. Watson (1985), pl.45. The Metropolitan Museum in New York displays a metal and a ceramic example side by side, nos.59.53 and 19.105.1

4. Watson (1985), pl.73.

5. Melikian-Chirvani (1982), fig.26.

ure 5. Jug, inlaid bronze. 12th-13th century. Ht. m. Photograph courtesy of Sotheby's. Published: mic *Works of Art*, lot 187, 15th October, 1985, heby's, London.

Figure 5a. Jug, turquoise fritware. c.A.D.1200. Ht. 17cm. Victoria and Albert Museum, Clement Ades Gift, C153-1977.

Albert Museum, is one of the very few pieces of silver known from the period. The form of the dish, with or without legs, is known in cast brass throughout the 12th and 13th century. Ceramic versions of it are known in a variety of techniques, including *mīnā'ī* enamel painting, and lustre painting of the early 13th century. The feet on both ceramic and metal examples vary: one lustre dish has feet in the form of sphinxes;[6] another silver dish has "ball" feet similar to the ceramic pieces shown here.[7]

Figure 4 and 4a. The metal tray does not provide a very close prototype for the lustre dish, but shows the general form—a flat dish with shallow fluted cavetto and narrow rim. In this instance the skill of the lustre painter is infinitely greater than that of the metalworker, though what the relative cost was of an inferior piece of metal, and a superior piece of pottery is not known. Closer parallels in metal are known.[8]

6. Watson (1985), pl.74. For other metal versions see Melikian-Chirvani (1982), nos.36-38, 66 and 73.

7. Pope (1939), pl.1351b.

8. Pope (1939), pls.1315 and 1331.

Figure 5 and 5a. The ceramic copies the shape of the metal piece closely, but relies on the form and the quality of the glaze alone for its decorative effect. An even closer metal model for the ceramic shape is found in a jug from the Museum at Ghazni, Afghanistan.[9]

9. Melikian-Chirvani (1982), fig.31; see also Pope (1939), pl.1317a and b.

Bibliography

Allan (1982)	Allan, J., *Islamic Metalwork*, London, 1982.
Kelekian (1910)	Kelekian, D., *The Kelekian Collection of Persian and Analogous Potteries*, Paris, 1910.
Lane (1957)	Lane, A., *Later Islamic Pottery*, London, 1957.
Melikian-Chirvani (1982)	Melikian-Chirvani, A.S., *Islamic Metalwork from the Iranian World*, London, 1982.
Pope (1939)	Pope, A.U., *The Survey of Persian Art*, Oxford, 1939.
Raby & Yücel (1983)	Raby, J. and Yücel, Ü., "Blue-and-white, Celadon and Whitewares: Iznik's Debt to China", *Oriental Art*, 29, 1983, pp.38-48.
Watson (1985)	Watson, O., *Persian Lustre Ware*, London, 1985.

Notes on the Colloquium on Ceramics and Metalware, Oxford, March 1985

ALAN CAIGER-SMITH

One of the objectives of the colloquium was to examine "the dependence of the potter's craft on that of the gold- and silversmith". Instances of really close dependence turned out to be surprisingly elusive. The closest derivations appeared to be the black-glaze *kylikes* of the 5th-4th centuries B.C. from Athens, and the Sāmānid epigraphic platters of the 10th century A.D., shown by Michael Vickers and Julian Raby. These pottery vessels really do seem to have been a ceramic substitute for metalware. In other examples, such as the Yueh stoneware ewers shown by Mary Tregear and the jewel-style Tang earthenware of the 8th century, shown by William Watson, the pottery was a re-interpretation of a recognized metal form rather than a replica in cheaper material. Suggestions from metalware were being absorbed into the potters' repertoire, but the pots do not seem to have been intended as substitutes for metalware. These two kinds of derivation are subtly different. The word "dependence" could be applied to the former but hardly to the latter.

Since pottery and metalware are capable of serving the same functions, one might expect to discover a multitude of resemblances, but the proceedings of the colloquium suggested that in fact close resemblances are few and far between. The vast majority of common wares seem to have no obvious relation to metal forms even though they may have served similar practical purposes. The pots most closely related to metalware seem to have been fairly unusual "up-market" wares, requiring an experienced and attentive hand, and sometimes extra colour, ornament and imagery. It seems likely that the ordinary potter was too unadaptable or too hard-pressed to be able or willing to work from a metal prototype.

The photographs (**Figs. 1 and 2**) of unglazed pots in present-day kilns at Fusṭāṭ may indicate another reason why derivations from metalware were limited. The forms of common pottery have evolved not only because of their utility but because of considerations of manufacture and convenience of firing. Forms likely to warp in drying or firing, and forms that were difficult to accommodate in kilns, were avoided as far as possible. The photographs show how neatly certain types of pot can be set in a kiln, as a result of years of

Figure 1. Unglazed pots in present-day kilns at Fusṭāṭ.

Figure 2. Unglazed pots in present-day kilns at Fusṭāṭ.

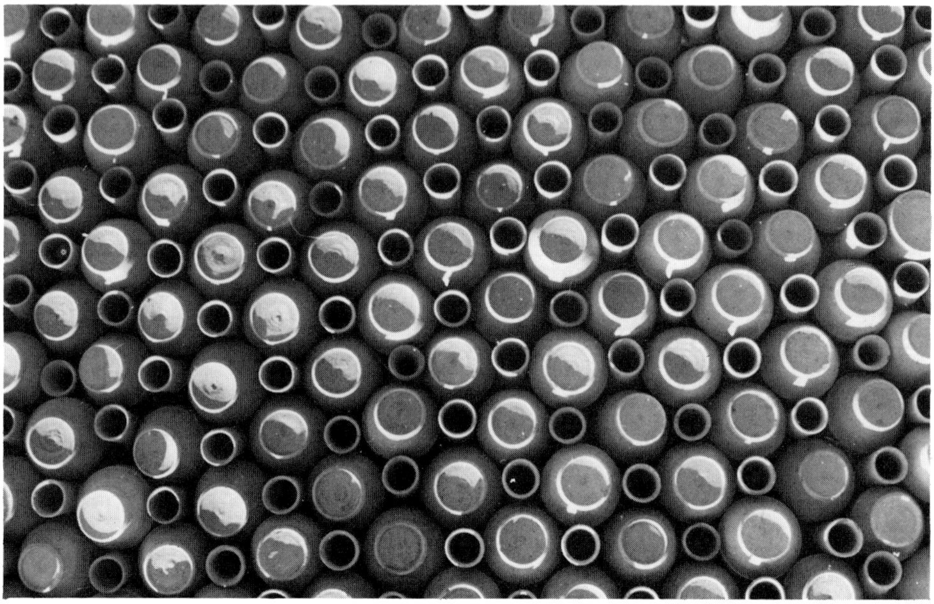

manufacturing-evolution, a consideration that did not apply to metalware. Large platters and stemmed-forms such as the *kylix* are forms obviously liable to crack or warp and would have been relatively difficult to place, and costly to fire.

Thus derivations from metalware are likely to have occurred only when the potters were skilled enough to modify their forms and decoration, and could be sure of being paid for the extra work and kiln-space.

There was some discussion of the age-old tendency for objects made in cheaper materials to borrow forms and imagery from those of more costly material. Some potters today find this distressing, as if it devalued their craft. It does not really do so. The one-way borrowing seems quite natural. By and large, the cheaper a product, the more quickly it has to be produced. Therefore the development time matters a great deal and is usually kept to a minimum. Design decisions can take far longer than following an existing model in which the decisions have already been made. In my own workshop we estimate that on average it takes five times longer to plan a commissioned design than to carry it out. If an object is made of valuable material the cost of design-time is only a small proportion of the finished piece, but the cheaper the material the greater the relative cost of design-time. Only in exceptional cases have potters ever been sure of recovering the cost of time spent on devising new forms, imagery, or inscriptions. So it is not surprising that a close relation between pottery and metalware occurs only where potters were able to command prices beyond the ordinary, as happened for instance at Kāshān in the late 12th and early 13th centuries, in the foremost Italian *botteghe* of the *cinquecento*, and in many of the factories under royal or noble patronage in 18th century Europe.

The Kāshān wares might perhaps have deserved more comment than they received at the Colloquium. They are specially relevant to its theme not only because many of the forms echo metalware, as does the lustre decoration, but because the techniques of forming the clay appear to have followed a sequence similar to the making of metal vessels. Because the siliceous paste lacked plasticity and steadiness, many of the Kāshān forms were composites, made by luting together units which had been made separately, and finally inverting the completed form to throw the base inwards and fashion a foot-ring, a forming-method still current in the Middle East. The procedure has obvious affinities with the making of metalware, and Kāshān bottles and ewers are often remarkably close to vessels of brass or bronze.[1]

1 The process is described in a little more detail in my book *Lustre Pottery*, London, 1985, 74-75.

Puritanism and Positivism

JULIAN RABY & MICHAEL VICKERS

It has emerged from many of the papers given here during the past two days that it is not an unusual practice for vessels made in precious metals to be evoked by craftsmen working in less costly materials. Where few precious metal objects have survived, we have resorted to texts and argument by analogy to make good the loss, texts providing an idea of quantity and types, pottery analogues an image of the forms and decoration. The implications go beyond enabling us to visualize an individual artefact; we might, if we are bold, visualize an entire category of craft, and from there delve into the realms of consumption and economics.

Many of the speakers appear to have been excited by this discovery. The examples they have cited should not be taken as providing a universal principle—that ceramic is *always* subservient to precious metal. But the examples do raise the question why the simple hierarchy which often prevails has not received more attention from scholars.

What we should like to do now is to widen the discussion. Let us turn away from the Chinese, Muslim and Graeco-Roman cultural contexts and consider instead factors that may prejudice *our* view of those cultures. Two trends seem to us to have clouded understanding of the ways in which pottery and metalwork can interrelate: Puritanism and Positivism.

Puritanism can be seen to have operated on two levels. In the first place, critics of luxury have frequently railed against gold and silver. At Rome, for example, the advent of great amounts of gold led to a transformation of manners and values during the first century B.C., and caused traditionally-minded Romans to voice the kind of criticism still being expressed by the elder Pliny a century later:

" How innocent, how blissful, nay even how refined life might be, if it coveted nothing from any source but the *surface* of the earth... " Gold, by contrast, had to be extracted from the earth at great cost and quickly led to luxuriousness and every kind of avarice.[1]

Moralists have long observed how foolish it is for men to lust after a metal which merely serves as a badge of rank and wealth, but which cannot be eaten or worn or used for any utilitarian purpose which other, less valuable, substances will not serve as well or better. There have thus been many attempts to devise social systems in which the roles of gold and silver were

1. Pliny *NH*, 33.3ff.

diminished. A corollary of such attempts has been the enhancement of the role of ceramics.

The discovery of America at the end of the fifteenth century gave a great impetus to philosophical speculation of this kind. The first reports of the New World to reach Europe suggested that there were people in the West who placed no value whatsoever on gold and jewels.[2] It matters little that such reports were exaggerated. They contributed to the society which Thomas More invented as an oblique criticism of the luxury of the court of Henry VIII. More's Utopians were systematically conditioned to despise precious metals:

" Inasmuch as they eat and drink from vessels fashioned out of clay and glass which, though handsomely shaped, are nevertheless of the cheapest kinds, they...make night jars and all kinds of squalid receptacles out of gold and silver.[3] " In an emblem devised by Alciati in criticism of such an attitude and entitled "Those who sin against Nature", we see precisely this: an earthenware pitcher and a glass goblet on a table, and a naked man emptying his bowels into a golden vessel.[4]

More's "provisional blueprint for a perfect society"[5] was in the long term extremely influential on both the ethical and aesthetic planes. In the sixteenth century, however, it was such a challenge to accepted material values that many were scandalized. But others echoed this critique of luxury. In about 1550 Pierre de Ronsard wrote an ode in praise of glass. He was consciously imitating Pindar. Yet whereas for Pindar "gold gleameth more brightly than all other lordly wealth",[6] Ronsard recites a long list of mythical quarrels which broke out over gold. He then contrasts it with the simplicity of glass and thus reverses Pindar's scale of values.

> ...Mais toy verre joly,
> Loin de tout meutre en te voyant poly,
> Net, beau, luisant, tu es plus agreable
> Qu'un vaisseau d'or, lourd fardeau de la table.[7]

If the discovery of America and the West Indies brought Europe an unprecedented influx of precious metals, the discovery of the East Indies ensured the import of a viable substitute for gold and silver plate, namely porcelain. Let us take two examples of the way in which porcelain was contrasted with plate in the sixteenth century. In 1562, a Portuguese delegate at the Council of Trent was shocked to see the array of gold and silver on the papal table. He recommended to his Holiness "a type of baked earthenware

2. Vespucci (1505/6), fol.4v; cf. Slavin (1976).

3. Translated by Heckscher (1981), 297; (1985), 487.

4. Alciati (1621), 353; Heckscher (1981), 292; (1985), 482.

5. cf. Turner (1965), 13.

6. Pindar *Olympians*, 1.1ff.

7. Ronsard (1967), 346-7.

which is far superior to silver in elegance and neatness" called porcelain, from China. Its lustre surpassed that of both crystal and alabaster, while its relatively low price compensated for its fragility. The Pope responded by ordering a porcelain service for the Vatican.[8]

Here the Bishop of Braga's criticism of the papal plate had a moral basis. Our second example illustrates how porcelain could be preferred on physical grounds. It was, quite literally, a matter of good taste. Aldrovandi's *Museum Metallicum* describes how "many princes" had abandoned silver services in favour of foreign porcelains because food tasted better when served in ceramic rather than metal vessels.[9]

So far, the Puritan criticism of gold and silver plate has been on a moral rather than artistic plane. One option suggested by the Puritan attack on precious metal was to make substitutes in ceramic. This leads us to the second aspect of our Puritan theme, namely the problem of copying the characteristics of one medium in another. Some have seen this as a question of deceit.

If we return to the Elder Pliny we find frequent criticism of the luxury of imperial Rome. This luxury was a relatively new phenomenon, having come about as a consequence of the Roman conquest of the Hellenistic East. The use of veneer, "of covering up one tree with another and making an outside skin for a cheaper wood out of a more expensive one", he found offensive; even more so the practice of "causing (turtle-shell) to lose its natural appearance by means of paints and to fetch a higher price by imitating [exotic] wood".[10] More recently, we can find a similar view expressed by the philosopher and statesman Francis Bacon. He took a firm stand on this issue, and since his *New Atlantis*, which was published in 1627, was in many respects a blueprint for the Royal Society, the fountainhead of scientific research in the modern western tradition, his strictures merit attention:

" But we do hate all impostures and lies, insomuch as we have severely forbidden it to all our fellows, under pain of ignominy and fines, that they do not show any natural work or thing adorned or swelling, but only pure as it is, and without all affectation of strangeness.[11] " "Pure as it is" is a concept which on any grounds comes close to the values expressed in the seventeenth century by Puritans: those who consciously rejected the flamboyant luxury prevalent in Caroline England. The equivalent today might be the view that woodwork in scrubbed pine is somehow more "honest", somehow more "worthy", than wood finished in formica or painted woodgraining, or even veneer.[12]

So much of our modern attitude has been formed by nineteenth-century

8. Lach (1970), 41-42.

9. Aldrovandi (1648), 231.

10 . Pliny *NH*, 16.223.

11. Bacon ([1627] 1922), 158.

12. cf. Sir Terence Conran: "To be simple in decoration is always to be in good taste." (quoted in *The Times* Saturday section 19-25, May 1984).

criticism, expressed in its most characteristic form by John Ruskin:
" Nobody wants ornaments in this world, but everybody wants integrity. All the fair devices that ever were fancied, are not worth a lie. Leave your walls as bare as a planed board, or build them of baked mud and chopped straw, if need be; do not rough-cast them with falsehood...You use that which pretends to a worth which it has not; which pretends to have cost, and to be, what it did not, and is not; it is an imposition, a vulgarity, and a sin. Down with it to the ground, grind it to powder, leave its ragged place upon the wall...[13] "

Most books on ceramics were written after 1850,[14] and most students, certainly of Greek ceramics, possessed a cast of mind which tended to make them look at their material in a way of which Ruskin would have approved. It is only very recently, for example, that Greek South Italian pottery, rather florid and ornate for the most part, has been brought to the attention of a public wider than a very limited number of scholars.[15] It has been the simpler, more "refined", Athenian ware which has received most attention, and even within this category those pieces with the simplest painted decoration have been most highly prized by the *cognoscenti*.[16] Indeed, J.D. Beazley, one of the leading lights in the study of Greek pottery in this century, occasionally used language which smacks of Ruskin's in his condemnation of industrialism or of what he regarded as falsehood in art.[17] The notion of craft integrity, of *Materialgerechtigkeit*, had also taken root by the early twentieth century. This was the view that objects should obey the aesthetic of the material of which they were made, otherwise they were in bad taste or even "Kitsch".[18]

13. Ruskin ([1849] 1903), 83; cf. Pevsner (1937), 11. "In a cardboard travelling-case made to imitate alligator skin, in a bakelite hairbrush made to imitate enamel - there is something dishonest. A pressed-glass bowl trying to look like crystal, a machine-made coal-scuttle trying to look hand-beaten, machine-made mouldings on furniture, a tricky device to make an electric fire look like a flickering coke fire, a metal bedstead masquerading as wood—all that is immoral. So are sham materials and sham technique. And so is all showy, pompous, blatant design." See too, Watkin (1977), 98, *et passim*.

14. e.g. The great majority of the titles in the bibliography to Fortnum (1872), 657-65, were published after that year.

15. Mayo (1982). Cook (1972), 191, claims that "strong stomachs" are necessary for the study of South Italian. Braun (1849) explicitly, but anachronistically, associated South Italian pottery with the values of the *ancien regime*; see further Vickers (1986).

16. e.g. Dennis (1848), lxxxii; cf. Vickers (1987).

17. e.g. Beazley (1945), 158; cf. the following, taken from a letter from J.D. Beazley to Paul Jacobsthal written in 1931 and preserved in Oxford: "Flaxman is to me the Beast. He, Thorwaldsen and Wedgwood are the Bogus classic, as the English Pre-Raphaelites are the Bogus Gothic and early Renaissance. And nothing more". Thanks are due to Professors Bernard Ashmole and Martin Robertson for granting access to the correspondence between Beazley and Jacobsthal and for permission to publish this extract.

18. cf. Pazaurek (1912); Giess (1971); Richter (1972).

So far then we have been dealing with *idealistic* arguments. The criticisms of gold and silver, or of ceramics plagiarizing precious metal, have been voiced in the context of wider considerations of social justice and of truth. In contrast, the second theme we wish to isolate has an *empirical* premiss. In the context of this conference, Positivism holds that one can only discuss matters for which one has physical evidence.[19] Positivism plays an important rôle in traditional archaeology, so much so that it has been claimed that "in all archaeological studies we are restricted to consideration of what has survived".[20] For archaeologists pottery holds a special place. This is understandable, since pottery is ubiquitous. Not only is pottery common to most cultures, but it can also be found in most phases of a culture. In other words, it is widespread geographically and chronologically. What is more, it survives. Unlike precious metal, it cannot be reduced to its raw form. It can be broken, but the fragments endure. Pottery's prevalence has meant that ceramic chronologies, for example, are frequently used to date other materials whose survival is more sporadic. No-one here needs to be reminded after the past two days that few silver and gold vessels survive, nor of the reasons why. The result is that we have two very different survival rates for ceramic and precious metal. Take the example of the Anglo-Saxons. Their pottery survives in quantity; the number of extant gold and silver objects is minimal. The tendency, then, has been to measure Anglo-Saxon culture by a pottery standard. Yet the recent textual research of C.R. Dodwell has revealed an Anglo-Saxon society which revelled in gold and silver, a society with very different tastes from the traditional image. The lesson, clearly, is not to put total trust in what has survived, for, as Dodwell has seen:

"If the survival pattern of the various crafts of the Anglo-Saxons has distorted our knowledge of their arts, it has also falsified our understanding of their tastes.[21]"

By concentrating our attention on pottery, whether for reasons of puritanism or positivism, by neglecting the problem of precious metal, we are in danger of distorting the historical relationship between these media. First in terms of artistry, secondly in terms of status, and thirdly in terms of statistics. By failing to see the relationship between crafts, we do a disservice to both the goldsmith and the potter. The goldsmith because we ignore him; the potter because we underestimate his skills. These can be skills of imitation—and let us not dismiss out of hand all imitative works of art—and they can be skills of independent invention. The other distortions are in terms of status and

19. cf. Hermerén (1984), 19-20: "To say that 'only what can be measured can be known', or that one's ambition should be 'to measure everything that can be measured, and to make everything measurable that cannot now be measured' is to express an ideal of science which has consequences for what kind of concepts are regarded as 'scientific'."

20. Kurtz and Boardman (1971), 203.

21. Dodwell (1982), 12.

statistics. The consequences are obvious for both the social and economic historian.

Bibliography

Aldrovandi (1648)	Aldrovandi, U., *Musaeum Metallicum in Libros iiii Distributum*, Bonn, 1648.
Bacon (1627)	Bacon, F., *New Atlantis, a Worke Unfinished*, London, 1627, quoted from P.E. and E.F. Matheson, eds., *Francis Bacon, Selections*, Oxford, 1922.
Beazley (1945)	Beazley, J.D., "The Brygos Tomb at Capua", *American Journal of Archaeology*, 49, 1945, pp.153-8.
Braun (1849)	Braun, E., *Le Dipinture di Clizia Sopra Vaso Chiusino d'Ergotimo, Scoperto e Pubblicato da Alessandro Francois, Dichiarate da Emilio Braun*, Rome 1849.
Dennis (1848)	Dennis, G.T., *Cities and Cemeteries of Etruria*, London, 1848.
Dodwell (1982)	Dodwell, C.R., *Anglo-Saxon Art, A New Perspective*, Manchester, 1982.
Fortnum (1872)	Fortnum, C.D.E., *A Descriptive Catalogue of the Maiolica in the South Kensington Museum*, London, 1872.
Giess (1971)	Giess, L., *Phänomenologie des Kitsches*, Munich, 1971.
Heckscher (1981)	Heckscher, W.S., "Pearls from a Dungheap: Andrea Alciati's 'Offensive' Emblem, 'Adversus Naturam Peccantes'", in *Art the Ape of Nature, H.W. Janson Festschrift*, New York, 1981, pp. 291-311. Reprinted in W.S. Heckscher, ed. E. Verheyen, *Art and Literature. Studies in Relationship, Saecula Spiritualia*, Baden-Baden, 17, 1985, pp.481-501.
Hermerén (1984)	Hermerén, G., "Positivistic and Marxist Ideals of Science and Their Consequences for Research", *Perspective on Archaeological Theory and Method*, University of Lund, Report Series No.20, 1984.
Kurtz and Boardman (1971)	Kurtz, D.C. and Boardman, J., *Greek Burial Customs*, London, 1971.
Lach (1970)	Lach, D., *Asia in the Making of Europe, Volume II. A Century of Wonder. Book one: The Visual Arts*, Chicago, London, 1970.
Mayo (1982)	Mayo, M.E., *The Art of South Italy. Vases from Magna Graecia*, Richmond, Va., 1982.
Pindar	Pinder, (Loeb Classical Library).
Pliny	Pliny, *Natural History*, (Loeb Classical Library).
Pazaurek (1912)	Pazaurek, G.E., *Guter und Schlechter Geschmack im Kunstgewerbe*, Stuttgart/Berlin, 1912.
Pevsner (1937)	Pevsner, N., *An Enquiry into Industrial Art in England*, London, 1937.
Richter (1972)	Richter, G., *Kitsch-Lexicon von A bis Z*, Gütersloh, 1972.
de Ronsard (1967)	de Ronsard, P., "Le Verre", in I. Silver, ed., *Les Oeuvres de Pierre de Ronsard*, Paris, 4, 1967.

Ruskin (1849) — Ruskin, J., *The Seven Lamps of Architecture*, London, 1849, quoted from E.T. Cook and A. Wedderburn, eds., *The Library Edition of the Works of John Ruskin*, London, 8, 1903.

Slavin (1976) — Slavin, A.J., "The American Principle from More to Locke", in F. Chiappelli, ed., *First Images of America*, Berkeley, 1976, pp.139-64.

Turner (1965) — Turner, P., *Thomas More, Utopia*, Harmondsworth, 1965.

Vespucci (1893) — Vespucci, A., *The First Four Voyages*, (Florence, 1505/6), London, 1893.

Vickers (1987) — Vickers, M., "Value and Simplicity: Eighteenth-Century Taste and the Study of Greek Vases", *Past and Present*, 1987.

Watkin (1977) — Watkin, D., *Morality and Architecture*, Oxford, 1977.